THE RELUCTANT MIGRANTS

THE RELUCTANT MIGRANTS

Migration from the Italian Veneto to Central Massachusetts

Teresa Fava Thomas

<teneo> //press
AMHERST, NEW YORK

This book has been registered with the Library of Congress.

The Reluctant Migrants:
Migration from the Italian Veneto to Central Massachusetts
/Teresa Fava Thomas

pages cm. --

Includes bibliographical references and index.

ISBN 978-1-934844-71-7 (alk. paper)

TABLE OF CONTENTS

LIST OF FIGURES

ACKNOWLEDGMENTS

This book examines the transnational experience of migrants from the Italian Veneto who lived and worked in central Massachusetts. As their experience spanned two worlds, so did the research for this book. Throughout the years I have delved into archives across Massachusetts, New York, and Washington, DC, as well as throughout the Veneto region. I have spent years studying a language that came naturally to my grandparents and parents. Although I grew up hearing the Venetian dialect spoken, after extensive study I finally developed some skill in reading Italian and Venetian dialect sources. Exploring the Veneto was a wonderful experience and allowed me to sample life in the mountains. To better understand the transatlantic voyage, I booked my return home on a modern passenger liner. Even though the ship was equipped with the latest amenities, a three-day Atlantic storm turned the trip into a more exact replica of the immigrant experience than I had intended.

My earliest contact with immigration studies occurred at Clark University, where I was a teaching assistant in Professor Janette Greenwood's course Race and Ethnicity in American History. My research concentrated more broadly on American foreign relations when I studied with

Professor Douglas J. Little, who guided my dissertation research on language and area studies training in the US State Department.

After receiving my doctorate from Clark, I began teaching at Fitchburg State University (FSU) and was invited to join the Advisory Board of the Center for Italian Culture (CIC), which was generously supported by the Amelia Gallucci-Cirio Endowment. Amelia V. Gallucci-Cirio, an FSU alumna, established a foundation to encourage Italian and Italian American studies through a series of amazingly liberal financial gifts. It is no exaggeration to say her generosity altered the trajectory of my career and changed my life. The CIC has supported both faculty and students in pursuing Italian-language studies and research trips, promoted cultural programming and an oral history project, and established FSU's study abroad program in Verona, Italy. CIC Advisory Board members have all been wonderfully supportive of my project, and very special thanks go to Anna Mazzaferro, Anna Maria Clementi, Henry and Loretta Lisciotti, Dr. Joseph Addante, and Rose Anne Addorisio. The CIC and the FSU foundation have supported and encouraged this work from the very beginning. The university granted me a sabbatical in 2006 with support for Italian-language and historical studies, and its support continued for successive years of language study at the Istituto Venezia, as well as for research in Venetian archives. During my sabbatical I explored Italian American immigration history with Professors Elvira DeFabio and Carol Bonomo Albright at Harvard University. Their encouragement was a wonderful example of the scholarly ideal.

This book has developed with the generous aid of many other scholars' comments. Early versions of the manuscript were presented to the Robert Dombrowski Conference on Italian studies at the University of Connecticut, at Storrs, as well as to the American Italian History Association and its new iteration, the Italian American Studies Association (IASA). Comments and suggestions from many scholars, especially from the Italian American specialists of the IASA conferences, have greatly aided its evolution and expanded its focus.

Thanks to the library and archival staffs of Harvard University, espe-
cially the Houghton and Widener Libraries, for access to materials on
the Society for Protection of Italian Immigrants (SPII) and its rival, the
Immigration Restriction League (IRL). Thanks also to the New York Public
Library's Italian-language newspaper collections, the George Washington
University Gelman Library archives' special collections of materials on
the Italian ambassador's conflict with Cesare Celso Moreno, the Yale
University Library, and special collections librarian Debra Kimok of the
University of Plattsburgh's Benjamin Feinberg Library for access to the
family letters of the young Sarah Wool Moore.

The Boston Public Library's special collections staff located a rare
publication by Cesare Celso Moreno. The Massachusetts Historical
Society's materials on Reverend Gaettano Conte were especially helpful
in detailing the origins of the SPII and in tracing Conte's connection to
the New York branch, as well as to Sarah Wool Moore.

Closer to home, archivist Sean Fisher of the Massachusetts Department of Conservation and Recreation (DCR) and the Massachusetts State
Archives greatly assisted in tracking down government documents and
rare photographs pertinent to the experience of Italians in the construction of the Wachusett Dam and Reservoir project. DCR Rangers at the
Wachusett Reservoir Rebecca Baranowski and Kelley Freda generously
shared advice about the photographic materials documenting Italians
working on the dam project. Thanks to the West Boylston Historical
Society and also to Louise Howland, director of the Beaman Memorial
Public Library, for allowing access to James F. Higgins's photographs of
Italian workers in the reservoir project's camps. And my appreciation goes
to Michael Ruocco of Ruocco Designs for creating the map of the Veneto.

The Fitchburg Historical Society's director, Shirley Wagner, offered me
access to its local history collection, which provided vital information on
the experience of immigrants in Fitchburg's industrial sector, especially
the Water Street foundries and the Rollstone Hill quarries. The society's
biographic files offered details on the career of Margaret Kielty and

the development of Americanization programs for Italian immigrants. The Fitchburg Public Library special collections and clipping files were especially helpful regarding material on World War II–era enemy alien registration and the development of Italian American businesses. Saint Anthony of Padua Church, the first Italian parish in northern Massachusetts, provided access to its historical materials, and special appreciation goes to Betty Pagnotta for her special role in preserving that history.

The Leominster Historical Society is home to a valuable collection of materials on Italian social clubs, as well as to oral history interviews with Italian Americans in the area. The Italians of Leominster, especially the Avellinese families, built a strong foundation of materials on the history of their community and Saint Anna's Church. Special thanks to the Women's Society of the church for inviting me to discuss Italian American history and for telling me about their role in establishing Saint Anna's.

While teaching at FSU, I have profited greatly from interaction with students and faculty as I made a number of presentations on my research. Assistant vice president Paul Weizer invited me to discuss Italian American immigration at the Citizenship Day conference and has always supported my research initiatives. FSU's Study Abroad in Italy program allowed me to spend a wonderful summer teaching modern Italian history to our students in Verona and guiding their exploration of the Veneto. The CIC's collection of Italian materials, especially the Sogni d'Oro Oral History interviews located in the FSU archives, has been a very useful resource. Most of all, I am thankful for the support of FSU's head librarian, Robert Foley, and his staff, especially Mark Melchior and Kathryn Wells at the Amelia Gallucci-Cirio Library, who patiently fulfilled reams of requests for interlibrary loans and Italian-language materials. Professor Michele Caniato of the humanities department offered access to the Italian-language materials in the Belding Music Collection and patient advice about the Venetian experience. FSU's president, Robert Antonucci, gave most generously of his time for an interview about Italian American life in central Massachusetts and about his father's special role in the establishment of the Italian American Citizens Club (IACC).

Research in Venice and the Veneto has been a wonderful experience. My earliest explorations in Venice were greatly eased through help from the Bianchini family, especially Thomas Tortorella and everyone at the Campiello. The Fondazione Cini's Vittore Branca Center generously provided a home away from home in its scholars' residence and access to its research libraries on the Isola San Giorgio Maggiore. The combination of a fine archival collection on the Veneto and the quiet life on an island in the Venetian lagoon certainly concentrated the mind. The Branca Center is a wonderful place where the plan for this work germinated and grew over several years. Special thanks go to Marta Zappetti and Massimo Busetto for their support, as well as to the Vittore Branca Center's archivists.

Venice's archives hold a wealth of materials that shaped this project: the Biblioteca Nazionale Marciana, the Archivio d'Stato in Venice as well as in Treviso, and the Ateneo Veneta. The Biblioteca Querini Stampalia offered access to Italian government documents and materials on the Veneto, along with a quiet place to work on a Venetian evening. Libraries throughout the Veneto, especially the Biblioteca Civica at Belluno and at Vittorio Veneto, offered access to unique local materials. Special thanks are due to the Grava family at the Ca De Lach in Revine Lago for access to Osvaldo Grava's memoirs and other Grava family materials. Appreciation goes to scholar Giulio Bobbo of the Museo della Storia Contemporanea e Resistenza in Venice for a lively afternoon discussing the experience of Venetians and the life of the city during the Second World War. Special thanks to scholar Alessandro Paglia of Venezia for his encouragement and for sharing materials on Luigi Einaudi's interest in Massachusetts. Deepest appreciation to Paul Moretto, whose lifelong interest in preserving the history of his family and the story of their migration from the Veneto inspired my work.

Great appreciation goes to Maddalena Tirabassi, director and editor of *Altreitalie* journal in Turin, Italy, for granting permission to reprint parts of "Arresting the Padroni Problem" and to editor Eric Dursteler for permission to reprint parts of "Retrospective Review: Giuseppe Grava and Giovanni Tomasi" from *News on the Rialto*. In addition, most gracious thanks to George Guida, editor of the IASA anthology *What Is Italian American? Selected Essays from the Italian American Studies Association*.

Finally, the most important support has come from my parents, John and Bianca Fava, especially my mother, whose incredible memory offered invaluable leads that helped gather the threads of many personal histories. To my husband, Arthur Frank Thomas, and my daughter, Ann Emily Thomas, go my most devoted and unending thanks for all of their kindness, patience, and support through every step of the journey.

THE RELUCTANT MIGRANTS

INTRODUCTION

From Reluctant Migrants
to Birds of Passage

This book describes the economic and social changes in postunification Italy that drove migration from the Veneto between 1880 and 1920. It also explores the strategies migrants used to hold on to their homes and what finally led many to settle in central Massachusetts. The study seeks to determine how northern Italian migration was distinct from the waves of southern emigration. What strategies did they develop, and how did social networks help them to gather information about migration? How did modern rail and steamer transport systems lead to more complex migration patterns? Why did central Massachusetts attract migrants, and in what respects did its economy fit their needs? How did immigrants integrate into American society, and what problems ensued? How did members of the second and third generations fit into American society and accept or reject the social and linguistic traditions of their ancestors?

The analytical framework that shapes this study is the "village-outward approach" of Samuel Baily. He has argued that one should examine migration at the village level and then explore the complex migration patterns that emerged over long periods. Baily emphasized "the centrality

of social networks to the migration process" and "expanding our defi-
nitions of time and space."[1] In other words, this approach examines
the strategies and the many destinations of migrants from one village
in order to understand the reasons why new labor opportunities were
chosen. Baily focused on what attracted laborers and on how "emerging
industrial regions created a demand for immigrant labor."[2] Baily's multigenerational study explores how migration worked on three levels: the
global, the community, and the family level. His study began in Agnone,
a tiny mountain village east of Rome, and then traced the global migrations of Agnonesi laborers, and finally the history of four generations
of the Orlando family. By examining immigration to America from the
village-outward perspective, scholars like Baily and Donna Gabaccia
have broadened the scholarly perspective. Immigration to America was
not always a single, one-way voyage. Such scholars view *migration* as a
more complex process that involved generations of migrants traveling
across the globe over a long span of time. Cheap and efficient transport
systems linking northern Italy and Europe made higher levels of mobility
possible in the 1870s.

This volume discusses the Veneto as a whole but also focuses on
migration from several villages: Revine Lago, Treviso, Rovigo, Vittorio
Veneto, and Belluno. Migrants from these areas first traveled within
Italy and across the border into Austria for seasonal work. Later they
traveled to Brazil and Argentina as the migration network grew and
crossed generational lines. Construction projects in central Massachusetts,
especially the massive Wachusett Dam and Reservoir project, attracted
legions of stonecutters and quarry workers, including Veneto families
like the Cassinaris and the Gravas. This study addresses the Veneto
migratory experience across several generations.

The opening chapters explore Italian and Venetian sources to describe
mountain life in the Veneto *prealpi* (alpine foothills) as it had always
existed until the economic and social disruptions that followed unification in 1870. Investment in large-scale agriculture reduced indepen-

dent farmers to temporary day laborers, and they struggled to survive; malnutrition, disease, and unemployment forced thousands from the Veneto to become reluctant migrants far earlier than others elsewhere in Italy did. The central chapter of this study deals with the diplomatic conflict between Rome and Washington regarding the security of Italian nationals who lived and worked in America between 1881 and 1901. The second half of the book explores why many of these migrants were drawn to permanent settlement in the booming industrial economy of central Massachusetts and how they built a network of family and friends into a community. The foreign born and their children comprised nearly three-quarters of the region's population in the 1910s. Anti-Italian hostility in Massachusetts escalated to a fever pitch during the trial and appeals of Nicola Sacco and Bartolomeo Vanzetti of the 1920s and never abated into the 1940s, when Italian nationals were categorized by the federal government as enemy aliens under the Smith Act. During the Second World War Italian American men and women served in the armed forces, and this experience altered their Italian identity. And after the war, the *Veneti* (people of the Veneto) in central Massachusetts struggled to find strategies that would preserve their links to their home region's culture and language as Italian corner markets gave way to supermarkets and their children abandoned the familiar neighborhoods for newly constructed suburbs.

My research shows a complex migration pattern among mobile northern Italians to central Massachusetts that began emerging earlier than movements from other regions of Italy and that reached its peak in 1909. Unlike movement away from southern Italy, which was largely undertaken by the young, single, and male, these networks of northern migrants were more often multigenerational and even included women. The travelers returned to the Veneto in winter and emerged to try new routes the following spring. Those who left the Veneto pursued these strategies because they were deeply attached to their *paese* (hometown) and had a steadfast desire to hold on to the land despite hardships and the lack of work. Many had struggled for decades to supplement dwindling wages and to stave off worsening social conditions. Small-scale rural farmers who worked the alpine hillsides, as their ancestors had done since the fifteenth century, were forced to sell their livestock and abandon their farms. After the unification of Italy, efforts to foster modernization and large-scale agriculture threatened to make life in the mountains unsustainable. The men and women of northeastern Italy became reluctant migrants.

At first they traveled within Italy to newly irrigated farms or urban areas seeking supplementary income and returned in the fall to their mountains. But by the 1880s that strategy no longer worked. As Italian government improvement projects encouraged private investment in large-scale Po River valley agriculture lowered wages, it also made the alpine economic model of small farms, with their *fienagione* (haymaking) and wood gathering, untenable. Falling wages left the impoverished with less food and led to malnutrition. Children suffered from epidemic levels of pellagra, and contagious diseases like cholera killed people and animals. A perfect storm of suffering drove the people of the Veneto to migrate sooner than residents of other Italian regions did, and the development of new transport systems made this movement easier. By the time that Rome dispatched the Jacini Commission to investigate the condition of the agricultural sector in 1882, many of the Veneto's people, however reluctantly, had already embarked on the path to migration.

These individuals used the new national and international transportation system so often that it is difficult for immigration historians to calculate how many left temporarily and how many permanently. Women traveled first within northern Italy but soon took new railroad connections to Austria to work as housekeepers and farm laborers. Men found new opportunities in Switzerland, France, Germany, and Belgium working on mining and railroad projects. The Italians called these seasonal migrants *uccelli di passaggio* (lit., "birds of passage" or "migratory birds"). Living frugally, they returned home in late fall with savings to help their families survive. Immigration historian Donna Gabaccia, author of *Italy's*

Many Diasporas, termed this new form of existence *transnationalism* and defined it as "a way of life that connects family, work, and consciousness in more than one national territory."[3] For Veneto migrants, the shortest transatlantic voyage was to Boston, and from there they found seasonal work in central Massachusetts. This path fit their transnational goals.

The old model of immigration studies described migrants as "the uprooted." That term has a finality to it. The image of an Italian immigrant making one dramatic crossing of the Atlantic to land once at Ellis Island is deeply ingrained in the American psyche. Seasonal migration, however, was a strategy to earn money abroad but to return, for at least part of the year, to the Veneto (though eventually, many found that Massachusetts offered more permanent work in foundries and factories). Social networks provided information about boardinghouses, jobs, and survival strategies as migrants repeatedly crossed the Atlantic. These reluctant migrants preferred seasonal migration as they struggled to retain a foothold and to support their families in the Veneto until conditions finally forced them into permanent settlement abroad.

First-time travelers were naïve immigrants, often called greenhorns, but not all of them settled permanently after their first voyage to America. Nor did they remain greenhorns. They often ventured on a series of voyages to explore the opportunities in a variety of destinations. Once these Veneto migrants began to move, they became highly mobile migrants who traveled to an amazing array of destinations where they worked —on railroad tunnel projects in Switzerland, in the mines of Belgium, on farms in Brazil, on construction projects in New York State, and in similar jobs (construction projects, quarries, foundries, and textile mills) in Massachusetts.

During the work season they saved every possible cent and returned to the Veneto with a substantial nest egg. Immigration restrictionists did not praise their thrift but argued that their frugality deprived the United States of their earnings. Labor leaders protested that these workers accepted the lowest wages and so undercut skilled union labor. Others argued that they clogged the urban slums because the American dream of owning a farm did not appeal to these new arrivals. But those who had been starved into migration by the rapid decline of farm wages in the Veneto were not eager to repeat the adventure in the American farm sector.

From the perspective of the Veneti, America was a place where their dreams, or *sogni*, could come true, but they had a variety of different dreams. In America many diverse dreams could be pursued. But what they most needed was information that would allow them to navigate these far-flung destinations, and they developed social networks of experienced family and friends to advise them. They extended these networks to more distant friends and acquaintances in boardinghouses and factories, then returned home and brought new Veneto migrants with them to traverse new routes. Sophisticated strategies developed that made subsequent trips easier and more lucrative.

A boardinghouse in one city might see dozens of people from the same region with the same last name arrive every year, but the first names and the faces would be a bit different each time. An uncle, a father, a cousin, a brother, a sister, or a friend may have lived and worked in one place and then encouraged other friends and relatives to accompany them the following year. Migrants heard of better opportunities and abandoned old destinations for new ones. Italian laborers on the Wachusett Dam project were so badly treated one summer that they walked off the job, and the following year contractors complained that they could not find Italians to work on the project. Laborers had surely spread the news of their maltreatment along the migrant network, and as a result few returned to that project the following spring. Even if workers were content with these construction projects, most lasted a few years at most. As a project drew to a close, its workers went home and advised their friends of new opportunities in neighboring towns. As the Wachusett project was ending in Clinton, it became known that a half-dozen quarries in nearby Fitchburg needed stonecutters.

Such workers often left their small *paese* with *paesani* (trusted friends) and crossed the ocean together. The phenomenon of returnees makes it is difficult to estimate how many took part in these human migrations. Historian Mark Wyman has estimated that returning migrants were so mobile that many Italian towns had "from 16 to 37 percent of their twenty-year-old men away from home at any time," from 1820 to 1900.[4] But once in America they scattered like leaves in the wind to different destinations: digging ditches in New York, driving a delivery truck in Chicago, cutting stone in Massachusetts, pouring molten brass in a foundry, or doffing bobbins in a cotton mill. Having once taken wing, they remained highly mobile and pursued their global strategy; many migrants undertook new and different journeys year after year. This could go on for a decade or more. The expansion of the European and American rail networks and cheaper steamship fares made global commuting a practical alternative to struggling in the Veneto.

The Veneti often left from the port of Genoa on the northwest coast of Italy, but some found that a rail journey through France to Le Havre made the sea voyage even shorter. Boston, as the closest arrival port after a transatlantic voyage, had a particular advantage, and the establishment of many Italian American businesses in the city's North End made arriving and leaving easier. Having family or friends from one's *paese* in Massachusetts made it an extension of home. Over time, some migrants established their own importing businesses farther inland as they developed small enterprises that served the special interests of Italians in America.

Unlike numerous southern Italians, who were recruited by *padroni* (labor bosses) and settled in major cities like New York and Chicago, many northerners traveled independently in smaller groups and chose smaller industrialized towns as their destinations. They commuted to Massachusetts, where opportunities on massive public-works projects offered seasonal work; then they moved to work in quarries, foundries, and factories, which offered more dependable year-round work. As one of America's most highly industrialized regions, with a strong demand for labor, this area offered many reasons to settle there. By 1910 first- and second-generation Europeans constituted 74 percent of the population in central Massachusetts (but this led to a backlash when anti-Italian hostility intensified a decade later).

The networks Italian migrants developed became a source of support and kinship, but most of all they offered some sense of security. People rented rooms or boarded with *paesani* whom they knew and (hoped) they could trust. The tradition of *campanilismo*, or trusting people from one's hometown—literally, those who lived within the sound of the town's *campanile* (bell tower)—was stretched to include people more distantly connected within one's social network. Gradually, Veneto women joined the international migration as well, often traveling with kin and settling with friends and relatives where work could be found. Their presence made more permanent settlement viable. Whereas padroni recruited entirely male work crews from southern Italy for large projects, thus excluding women from the initial migration waves, the smaller, more personal scale of Veneto migration opened the possibility of migration to more women earlier in the process.

By the early 1900s, the economic and social problems of the Veneto had worsened to the point that labor unrest and hunger propelled new, larger waves of more permanent emigration in the peak years of 1907–1909. Over time, those in Massachusetts found better jobs, settled in tenements, established social clubs and churches, and solidified their social networks. They also expanded the definition of family to include friends and *paesani*. The Italian terms for godparents, *comare* and *compare*, signify a relative who pledges at baptism to take responsibility for a child. But these words came to apply to people who replaced blood relatives, who were thousands of miles away. Someone termed a *comare* might be a real godparent or a friend from the Veneto who lived in America and was as close to her friends as a blood relative might be.

As more Italians, whether from north or south, settled in Massachusetts, hostility toward them escalated. Historian Joseph Cosco has divided Americans into two groups, the first of which held a positive, even romantic view of Italians, often stemming from having traveled to Italy or from an appreciation of its art and music. These people looked upon Italian immigrants with what Cosco termed *Italophilism*. They supported Italian immigrants' assimilating into American life and worked to help educate and encourage them to become naturalized citizens. But a larger group, especially American nativists and immigration restrictionists, viewed the influx of Italians as a threat. Anti-Italian hostility, driven by a sense of economic menace as well as by racial and cultural anxieties, intensified in the 1920s. Cosco labeled this hostility *Italophobia*.[5] The reluctant migrants from the Veneto had blended with the larger flow of immigrants from the Italian peninsula, and once in America all were regarded as "Eye-talians," sometimes called by even more derisive terms like *dago* and *wop*.[6]

Unionized American laborers were threatened by low-wage, non-union workers who were willing to work on almost any terms, no matter how difficult. Day labor in the Veneto paid what were literally starvation wages, but the meager earnings of day labor in America could be husbanded into substantial savings. American labor organizations were joined by a small group of elites who used scientific racism to argue for immigration restriction and even deportation. The immigration restriction movement developed a strong base in Massachusetts. The leadership of the movement's most prominent group, the Immigration Restriction League (IRL), was almost entirely drawn from Harvard University professors and alumni. The IRL's small but powerful cohort finally succeeded in its aims: efforts to restrict immigration culminated in the 1920 and 1924 Quota Acts, federal legislation that cut off the flow of Italians and southern European immigration to America. Among the most vocal restrictionists was the senator from Massachusetts Henry Cabot Lodge and IRL leader Prescott Farnsworth Hall.

Other Americans, called assimilationists, admired Italian language and culture and did not view Italians' presence as a threat. Among them were social reformers like Jane Addams, who welcomed immigrants to Hull House in Chicago. But assimilationists pointed to the need to fully integrate newcomers into American society, arguing that the public authorities should assist them in learning English and earning citizenship. Reverend Gaettano Conte of Boston and Sarah Wool Moore of New York established the Society for the Protection of Italian Immigrants (SPII), which sought to protect, educate, and integrate newcomers throughout Massachusetts and New York State. In Massachusetts, first the Fosdick family and the Young Men's Christian Association (YMCA) and then other groups carried forward educational programs to integrate immigrants that ultimately were adopted at the state and the national level. Eventually, the YMCA built an international network of volunteers to contact migrants before they left Europe and to provide linkage at the ports of entry in America.

Many migrants found better work and established homes and families in what they viewed as an Italian colony. Some worked in foundries or cut granite for the rest of their lives, unable to escape the most grueling jobs. Some spent their lives in crowded triple-decker tenements where diseases spread. Others established small businesses, like corner markets, and eventually bought their own homes. The social and *mutuo soccorso* (mutual benefit) clubs often organized by small groups from a particular town or region, like Fitchburg's Venetian Club and Carlo Alberto Society, offered some small comfort and sometimes financial assistance (including health and life insurance). For the second generation, work in foundries and quarries often gave way to better jobs in factories and mills, but only the few able to complete their education reached the professions. Desperate immigrant families most often demanded that their sons and daughters work to support the family's economy from as young as fourteen years of age.

Learning English and studying for naturalization exams offered an opportunity for the first generation to participate fully in American life as citizens. But that was not easy, and some migrants refused to abandon Italian citizenship. Although Veneto migrants arrived with a higher level of literacy than many other newcomers, not all were able to learn enough English to clear all the hurdles to US citizenship. Assimilationists helped ease the way for many in some periods, but in the 1920s Massachusetts became a tense, violent place where Italophobia exploded in the era of the Sacco and Vanzetti trial.

The hardships of the Great Depression only intensified economic competition for access to jobs as Benito Mussolini's Axis alliance with Adolf Hitler put Italian immigrants to the United States in jeopardy. Those who had not previously applied for citizenship found themselves categorized as enemy aliens in 1940; the Smith Act required them to be fingerprinted and to carry identification cards. It fell to the second generation of Italian Americans to serve the country they had been born in as members of the American armed forces and to win new respect for Italians in Massachusetts.

Only in the post–World War II era did the second and third generations of Italian Americans achieve the American dream of financial security and upward mobility. Among these success stories were many Veneti in Massachusetts. Those generations often married non-Italians and moved to the suburbs. The Italian American parish of Saint Anthony's Church bought land and constructed its own housing development (married couples could buy a home as long as one partner was of Italian heritage) in an effort to keep the second generation literally closer to the church. The struggle to preserve the Italian language was made much more difficult in the wake of Mussolini. American public schools closed Italian-language programs after the government rounded up many instructors as enemy aliens in 1942 and launched a "Don't Speak the Enemy's Language" campaign. After the war, the effort to rebuild these programs was centered in Italian Catholic parishes and social organizations that promoted Italian-language instruction, which was not reinstituted by public schools. But the damage had been done, and many second-generation Italians distanced themselves from their heritage while the older first generation feared for the survival of their social clubs and even parishes.

For the people of the Veneto, beginning in the 1880s, migration was a survival strategy. It was not taken up easily or on the spur of the moment but was driven by extreme hardships. They first tried seasonal migration within Europe, then to South America, and eventually to North America and central Massachusetts. Along the way, they depended on networks of fellow migrants to gather information and to decide which labor markets they would explore. The process involved many journeys and wove a complex pattern of migrations that spanned the globe. From the perspective of the Veneto, those migrations continued even after America restricted immigration in 1924. The Veneti simply altered their strategy to explore new destinations, especially in Canada and Australia. From the American perspective, many of the third and even fourth generation lost their connection to the mountains their ancestors had once farmed and the dialect they had spoken.

In the Veneto there is still a desire to migrate.[7] In the 1950s new generations who could not enter America chose to settle in Canada and Australia, where new immigrants were welcomed. In the jet age, nearly anyplace on the globe is accessible. Residents of Revine Lago and other Veneto towns regard those who left and their descendants as Italians abroad and welcome them to annual festivals celebrating the lost arts of haymaking in the Alps and to family reunions of Veneti from around the globe. On a research trip to the Veneto in 2013, I found that a family of Chinese immigrants had recently purchased a shop in Revine Lago, pursuing their own dream of immigrating to the Veneto.

NOTES

1. Samuel Baily, "The Village Outward Approach to the Study of Social Networks: A Case Study of the Agnonesi Diaspora Abroad, 1885–1989," *Studi emigrazione/Etudes migrations,* volume 15, (1992): 43.
2. Ibid., 44.
3. Donna R. Gabaccia, *Italy's Many Diasporas* (Seattle: University of Washington Press, 2000), 11.
4. Mark Wyman, *Round-Trip to America: The Immigrants Return to Europe, 1880–1930* (Ithaca, NY: Cornell University Press, 1993), 17.
5. Joseph Cosco, *Imagining Italians: The Clash of Romance and Race in American Perceptions, 1880–1910* (Albany, NY: SUNY Press, 2003), 8, 17.
6. See Salvatore J. LaGumina, *Wop! A Documentary History of Anti-Italian Discrimination* (Toronto: Guernica Editions, 1999).
7. This refers to the desire to leave and return, hence my use of migrate, reflected in 1950s where it was easier to travel seasonally. Recent studies of Veneti in Australia reveal a strategy to maintain residence in both places

CHAPTER 1

MOUNTAIN LIFE IN THE VENETO

Northern Italians, among the first emigrants from their home country, were forced to leave by a number of factors that shook the population and changed forever their ability to live on the land as they once had. A people who rarely strayed far beyond the sound of their town's *campanile* became sojourners and established themselves as transnational migrants, even seasonally commuting across oceans in a desperate effort to hold on to their Veneto homes. In this chapter I first explore the traditional mountain life of northeastern Italy's Veneto region and that of its people, the Veneti, in order to better understand how it was abruptly transformed as the nineteenth century drew to a close. Up to that time the fundamental way of life based on agriculture in the alpine mountainsides and valley marshlands had continued with little alteration.

The earliest evidence of human settlement in the Veneto dates to the Bronze Age. The ancient Veneti constructed *pallefitte* (hay and reed homes on stilts) along the marshy shores of lakes. At one of these sites, Revine Lago in the *prealpi* region, a Bronze Age sword and other materials have been excavated.[1] Today the spot, known as Livelet or Parco Archeological Didattico del Livelet, is an educational center that boasts reconstructions of typical housing and crafts of the ancient era. The *capanne* (huts) have been reconstructed and sit directly over the water on wooden pilings of larch, chestnut, oak, and other wood. The roofs are covered with marsh reeds, and the structures are coated with a mixture of clay, chopped hay, sand, and lime. The community may have been settled as early as the Neolithic era (4500 BC) as a farming and fishing site, based on stone flints and ceramic evidence found there.[2]

The twin lakes, Lago Santa Maria and Lago di Lago, still yield fish and waterfowl to residents, whose grapevines run down to the water's edge. Elevation at the lakes is 224 meters but rises sharply to over 1,200 meters on the hillsides above,[3] where a population of 2,244 residents (in 2011 census) live in homes built of tufa stone, raise small animals, and farm extensive gardens and hayfields. Local quarries yield stones for constructing homes and farm structures. The earliest quarrying is estimated to have begun in the Roman era, when stone was shipped down the Piave and Brenta Rivers. In most Veneto towns there have always been stonecutters skilled in shaping blocks for construction but also more sophisticated carvers who produced decorative and memorial pieces. As with other forms of labor, most of this was done by hand, and *slitta* or *mussa* sleds were used to move the blocks. Stone was excavated in small quantities and hand laid to construct one- or two-story homes with wooden porches and staircases. Even in town centers, most have a courtyard and connected buildings for hay storage and animal husbandry.

Geography is destiny. The Veneto region stretches north and west from Venice as far as Lago di Garda and borders Austria. It is washed on the south by the Po River valley and to the east by the Adriatic Sea. The Veneto is spanned by numerous rivers draining from northwest to east: the Po, the Adige, the Piave, the Brenta, the Polesine, and the Sile create a verdant flat valley ideal for cereal crops and rice fields. Eons ago the Po valley was beneath an inland sea that divided the alpine regions from Tuscany. The Po eventually developed into a river that drained from west to east into the Adriatic Sea, south of the Venetian lagoon, as the Po River delta. Early human settlers along the river valley built huts from reeds and lived on the abundant fish and waterfowl. There are unique varieties of shrimp, mussels, and eels and a vast variety of fish to be harvested from the rivers and the lagoon, as well as from the Adriatic. Venetians still farm and harvest fish within the lagoon itself, and the islands surrounding Venice provide flat, marshy lands suitable for crops.

Farther inland, many Veneto cities were established where rivers created natural moats for urban settlements; inhabitants constructed defensive stone and brick walls to further protect themselves. The city of Verona is an excellent example of the defensive river-and-city-wall construction: the historic center was built within a deep curve of the Adige River, which surrounds Verona on three sides. The city has two layers of defensive walls that offered protection as the city expanded outward. Even today access to Verona exists only through its gates. Stone and brick walls line the surrounding hilltops as a first line of defense, much like Hadrian's Wall or the Great Wall of China. A second line of defense protects the center: the historic castle of the ruling Scaglieri family, known as the Castelvecchio (old castle), guards the city's western flank on the far side of the Adige, a broad defensive bridge spanning the river. Farther to the east, large urban centers like Treviso and Padova (Padua) were built where the oldest settlements could be moated by rivers (in the case of Treviso, these were diverted into manmade moats that surrounded their historic centers) and supplemented by protective gates and walls.

The Dolomite Mountains rise sharply to form the Veneto's northern border with Austria, and below the central region, the *prealpi*, of the Veneto lies the locus for raising hay and animals, as well as for growing cereal and vegetable crops. Alpine slopes rise sharply from verdant valleys. Life in the central Veneto is different—and distant—from the flat plains of the lower Veneto, where the urban centers of Verona, Treviso, Padova, and Rovigo developed along the river valleys. These cities, surrounded by their ancient walls and moated by the rivers, were trading centers, and their fields were irrigated to produce vegetable crops.

Rovigo, situated on the flattest part of the plain, draws irrigation water from the Polesine River and is crisscrossed with canals that water its crops. With river branches passing to its north and south, in ancient times the people of Rovigo dug north-south canals on both sides of the city, thus creating a defensive box of water around the city while ensuring that its flat fields could easily be irrigated.

Venice, the largest city of the Veneto, was established on marshy islands more than two miles from shore to isolate its population following the Lombard invasion of 568 A.D.[4] Venetians developed defenses along the openings to their lagoon and at Chioggia; they also established the Arsenale, a shipbuilding center whose highly skilled teams of workers could produce a warship in a single day. Fleets of merchant trading ships plied the eastern Mediterranean beginning in the thirteenth century and brought wealth to the city. Venice's sea empire fostered a land empire as the city dominated the region, establishing the Veneto as its heart.

The urban complex of Venice, or Venezia, developed an early economic reliance on trade and even tourism. Its more remote lagoon islands provided (and still provide) arable land for grapevines and vegetable crops; even today the produce is transported to Rialto and other city markets. Residents of fishing villages like Chioggia, as well as of the islands of Murano and Burano, harvested the riches of the Adriatic and the Venetian lagoon to provide sustenance, selling the excess inland. By the twentieth century, industrial investments had made the port of Marghera into a coastal maritime and industrial center, along with neighboring Mestre. The contemporary maritime economy of Venice remains unique: an awkward blend of tourism, fed by the arrival of large cruise ships, and Marghera's rampant industrialism as a central port for petrochemicals and shipbuilding.

Within the Veneto region there has always been a historic pride in and identification with the ancient Venetian Republic, a citystate that once dominated the eastern Mediterranean. But the Venetian Republic's maritime trade withered as new competitors took over the spice and silk trade with Asia, and its land empire was first crushed by Napoleon's armies in 1797 and then subsumed into the Austrian Empire. Austria's military controlled the Veneto, exerting its power across northern Italy, between 1814 and 1870. The wars of the Risorgimento liberated the Veneto from foreign control and unified Italy, but conflict with Austria would remain a persistent threat to the region into the twentieth century.

Life in the Veneto's mountains begins with the ringing of church bells in the *campanile*. The bells ring from morning to evening today as they have for hundreds of years. The Veneti have long lived and worked within the small scope of their *paese*, building their homes of local tufa stone and wood; women have labored in the *cortile* (farmyard); sons and daughters have worked on the farms and settled in the same *paese* as their ancestors. Animals would be taken to pastures, drinking water hauled from courtyard wells or streams; work was done in hayfields, and the *orto* (vegetable garden) was tended.

The dialect the people have long spoken[5] here is broadly described as *Veneziano* (Venetian), a language whose many loanwords reflect Venice's lost maritime empire, but in the mountains and valleys of the Veneto, localized subdialects grew more distinct. The isolation created by the Veneto's mountainous topography bred linguistic differences. There are notable divergences between the dialects spoken even in neighboring towns like Belluno and Revine.[6] On either side of the Polesine River near Rovigo, two distinct dialects are spoken that are so different they have been codified in separate dictionaries. There are even greater differences between dialects of the Veneto and modern Italian (drawn from the Tuscan dialect). Mountain dialects often lack the vowel suffixes of Italian, doubled letters are often represented as single with significant differences in accent, and the letter *k* is quite common in dialect, whereas it is absent in modern Italian. *G* sounds are often converted to *z* sounds. Both words and names are shortened; more have consonant rather than vowel endings.[7]

The life of *contadini* (farmers; sg. *contadino*) in the Veneto was attuned to the seasonal rhythms of agriculture. Contadini rose early to tend animals. Chickens and roosters made noise throughout the day from nearly every courtyard. Men worked in the fields. They traditionally wore simple clothing for daily work: pants, shirt, and waistcoat, heavy nailed boots, rough hand-knit woolen socks, and a broad-brimmed straw hat for working on the sunny and often cold mountainsides. Women not only managed the household but also tended the animals in the courtyard, in addition to producing yarn, wool, and silk thread for home use. They wore blouses with knit scarves, long skirts protected by aprons, and they covered their hair with kerchiefs. They wore soft slippers in the house and heavy sabots, or leather shoes, to work in the fields.[8] The family was dominated by the oldest male, but gender divisions in the world of labor were, according to a study of rural Veneto life by Alessandro Baldan, less obvious. Baldan found that men generally considered women inferior only in physical strength. Men usually did the field work on the mountainsides, and women raised animals and processed all the foodstuffs while managing the farmhouse, along with its gardens and vineyards.[9]

Economic and personal hardships, especially the loss of a spouse, could blur those gender divisions. When men and youths began to emigrate, whether seasonally or for longer periods, women took over the management of fields and farms in hopes of a reunion. Veneto women were, and remain, resilient individuals who have managed farms and small shops alone. But the sharpest social divisions arose between those who owned land and those who labored for others. The *padrone*—in the Veneto, the term padrone in this era signified a field boss or estate manager rather than a labor recruiter from America, its primary meaning in southern Italy—emerged as a hated figure as economic development in the late nineteenth century drove the consolidation of smaller holdings into larger estates. The result was a drastic reduction in independent farming as landowner-farmers were forced from their own lands into seasonal day labor. A Venetian phrase, *la mosca e il ragno* (the fly and the spider), vividly illustrates the relationship between day laborers and the landlords and padrone: the contadino is the fly, and the padrone is the spider that eats the fly when it falls into the web. A local proverb illustrates the lack of sympathy for the economic suffering of the impoverished: *The one who feasts does not believe in hunger.*[10] Other proverbs reflect the disdain of the padrone for the contadino: *Neither a dog nor a contadino ever closes the door. The contadino is wide in the mouth and tight in the fist. The contadino, like a dog hit with a stick, licks the hand.* The contadino's opposing view across the social divide was similarly blunt: *Better low and sensible than high and stupid.*[11]

With little money to afford manufactured products and little industrial production in the mountains, self-sufficiency was key to survival for the contadino. Clothing, hats, shoes, and boots were all made at home. Women spun, knit, and sewed for the family, and men did carpentry, cut stone for building construction, and produced any equipment needed for agriculture. Both men and women could weave baskets, carve wooden implements, and make the lightweight sleds and baskets needed for moving hay and produce. Veneto ethnologists Giuseppe Grava and Giuseppe Tomasi have carefully recorded and illustrated the material culture, agricultural methods, and the dialect of the central Veneto in number of books, including *Dizionario del dialetto di Revine, Revine: Storia di una comunitá, La fienagione nelle prealpi venete,* and *Topografica antica.* The dictionary constitutes much more than a list of terms, for Grava and Tomas's research defines and explains the dialect names for farm implements, kitchen tools, clothing, and other elements of material culture. As a whole, their research documents the ethnology and anthropology of the area, including farming tools and techniques, food production, and hunting practices, all of which are illustrated with line drawings by Grava detailing every aspect of contadino life. In addition, their works compare the dialect differences in the nomenclature for these tools and the differences in their construction across the central Veneto.[12]

The people of the Veneto lived surrounded in their home *paese* by people they knew. Large cities were often dominated by the *signori* (lords) of a single clan, like the Scaglieri of Verona and the dogal families of Venice, but the leadership of long-resident families was also a social and political factor in smaller Veneto towns. A town might be dominated by four or five extended family clans. Until the 1870s, most Veneti lived in an area where their families had worked the land for generations and where the traditional *signori* and their land-owning families also had a long history. The historic linkage between family and place remained until it was disrupted by migration. Ancestral names often extend back into a village's earliest written records; landholdings were mapped as early as the fourteenth and fifteenth centuries, and church and tax lists attest numerous generations. The origin of some family names can be traced to a single town.

A town might have four or five men with identical first and last names born in the same generation. A handful of these families usually constituted a substantial portion of the population at the end of the nineteenth century. Family groups often have a *soprannome* (nickname), an additional name that identifies their clan. In one Veneto town there were 168 families but only forty different family names. With twelve families of Carlet, twenty-five of Carpene, twenty-three of De Noni, and so on, it was natural for the more closely related to take a distinctive *soprannome*. In another town the Gandin family was subdivided into the Cet, Iovanin, and Roc clans. Among the Grava of Revine[13] were seven Antonios divided by *soprannome* into the Grando, Pupol, Soldado, Carli, Scarset, and Testa clans. A person's name and *soprannome* followed him or her from birth and might even appear on a war memorial identifying the fallen or be incised on a gravestone.[14] Church records reflect these family names in their lists of parishioners, and the same names were carved on pews marking donations to the church and on memorial plaques.

Local churches honored patron saints; artists and stone carvers decorated these edifices, and the best of these worked in Venice as well. The calendar was divided by saints' days and the celebrations linked to them. Loyalty to patron saints was strong among the Veneti, especially for Saint Mark, honored at the Basilica San Marco in Venice, and for Saint Anthony, interred in the Basilica di San Antonio in Padova. Reverence for these saints remains very powerful throughout the Veneto even today. In Padova the June pilgrimage in honor of Saint Anthony can draw thirty-five thousand people per day, and residents of an entire town may travel together to the basilica for their pilgrimage. Venice's Basilica San Marco was a powerful destination for the faithful as pilgrims arrived to pray and to view Saint Mark's relics.

Carnevale, marking the last days the faithful may eat meat before Lent, became a reason to celebrate by feasting and wearing masks and capes, like the traditional Venetian *bauta*. The masquerade served to release class tensions, for masks allowed Venetians and the people of the Veneto to temporarily cross social divides; for a brief respite the masquerade erased class distinctions. The privations of Lent also leveled the eating habits of the rich with those of the contadini, who could not afford meat for most of the year. During the Austrian occupation of the Veneto (1815–1870),[15] Carnevale was suppressed owing to fears about its power to unify the Venetians in a nationalist revolt. Historian Alessandro Baldan observed that the Austrians were always fearful of popular assemblies, and as a result the celebration of Carnevale was stifled by the occupying Austrian military.[16]

Religious holidays like Saint Martin's Day, November 11, marked the end of the agricultural season and allowed farm laborers to take a break from the hard routine of farm work as the agricultural season drew to a close and labor contracts expired or were renewed.[17] La Canderola (Candlemas) in February marked the changing season and a break in the hardships of winter. Spring's Pasqua (Easter) was celebrated with religious observances, special cakes like *fugassa*, and children's rhymes. These events also gave women a reason to serve the richest meals they could manage and to prepare special holiday treats—cookies shaped like

Saint Martin on his horse or ribbon-like fried cookies (*galani* or *crustelli*) at Easter, Christmas, and other family celebrations. Such festivities were eagerly anticipated because they were among the few times during the year when meat was served in any substantial quantity.

The food culture of the mountains centered on polenta, ground corn meal cooked with water or milk until thick. Originally, the term *polenta* identified any boiled grain preparation, but it became exclusively linked to ground corn, whether yellow or white, boiled with water and salt, in the 1600s. Elsewhere in Italy polenta is cooked and served soft, but in the Veneto it is usually boiled in a copper *paio* for nearly an hour; then the pot is sharply turned onto a wooden *panaro* (board). Striking the pot's rim on the board separates the stiff mixture from the sides of the pot and drops a round, firm mass onto the board that is then cut into slices using a piece of string drawn from the bottom of the cake upward. It is best served hot, or it can be cooled and then reheated with a little butter or olive oil.

Ground corn first arrived in the Veneto around 1600, and its original name, *granturco*, derived from the first supplies, which arrived from Turkey. Because polenta was inexpensive to make and filling, it quickly was accepted by contadini, who found any number of uses for it at every meal from breakfast through dinner. Contadini began planting their own corn and cultivated strains that were better suited to the region. In 1890 Marano corn was developed, which yielded not one but two harvests in the Veneto. But repeated planting of a single crop depletes the soil of nutrients, and overdependence on polenta in the diet causes malnutrition and leads to the deadly disease of niacin deficiency, pellagra. Moreover, polenta must be carefully stored in a cool, dry place because dampness can cause poisonous toxins to develop in moist ground corn that will harm anyone desperate enough to cook with the spoiled grain. Roman Pascutto worked in the fields as a young boy in the 1910s and recalled the mixed blessing of a food that seemed to nourish even as it demanded hard labor and led to disease: "I don't know whether I should praise you like the soft rain in May when it brings out your buds or curse you like the drought in July ... broken backs, bare feet and hungry days ... with millions of kernels, it was pellagra."[18]

Local varieties of farm cheese were most often the accompaniment to polenta, especially the farmer's home production. In the central Veneto a soft, light-colored *skiz*, a specialty of Belluno, is melted on polenta. Cheese, primarily soft varieties that were not aged, was often produced daily in the home. Contadini typically ate polenta for breakfast with a little milk, and polenta again with beans or field greens at noon. In good times polenta might be supplemented with a few slices of dried sausage or a handful of mushrooms gathered from the woods. Mushroom hunting added flavor to the table at no cost, but the lore of identifying the safe, nontoxic fungi was regarded as a life skill. In hard times the poor ate plain polenta boiled in salted water at every meal. Coffee was rare, but a coffee-like drink was produced by roasting grain.

The contadini of the Veneto survived by growing and preserving a variety of agricultural crops on the mountainsides and in the valleys: cereals, maize, and subsistence foods like fava and lamon beans, as well as potatoes. Vines and fruit and nut trees provided substantial foodstuffs that were preserved to last through the winter. Orchards were extensively planted and yielded harvests of chestnuts, walnuts, apricots, and cherries. Chestnuts in particular provided sustenance and were roasted, boiled, or dried and even ground for use as flour. When flour was available, whether from wheat or other grains, bread would be made and stale bits later boiled to make a soup called *panada*.

Hay had an important economic value both as a cash crop in the market and as fodder for farm animals. Men cut hay on the steep mountainsides of the *prealpi* and brought it down to market on *slitta*. Women gathered wood to sell in the markets and to use in their home fireplaces. They raised small animals, especially chickens, turkeys, and rabbits, to supplement the family diet as well as to sell at the market. In lean times the supplies might not be enough to carry the farm family through the entire winter.

Even when food was stored away, an overreliance on a few foods could lead to malnutrition. In times of bad harvests or when diseases struck animals or plants, starvation was possible. But with a good harvest life held promise; a Veneto proverb defined a good year this way: *Fresh polenta and shore birds, wine in the cellar, and happy people.*[19]

The most basic foods were beans, dried or fresh, called *fagioli* (usually fava or borlotti/lamon beans). They were especially valued because they were inexpensive to grow and easy to dry and store. Carrots, onions, potatoes, radicchio, and other cold-tolerant vegetables were common for the same reason. Above all, beans were the survival food for the long winter; supplies of dried beans were either boiled in water for soup or served with polenta. *Signori* derisively referred to the poor who had nothing but dried beans to eat as *mangia fagioli* (beaneaters).[20]

Grapes were served on the table, often with cheese, but were mainly used to produce wine in the land of prosecco and soave. Wines were barreled for use throughout the year and in hard times diluted with water. Traditionally, after landlords had taken their portion of the harvest from the winepress, the remainder was left to the poor contadini, who soaked and distilled the pomace into an extraordinarily powerful, clear, brandy-like spirit called grappa. Production of this powerful drink has been traced back to 1200 in the Veneto; it was the favorite beverage of old men, who often drank a short glass of grappa in winter before going out to the fields or topped off an espresso with a splash of the stuff during a card game. Women favored grappa as a flavoring in holiday cookies like *crustelli*. In the Veneto, where medical care was nearly nonexistent, a shot of grappa was the prescription for a fever, and according to food historian Amedeo Sandri, it served as "a primitive anesthesia for children losing their first teeth."[21] Bassano del Grappa, the liquor's namesake town, is proud host to a museum filled with distilling equipment, and rows of plain bottles, some with handmade labels, line the shelves of Venetian bars. Grappa and prosecco, the Veneto's version of champagne, were produced for sale; urban wine shops in Venice found a steady market for both.[22]

In spring, rice cooked with fresh peas called *risibisi* (lit., "rice-peas") was a special treat and was often the first green vegetable, along with asparagus, to be consumed after a long, hungry winter. Access to fresh vegetables for proper nutrition lasted only as long as the growing season because fresh vegetables were not imported to the mountains. Contadini could rely only upon whatever foods they could raise themselves or harvest from the wild. Gathered *radici* (roots), most often dandelions, comprised a vital source of nutrition. Bitter greens gathered from hillsides were eaten from spring until winter's frost. Men and women still take pride in striding through the fields to pull up wild bitter greens that provide extra nutrients for their diet. During the decades when malnutrition stalked the Veneto, *radici* were especially valued for providing iron and other vitamins and minerals. As with hunting, knowledge of what was edible was passed from one generation to another.

Throughout the Veneto, contadini raised radicchio, a bright-red striped form of chicory that has been selectively bred into a green lettuce-like plant that turns a vivid magenta in the cold of December. In the seven provinces of the Veneto region one encounters very different breeds of radicchio and varied methods of preserving them after the crops have been harvested. Farmers roasted them with some olive oil over a fire or *ai ferri* (on the irons) to turn their bitter flavor mild. Even today, the people of the Veneto take pride in their local varieties of *radicchio*, which vary from tall, swirled, vase-like red leaves to plump rounded orbs dappled with red and tan. Treviso, Chioggia, and Rovigo all have very different types of radicchio. Like dialects, these regional variations remain a source of pride as Veneto farmers promote the "Strada del Radicchio," which runs from Treviso to Castelfranco, and hold celebrations of the harvest.[23]

Meat rarely supplemented the diet, and even on those occasions it was eaten in very small amounts—often wildfowl or small animals captured by hunters. Women raised and harvested the animals of the courtyard: rabbits, chickens, and turkeys. Rabbit was especially favored because the animals were quickly and easily raised within three months and produced meat and fur. Chickens could provide eggs that were bartered for other foods, including meat. Wild boar could be shot, and hunting them had the advantage of removing an animal that destroyed crops and raided gardens; in addition, its meat could be converted to dried sausage that lasted all winter.

The fortunate contadini fattened a pig and slaughtered it in fall, yielding a bounty of salami and prosciutto to carry the family through the long winter. Domesticated pigs could be fattened cheaply on wild acorns and then in autumn could be slaughtered for sausage and salami. The Venetian dialect term *norcino* identifies the man who arrived in fall to slaughter and hang the pig. One large pig could provide an enormous variety of products: dried sausages, salami, soppressata, pancetta cotechino, even lard and the blood were processed for consumption. Nothing was discarded as the entire family worked to process the meat. The people of the Veneto describe a long, difficult task as "taking more days than sausage."[24]

Storage of all of these products was the most important task. Late in the year, usually in December, radicchio was cut and preserved, along with the last carrots and other root vegetables, under sand in cellars. Grapes were grown on tall, horizontal wooden supports to produce the maximum yield and then harvested to be pressed into wine and grappa that would fill casks or bottles. Beans were hung to dry on tall, ladderlike outdoor racks called *arfa* and were then cellared for winter use. Rice, once produced only in the northwest valleys around Milan, was eventually also raised in the lower plains of the Veneto around Rovigo and was highly valued as the key ingredient in risotto, the symbol of Venetian cuisine but a rare treat on a contadino's table.

Hay was cut and dried in conical stacks called *meta* on mountainsides and then brought down on *slitta* to stables; the excess was sold at the market. In 1903 Alexander Robertson, a British hiker exploring the Dolomites, recorded that north of Belluno in Macchietto, the mountainsides were so steep that farmers strung wire across gorges and spanned rivers to transport the hay to markets: "Big bundles of hay, swung to the wire by hooks, were making a swift aerial voyage across the chasm. Sometimes, when the hay harvest is over, the more daring of the workers get into a basket and come down as their hay does."[25]

Harnesses for oxen, wagons, and tools were painstakingly carved and assembled by hand and carefully repaired. *Kop* (clay roof tiles) were formed in molds to cover roofs over the long winter. Women tended silkworms in warmer regions' valleys to supply the silk mills around Milan. In the alpine areas, sheep yielded wool to be harvested in January and August; it was then processed by women into yarn for knitting heavy work socks, mittens, scarves, and helmet-like head coverings for cold winters.

Hunting on the hillsides for wild game and fishing in the rivers and lakes supplemented the diet. The marsh-ringed lakes yielded ducks and other shore birds. Fish could be harvested in the rivers weaving through the Veneto; especially popular were the eels of the Po delta. Eel was considered a delicacy and served grilled or stewed year round, but it was always served at Christmas. Venice's lagoon yielded a variety of seafood, including fish, squid, numerous forms of shrimp, octopus, and sepia (a squid-like cephalopod whose ink sacks were harvested to produce sepia ink for newspaper printing and early movie-film dyes). Dried cod was sold in Venice, salted white, to be stored all winter then soaked in water and boiled to yield cheap protein. Today *baccalà* remains a traditional Christmas and Lenten dish because it is an inexpensive food that can be stored for a long time. Farm families could survive winters only by rationing small amounts of dried *baccalà*, beans, and other foodstuffs until the next year's harvest.

Farther south, in Verona's valley of the Adige River, the people ate a completely different diet; flour and eggs were used for gnocchi, and polenta was traditionally served with *pastissada* (stewed horsemeat). Pasta in rural areas was rarely purchased dry but rather was made with whatever form of flour was available. *Bigoli*, thick strands extruded from a press called a *torcio*, was made from coarse whole-wheat flour and eggs, if available. Most often *bigoli* was served with dried anchovies or, if the hunter was fortunate, bits of ground duck.

The lore of hunting, fishing, and gathering food for the table was a source of pride. The tradition of hunting for small birds, as portrayed by Papageno in Mozart's opera *The Magic Flute*, was practiced by contadini throughout the region. The *archet*, a light, handmade wooden trap, springs when a bird lands on its small horizontal stick. In Revine Lago the *arte da ośelàr* (art of bird hunting) includes devising elaborate traps using a *zevita* (decoy). Other traps comprised large walls of lightweight netting. The small birds were usually roasted and served with the ubiquitous polenta. A typical serving of *polenta e osei* (polenta with birds) required sixteen small songbirds.[26]

Scholar Sergio dalla Bernadina found that the Bellunese held a distinctive hunting ethos and passed their lore and traditions down through the generations, including their knowledge of bird communication. He discovered an 1856 Belluno manuscript that recorded "the harmonic language" of birds and described its influence on the Bellunese dialect. In Revine, hunters not only could mimic the birds but also hollowed out walnut shells to form whistles to call them. But there were conflicts between the way urban Italians viewed bird hunting, especially the killing of songbirds, and the cultural traditions of contadini. The Italian government banned bird killing in 1876. But despite these efforts, hunting small birds continued in the Veneto as a source of food rather than sport.[27]

In the 1870s concerns about malnutrition led Italy's new national government to an investigation of the contadini's meat consumption. Investigators in the Veneto found that farm workers had very little protein in their diet. The highest levels of consumption were found in Pieve di Cadore (.02564 kg daily per person) and in Belluno (.01310 kg daily), and the lowest were recorded in Feltre (.00439 kg daily). Thus, the highest meat consumption, in Pieve, averaged 9.35 kilograms per year, or 20 pounds, whereas in Belluno this was halved to 10.5 pounds per year, and in Feltre

3.52 pounds per year. Averaged out, the people of Feltre ate little more than an ounce of meat per week. The fundamental poverty of the Veneto contadini was starkly evident when compared with America's and even Italy's average national consumption. The United States Department of Agriculture calculated that American meat consumption in 1885 was 150 pounds per year; Italian national consumption averaged 18 pounds per year.[28] Worse yet, in subsequent decades as the farm economy collapsed, the contadini relied even more heavily on polenta as the staple food in the *cucina di povera* (food of poverty).

Along with the grain, dried fava beans could be stored over the winter when little else was available. One scholar has termed their cultivation "a dietary basic." From Feltre to Belluno, fava beans were ground to make bread and were even cooked with milk to wean calves in the barnyard. A sixteenth-century dialect proverb states that if one has fava beans, one does not need anything else. In Feltre the proverb "the one who has beans does not go hungry" emphasized their vital importance on the Veneto farmer's table. But impoverished and desperate contadini were forced to rely so heavily on them by the 1890s that malnutrition (especially niacin deficiency) and the resulting pellagra became endemic in the Veneto, bearing tragic human consequences.[29]

The economic development and political challenges that came with Italian unification, especially the integration of the Veneto into the new Italian republic in 1870, set off rapid changes that transformed the agricultural economy and threatened the ability of contadini to survive. Dramatic shifts in land ownership and investment created large lowland farms at the same time that imports of cheap American grains threatened the Veneto's traditional agricultural economy.

Plans were made in 1865 for an alpine railway linking Treviso and the northern towns of Conegliano, Ceneda and Serravalle (later merged as Vittorio Veneto), Revine, and Belluno. This promised to open up new markets, and the farmers in these areas, long isolated, hoped that better transportation would improve the quality of life. But the technical challenges of laying track along the steep mountainsides and bridging the valleys created unsolvable technical problems that slowed the expansion of transport systems into the most isolated areas, delaying their connection with the major cities of the Veneto. The original plan showed a straight northern line up the steep valley from Treviso to Conegliano and up to Vittorio Veneto, from which it took a sharp westward bend to reach Revine. To leave Revine, the track would have had to be laid in a sharp reverse-hairpin bend and then up a tight northward curve, to continue up the valley toward Belluno and Cortina d'Ampezzo. Ultimately, the railway was built but in a straight line from Treviso to Belluno. Revine and Lago (then two separate towns), as well as nearby Santa Maria and Tarzo, remained isolated. Even today, only regional buses serve the area. Similar technical challenges to extending electric lines up the steep mountainsides slowed the arrival of power lines until the 1920s—long after nearby Vittorio Veneto had been connected to the grid.[30]

Further, the steep mountain region of the central Veneto lies along a geologic fault line, making the area prone to earthquakes. In 1873 a devastating quake struck Belluno and destroyed more than half of the city, leaving forty people dead. Alexander Robertson, exploring the region in 1903, wrote that Belluno remained an agricultural center. Its Saturday marketplace was "a fair full of gaiety and picturesqueness" that featured livestock and foodstuffs. Farmers sold "butter cheese, eggs and fowls ... melons, peaches, apples, pears, nuts, garlic and vegetables of all sorts. Booths are erected in long rows for the disposal of scythes, sickles, knives, scissors, grinding-stones, barrels that the peasants use ... [while] a merry fellow standing in a little field of water-melons, is engaged busily disposing of them 'cinque schei la gondola'" (five coins per slice).[31]

As Robertson traveled farther north, he described fields of "tall green maize, interspersed with plots of barley and potatoes, and fields of grass ... men were busy cutting the hay, while women and girls, all looking bright and cheerful, with their colored dresses, white sleeves and gay handkerchiefs on their heads, were singing as they tossed up the mown grass." He observed heavy wagons loaded with logs headed for Belluno's rail station and noted that women hiked home with *gerla* (woven wooden backpacks) to carry produce from the fields.[32]

Thus, even in the twentieth century, throughout rural Veneto people continued to live and work as they always had. They quarried their own stone for houses, made their own farms tools, sleds, and even wagons in isolation. Farm equipment, work sleds, woven baskets, and tools of the area are often distinct from designs used elsewhere in the Veneto. As already mentioned, ethnologists Giovanni Tomasi and Giuseppe Grava have meticulously documented everyday life and material implements, as well as the linguistic distinctions strengthened by isolation, that characterized the area. These distinctions were also recorded in a comprehensive survey of the way of life and the dialect of the Veneto contadini conducted by Swiss linguist Paul Scheuermeier between 1921 and 1932. His work was an effort to record and preserve the last vestiges of the traditional ways, for emigration and economic development had already changed the region and its people forever. The northern Veneto was the focus of Scheuermeier's research, and his field notes and photographs provide an expansive and highly detailed town-by-town examination of life in the Veneto.

Scheuermeier's decade of field work as a graduate student served his mentors' creation of a linguistic atlas of the region and its peoples, but after its publication his original field notes were long forgotten in the University of Bern archives. Recently, these notes on the dialects of the region were deciphered and translated from German into Italian to be published along with photographs documenting the way of life and material culture of the Veneto's contadini.[33] The focus of his work was "words and things," the linguistic and ethnographic distinctions that defined the people's material culture, but as Scheuermeier's study progressed, his desire to document the contadini's life in photographs came to dominate his work—much to the dismay of his advisers.

Scheuermeier's research followed a specific pattern: he arrived in a community, selected one informant to be interviewed in detail with a questionnaire covering two hundred points. He not only recorded the informant's responses but also made notes of specific dialectic differences in the informant's responses using a linguist's phonetic code. He took photographs documenting farming techniques, tools, the use of animals, household equipment, farmhouse construction, kitchens, and work areas. He was particularly interested in documenting things that he found curious or unique, especially techniques of cultivation, creating objects, weaving, spinning, artisanal work, and so forth. His focus on photography distressed his mentors, who wanted the linguistic material secured for their own work on dialects and were less interested in Scheuermeier's obsession with visually documenting the last remnants of Veneto farm life.

The individuals Scheuermeier chose as informants had to have a good command of language in order for him to define the regional distinctions in the Venetian dialect. He summarized his "ideal informant" as someone who "makes a good impression, [is] intelligent … knows the plants and birds and summarizes things in a few words."[34] He interviewed people from all occupations: most often farmers but also a village priest and a hotelier. His normal questionnaire contained about two thousand words and dialect forms, with subdivisions on different objects, forms of labor, and the local methods of producing cheese, farming, and preserving vegetable crops. He tried to avoid large cities and politics, rejecting a visit to Piovene because he saw it as "an industrial center and headquarters of the Vicenza communists." He also avoided urban areas because his task was to record the genuine dialect that, in his words, was "not bastardized by the italianized venetian."[35]

The era in which Scheuermeier worked was marked by political and labor conflict and by the bitterness that arose in the aftermath of the Great War. Scheuermeier's visits began only a few years after the Veneto had fallen under Austro-Hungarian military occupation during World War I, which kept more than eight hundred thousand civilians in extreme deprivation and forced another five hundred thousand to become refugees. Those who remained suffered first the requisition then the pillaging of their livestock, farm produce, hay, wine, and even clothing. According to Homer Folkes's 1920 report for the Red Cross, in 1918 the Austrian military resorted to forced requisitions of bedding and finally even window glass for shipment back with the retreating troops. Perhaps as many as two hundred thousand homes in the central Veneto were left open to the winter winds in November of 1918. Folkes reported that women and children were emaciated, and when he questioned them, they told him that the Austrians had prevented them from harvesting even *radici*.[36]

In the central Veneto an estimated 10,000 civilians starved to death, and another 12,500 died from lack of medical care during the Austrian occupation of the Veneto (1917–1918). In Revine Lago forty-seven soldiers died, and the impact on civilians was even greater. Beyond the loss of soldiers' lives, an additional 115 civilians died from starvation in those two years. A nun in Revine Lago, Sister Elena, recorded in her diary that the church was confiscated and converted into a stable for the Austrian cavalry, and the school was taken over for use by the military as she watched parishioners starve.[37] Neighboring Ceneda and Serravalle constituted the site of the last battle of the Great War on Italian soil. The towns were unified and renamed Vittorio Veneto in honor of their role in forcing the Austrian armistice in November 1918. The Great War brought famine to a people whose existence had been based on the autonomous production of food.

Scheuermeier arrived as the Veneto was burning with political and economic turmoil. In April 1921 in Fratta Polesine he lamented "the red hot political climate."[38] His dialect informant failed to mention that he was the head of the local socialists and was allied with Giacomo Matteotti, an Italian senator and socialist from Rovigo, later murdered on Mussolini's orders. The informant also omitted that he had personally led a clash against the local *fascisti*.[39] After the interview was finished, Scheuermeier was rounded up for questioning by the carabinieri. They were curious about his research project and his Swiss origins and suspected that he might have secretly carried messages from Swiss socialists to the Veneto socialists. The experience left the researcher permanently on his guard. In January 1922 Scheuermeier mailed to his professor Jakob Jud a postcard portrait of an intense Mussolini, referring to him as "this fanatic" and writing, "Look at those eyes!"[40]

Many of Scheuermeier's informants told him that hardships had forced them to migrate, but they had struggled to return to their native Veneto. One explained how he had been trapped in Germany when the war began and struggled to return to Italy. Another detailed his repeated migrations to labor one year in Belgium then three years in Argentina, in addition to performing Italian military service in Piemonte—all before the age of twenty-five. He then professed his determination to remain in his home *paese* for the rest of his days. Another explained that he had spent seven years in America, four in Argentina, and three in Brazil but repeatedly returned home as one of the *uccelli di passaggio*, or migrant workers, until he could establish himself as a wine merchant.[41] Others recalled their migratory travels within Europe; many had worked in Germany and Austria prior to the war.

Scheuermeier viewed the conditions that forced such repeated migration as having a deleterious impact on these communities. He found that in some places all the men had emigrated at a single time and that "profound signs of abandonment" were evident in the Veneto's fields.[42] He observed the tenacity of the women to remain in their homes, preserving the traditions. He wrote that it was "above all the attachment of women to their *paese*" that had preserved the finer points of the local dialects.[43]

Scheuermeier's photographs are as important as his field notes in describing life in the Veneto. One image, taken in Belluno in the fall of 1921, shows the wood market in Piazza Santo Stefano. Contadini women had brought firewood down from the hillsides, and in the photo they stand beside their *slitta* on wheels, which are loaded down with piles of cut branches. Scheuermeier recorded the distance they traveled to gather the wood and that hay was loaded on the *slitta* and then taken down the mountainside. Having reached the road, the women put a set of wheels under the *slitta* and rolled their heavy loads to the market. The researcher's photographs document the techniques of viniculture and farming, including the methods of erecting *pai de frasca* (wood-and-wire frames) to support grapevines.

But earning the trust of poor farmers was not easy for a wealthy Swiss graduate student. He struggled to record an interview with one contadini whom he dubbed "the patriarch of the cowshed." The man, dressed in a waistcoat and a wool beret, sat on a stool milking cows surrounded by his children, who constantly interrupted Scheuermeier's work.[44] In Tarzo, a small village across the lakes from Revine Lago, Scheuermeier's frustration boiled over. His chosen informant, the village priest, was preoccupied with the consecration of a new church and had passed him off to a contadino. Although assured the farmer was "more intelligent than the others," the interview was a disaster, and Scheuermeier could not even get him to understand, much less complete, his questionnaire. The informant was unable to vocalize the distinctions in dialect and was apparently unaware of the differences between some common words. In a letter to his supervisors, Scheuermeier revealed not only his irritation with the rural farmers but something of his methods. He seemed unsympathetic to the recalcitrance of the farmer distracted from his work and pressed him to answer his long list of two hundred questions. The Tarzo contadino was not unworldly, describing his seasonal migrations to Switzerland and Germany for summer work, how he had been stranded in Germany at the start of the war, and "from then on never went far from his *paese*." The informant carved wooden sabots, or clogs, and spent his spare time hunting, claiming knowledge of the entire Veneto. In the end frustration got the better of Scheuermeier, who wrote to his university mentors, "It is useless to ask one who, different from the rough and stupid contadini, is able to speak better ... and to think he was recommended because he was more intelligent than the others." This crisis threatened to derail the research project, and Professor Jud arrived from Switzerland to personally advise Scheuermeier as he began again, moving up the valley into Belluno. The failed interview reveals hidden tensions between the urban Swiss and the Veneto farmers. To help defuse the problems, he shed his modern clothing and adopted a more traditional local costume that allowed him to, at least in dress, fit in with his Veneto informants.[45]

Scheuermeier turned increasingly to photography to document his interviews, concentrating on farm techniques, for he was especially interested in the methods of drying and preserving food—particularly fava beans (using *arfa*). As noted earlier, as the farm economy grew less profitable, overreliance on beans and polenta—sometimes polenta alone —fostered malnutrition. Pellagra creates permanent damage in children: it delays mental development, stunts growth, and eventually kills. It had been endemic in the region decades before Scheuermeier arrived, and it continued to take a human toll. Even though the Italian government and regional officials knew of its lethal effect and struggled to find a solution, the diet of poorly paid farm laborers and their children remained extremely limited, and pellagra continued to kill them. The prevalence of economic hardship and hunger had for decades been the key factor driving migration from the Veneto.

The least expensive and most traditional means of adding meat protein to the diet was hunting small animals—particularly birds, as discussed earlier. In Albisano, near Verona, Scheuermeier photographed a bird hunter's elaborate but illegal trap, used to capture *uccellini* (small song-birds). Hunting may have been outlawed a half century earlier, but its vestiges remained a key survival strategy for those contadini who strug-gled to put more than fava beans on the table alongside their polenta.[46]

The farm houses of the poor were strikingly similar to the ancient *pallafitte* of Livelet. Scheuermeier photographed not only stone but also thatch farmhouses (*cassone*). Typical farm housing in the early twentieth century consisted of a stone-and-mud base with a heavy wooden reinforcement and a roof thickly thatched with reeds. Outbuildings of similar construction housed animals. In small towns homes might be constructed of stone with mortar and have small wooden stairways and porches attached. Even in towns, adjacent outbuildings were used for raising small animals, as well as for hay and food storage.

But the housing of the poorest farmers was more often made of gathered sticks and reeds supplemented with mud, as the ancient Bronze Age constructions in the valleys of the Veneto were. Scheuermeier's photographs attest the persistence of the reed construction that the poor continually reverted to as a survival strategy to provide the rudest shelter. Historian Alessandro Baldan found that throughout the Veneto, the rural poor continued to use sticks, reeds, and mud to build these *cassone* without consulting health officials for permission to build or inhabit them.[47] Thus, over millennia the reed structure provided an inexpensive shelter but one that came at a heavy cost because its primitive sanitation posed a continuous health risk as cholera swept through the Veneto. But the central tragedy remained that the agricultural and economic hardships of the turn of the century had reduced the people of the Veneto to living as their Bronze Age ancestors had.

Scheuermeier also focused on similar farm buildings, including the *pollaio* (henhouse on stilts). This variation on the Venetian lake house was used by farmers to give their chickens a safe, high shelter away from predators and poachers; "only the chickens [could] get up" this structure. The Swiss researcher observed that raising the *animali da cortile* (animals of the courtyard) was designated as women's work. One woman managed a flock of ninety-five turkeys, along with numerous rabbits, doves, geese, and a herd of milk cows.[48] Veneto contadini often relied on small animals like pigs and rabbits for food, rather than going to the greater expense of maintaining cattle. Cows were almost universally used for milk and cheese production.

Of all forms of agriculture, the dominant task was *fienagione*, haymaking. Most of the labor occurred on the mountainsides and was limited to areas that were never suited to mechanization. From planting to reaping, haymaking was done by small teams of men. It was hard and even dangerous work. In some places Scheuermeier found that farmers harvested as many as three and even four cuts of hay per year. However, he recorded, that was done "in large measure by hand." The use of *slitta* was necessary to move heavy loads of wood and hay down the steep mountainsides and symbolized the most demanding type of manual labor.

Giuseppe Tomasi and Giuseppe Grava have recorded the persistence of traditional methods of growing, cutting, and drying hay, as well as the methods of constructing work sleds, the *slitta* and *mussa*, and the ways these activities vary across the Veneto region. Made from a variety of wood heated and curved into runners, the sleds are light enough to be carried up the hillsides on a man's shoulders. They can be used to skid heavy loads up to eight hundred pounds over rough ground and down hillsides. In the steepest terrain, *teleferica* (cable systems) were later used after being introduced during WWI to move hay and equipment.[49]

Women used *gerle* (large baskets) like backpacks to transport heavy loads between home and market. *Gerle* are tall, open-topped baskets handwoven of wood that can carry vegetables, hay, and even children up and down the steep mountainsides. Tomasi and Grava dubbed the *gerle* indispensable for agricultural labor in the Veneto.[50] Women carried the heavy loads of laundry to communal washing sites where water was available and returned with the wetter, heavier loads on their backs. The same *gerle* might be used to carry children or produce from the fields (bambini and radicchio do not mix).

But even as Scheuermeier photographed and interviewed farm laborers, the era of raising hay and crops on the mountainsides was drawing to a close. Emigration had reduced the number of fields worked, as noted earlier, but Scheuermeier's records show too how the distribution of land had changed for his informants. The era of the contadini and their families farming their own land, raising animals, and meeting their daily needs this way—supporting an independent life—had begun to fade decades earlier. Large-scale *bonifica*[51] (land-reclamation projects) in the Po River valley, begun by the Italian government in the 1880s, had already shifted landownership patterns. The independent contadini who had prospered on the yields of their own lands on the Veneto hillsides were reduced to *braccianti* (lit., "arms"; day laborers) long before the 1920s.

Scheuermeier's drive to record contadini life in the Veneto testifies to his recognition of its ephemeral nature; perhaps his fascination with photography as a documentary device was driven by his awareness that he had found the last vestiges of an entire way of life. He sought to preserve a way of life that was already coming to an end. Although the contadini had existed for thousands of years in the *prealpi*, they were unable to support themselves in the wake of such great change. Their descendants became landless laborers or permanent migrants. The Swiss researcher frequently encountered returned emigrants in his interviews, and the frequency demonstrates the determination of the contadini to cling to their mountains.

The traditional way of life in the northern Veneto had been in decline for half a century by the time Scheuermeier arrived. It had been unbalanced by economic and political changes that permanently altered the agricultural economy of the *prealpi* towns and made the traditional way of life untenable. Above all, these changes drove many individuals and families who had lived in the mountains for millennia to abandon the struggle for survival and to become reluctant migrants.

NOTES

1. A decorated bronze sword of forty-six centimeters was excavated in 1923, along with remains of the *palafitta* and a stag's horn; the blade is preserved in the Museo Civico di Conegliano, estimated date tenth century BC. *Il Veneto: Paese per paese* (Florence: Bonechi, 1982), 345.
2. Similar evidence has been discovered in surrounding areas: Montebelluna, Crocetta del Montello, and Cansiglio. See *Livelet parco archeologico didattico* (Treviso: Provincia di Treviso, with Comune di Revine Lago, n.d.).
3. Equivalent range in elevation: 800 to 3,960 feet of elevation. Revine Lago's highest point is at the Col de la Poiatte (1,344 meters or 5,100 feet) above sea level; its area is 18.66 square kilometers. *Il Veneto: Paese a Paese*, 345.
4. Frederic C. Lane, *Venice A Maritime Republic*, Baltimore: the Johns Hopkins University press, 1973, 4–5. On the actual construction of the city as well as pallefitte structures, Giovanni Distefano, *How was Venice Built?*, (Venezia, Supernova, 2014).
5. Local dialects survive today in rural areas, most often spoken by the elderly, but preserved in literature, comune records, and histories. See "patrimonio lessicale (fra dialetto ed italianismi)" in Giovanni Tomasi, *Dizonario del dialetto di revine*, 14.
6. Revine and Lago, once distinct communes, were unified in 1868 although local use of the individual names and the separate identities of each town very stubbornly persist.
7. The historic dictionary for the region is Giuseppe Boerio, *Dizionario del dialetto veneziano* (Venice, 1856); the facsimile reprint by Giunti is undated. Regional groups have published separate dialect dictionaries for most Veneto towns. For Revine Lago, see Giovanni Tomasi and Giuseppe Grava, *Dizionario del dialetto di Revine* (Belluno: Istituto Bellunese, 1983).
8. For illustrations of traditional dress, see Tomasi and Grava, *Dizionario del dialetto di Revine*, appendix, tavola V.
9. Alessandro Baldan, *La civilita rurale veneta* (Padua: Francisi Editore), 1988, 58. "L'oumo in genere ha considerato la donna inferior solo per forza fisica"; translation mine.

10. Proverbs in Venetian dialect; translation mine. For the original, see Baldan, *La civilita rurale veneta*, 18: "El contadin xe la mosca, el paron xe el ragno, che la magna quando la casca ne la so rete"; and "Chi xe passuo no crede a chi ga fame."

11. Giovanni Antonio Cibotto, *Proverbi Veneti* (Florence: Giunti, 2006), 87. My translation from bilingual Venetian/English text: "Né cane né contadino chiudano mai la porta. Il contadino è largo di bocca e stretto di mano. Il contadino, come il cane, a chi lo bastona lecca la mano." For the last quoted, "Meglio basso ma sano che alto e stupdio," see *I schéi no i ga ganbe ma i core: Selezione di proverbi e modi di dire nei dialetti del Veneto con traduzione in italiano* (Milan: Simonelli Editore, 2005), 21.

12. See the fifty-three tables of illustrations by Grava, in Tomasi and Grava, *Dizionario del dialetto di Revine*. For a detailed discussion of their decades of work documenting the history and material culture of the central Veneto, see Teresa Fava Thomas, "Retrospective Review: Giuseppe Grava and Giovanni Tomasi," *News on the Rialto: Newsletter for Studies on Venetian History* ((Provo, Utah: Brigham Young University, 2012): 14–15.

13. Here it is Revine only (not Revine Lago), as Grava have owned land there since 1426. The reference is to 1892 town tax records reproduced in the town history which deals with Revine only.

14. *Sopranomme* literally translates to "over name"—that is, "nickname." "Famiglie presenti nella parrocchia," in Luigi Carlet, *Lago ricordi* (Revine Lago: : Parrocchia di San Giorgio di Lago, 2005), 120; Giovanni Tomasi, *Revine: Storia di una comunita* (Belluno: Istituto Bellunese, 1984), 151.

15. Austrian land invasion was in 1814 but possession was made official at Congress of Vienna in 1815.

16. Baldan, *La civilita rurale veneta*, 39. Translation mine: "Sempre timorosa of assembramenti, il carnevale fu soffocato."

17. Ibid., 46.

18. Romano Pascutto (1907–1982), quoted in Amedeo Sandri and M. Fallopi, *Mangiare Veneto sette province in cucina / Veneto Cookbook: Seven Provinces, One Kitchen* (Vicenza: Edizioni Massimo Vicentini, 2009), 65; for Marano corn, see 226.

19. "Polenta nuova e uccelli di passo, vino di cantina e gente allegra." Cibotto, *Proverbi Veneti*, 48; translation mine.

20. Sandri and Falloppi, *Mangiare Veneto*, 218.

21. Ibid., 259.

22. See "Grappa Veneta," in Sandri and Falloppi, *Mangiare Veneto*, 259–261.

23. Inland breeds of radicchio are similar to the tall, slender striped Trevisan breed, while a shorter, round radicchio is bred in Chioggia that grows on the other side of the Venetian lagoon within sight of Venice. See *Strada del radicchio rosso di Treviso e variegato di Castelfranco* (Zero Branco: Provincia di Treviso, Provincia di Venezia, and Provincia di Padova, 2012). The 59-page booklet is available in Italian or in English at www.stradadelradicchio.it (accessed October 6, 2014).

24. For a detailed description with photographs of processing a pig, see "Il maiale," interview in Tarzo, Italy, by Scuola Media Statale (www.tragol.it/saperisapori/maiale.htm). For the proverb "Ci sono più giorni che salsicce," see *I schéi*, 39.

25. Alexander Robertson, *Through the Dolomites* (London: George Allen, 1903), 62–63.

26. The number of songbirds sacrificed for the table eventually led many to abandon the dish, but enterprising Veneto pastry chefs developed a dessert, *torta polenta e osei*, a yellow frosted cake in the shape of a round polenta with tiny chocolate "birds" on top. Today, Verona's La Pasticceria Cordioli and other shops still sell the sweet version.

27. "Il linguaggio armonico dei principali uccelli presenti nella region ... facesse parte integrante del dialetto bellune," 41; *archet*, 44–45. In Revine Lago bird hunters were interviewed in the 1980s about using what they termed the *arket*: *kaza ko la zevita* or "to hunt with the owl"; Tomasi and Grava, *Dialetto del Revine*, 28, and tavola XLIX. "Arket" is dialect and spelled differently in each commune; the word is derived from bow or archetto. See Sergio dalla Bernardina, *"L'innocente piacer": La caccia e le sue rappresentazioni nelle prealpi del Veneto orientale* (Feltre: n.p., 1989), 41, and illustrations of archet (spelling as in original Bellunese dialect) 44–45. In Tomasi and Grava, "arket" is the correct Revinese dialect term.

28. Sergio dalla Bernardina, *"L'innocente piacer": La caccia e le sue rappresentazioni nelle prealpi del Veneto orientale* (Feltre: n.p., 1989), 25. The Jacini Commission examined meat consumption during the 1870s; see *Atti della Giunta per la inchiesta agraria e sulle condizioni della classe agricola* (Rome: Forzani & C. Tipografi del senato, 1882), volume quarto, parte prima, Le condizioni dei contadini nel veneto, fasciolo I, capitolo VII, 147–149 (Hereafter, this source is cited as *Jacini Commission*; the massive Jacini Commission report was originally divided into fifteen large volumes but subdivided into tomi or volumes then into fasciolo or books with separate capitoli or chapters. Most references I have drawn from volume quarto, parte prima and parte seconda). On meat consump-

tion, see *The American Beef Supply*, United States Department of Agriculture Report no. 37 (Washington, DC: Government Printing Office, 1885), 7–8.

29. Ester Cason Angelini, "La coltivazione della fava nel bellunese," in *Fava, patata, papavero: Sistemi e tecniche tradizionali di coltivazione e di utilizzazione nel Bellunese*, by Daniela Perco (Feltre: n.p., 1988), 51, 64, 81; "che ghe ne fasoi no ghe ne fam," 133. Records of Revine Lago show "an explosion" of pellagra in 1900–1910; Bruna Berti Saccon, *Il comune di Revine Lago: Traccia storia-economica della origini al 1945* (Revine: Comune, 1997), 211.

30. G. B. Locatelli, "Progetto della ferrovia alpina da Treviso a Belluno 1865," reproduced in Giovanni Tomasi, *Topografia antica di serravalle e della val lapisina* (Pordenone: Grafiche editoriali artistiche pordenonesi, 1989), 147.

31. Alexander Robertson, *Through the Dolomites: A Practical, Historical and Descriptive Guide-Book to the Scotland of Italy*, (London: George Allen), 1903, 38–39.

32. Ibid., 52. On construction and use of the *gerla* see Giuseppe Grava and Giovanni Tomasi, *La fienagione nelle Prealpi venete*, (Vicenza: Neri Pozza Editore), 1999, 58–61.

33. Scheuermeier did field research for scholars Karl Jaberg and Jakob Jud's *L'atlante linguistico ed etnografico Italo-Svizzero*. He died in 1932, but his son assisted scholars in deciphering his field notes and the phonetic code he used to record dialect. The series of published field notes and photographs includes *Paul Scheuermeier, Il Veneto dei contadini 1921–32*, ed. Daniela Perco et al. (Vicenza: Fondazione Giorgio Cini, Regione del Veneto, Angelo Colla editore, 2011); and Paul Scheuermeier, *Il Trentino dei contadini 1921–31*, ed. Giovanni Kezich, et al., 2nd ed. (Trento: Museo degli Usi e Costumi della Gente Trentina, 1997).

34. "...Una buona impressione, sembrava intelligente e fedele ... piante e uccelli. Riaissumeno in poche parole"; Scheuermeier, *Il Veneto dei contadini*, 21–22.

35. Scheuermeier, *Il Veneto dei contadini*, 13: "un centro industriale e capoluogo dei comunisti vicentini"; translation mine: "Genuini ... non imbastarditi dalle koine veneziana italianizzante."

36. See the chapter "Italy: War Wipes Out Two Margins," especially "The Occupied Veneto," in Homer Folkes, *The Human Costs of War* (New York: Harper Brothers, 1920).

37. Mark Thompson, *The White War: Life and Death on the Italian Front, 1915–1919* (New York: Basic Books, 2010), 348–351. On Revine Lago, see Carlet, *Lago Ricordi*, 128.

38. "A causa del clima politico rovente"; Scheuermeier, *Il Veneto dei contadini*, 16.

39. "Cercassi un contatto con il noto capo socialista Matteotti." Ibid., 18.

40. "Questo fanatico ... gli stessi occhi!" Ibid., 327.

41. Ibid., 27.

42. "La lavorazione dei campi, che mostra proffondi segni di abbandono." Ibid., 21.

43. "Il dialetto locale si e tuttavia mantenuto con le sue caratteristiche particolari e con le sostanziali differenze tra le diverse frazioni ... soppratutto all'attaccamento delle donne al loro paese." Ibid., 21.

44. Ibid., 25.

45. Ibid., 122, report on Tarzo, Jan. 31, 1922; photos 613–615.

46. Ibid., 150, photograph and text no. 406.

47. Baldan, *La civilita rurale veneta*, 195: "senza ricore all'ufficiale sanitario per il permesso di abitabilità!"

48. Scheuermeier, *Il Veneto dei contadini*, 32.

49. Tomasi and Grava, *Il dialetto del Revine*, 126–127 (detailed description of sled and its uses, with illustrations in appendix, tavola XIV) and appendix, tavola XIV. For photographs of loading and transporting hay in the mountains, see Tomasi and Grava, *La fienagione nelle prealpi venete* (Vicenza: Neri Pozza, 1985), 131–137. On construction and use of the *gerla* see Giuseppe Grava and Giovanni Tomasi, *La fienagione nelle Prealpi venete*, (Vicenza: Neri Pozza Editore, 1999), 58–61. This includes photos of women and children with gerle Capitalization as in original.

50. Tomasi and Grava, *La fienagione nelle prealpi venete*, 58–59.

51. Bonifica were state-sponsored land-reclamation projects that led to the consolidation of small properties into large agricultural estates which need both flood control and irrigation to be profitable.

CHAPTER 2

RELUCTANT MIGRANTS ABANDON THE VENETO

The people of the Veneto took great pride in their long history—not as a region of Italy but as an independent republic. The Republic of Venice was a powerful city-state commanding a land and sea empire that stretched down the Adriatic coast and encompassed strategic possessions into the eastern Mediterranean. Historian Frederick Chapin Lane's *Venice: A Maritime Republic* describes the way that *la serenissima repubblica* (the most serene republic) began building its wealth in the eleventh century and then expanded its empire. Merchant traders sailed to the Levant and Asia while the Venetian navy secured strategic ports. Venetian dominance was exerted throughout the Adriatic, and by 1202 the republic had mounted naval expeditions in support of the Crusades; its possessions included Levantine ports and the island of Corfu. Ruled by an elected doge and managed by councils of elected officials, Venice was an example of republican government until the Napoleonic Wars.[1]

Venice also secured a land empire stretching from Mestre westward nearly to Milan, and north and east along the Adriatic; it was ruled through local *signori*, who held power in cities like Treviso, Verona,

Vicenza, Padua, Feltre, and Bassano del Grappa.[2] Today stone statues
of the winged lion of Saint Mark, last vestiges of Venice's land empire,
still look down upon many Veneto cities and memorialize the city-state's
former outposts along the Adriatic. Venice's lion stands atop a stone
column near the Doge's Palace, carved with his front paws symbolically
on land and his rear paws in the sea.

Venice's republic was crushed by Napoleon when his army occupied
and looted the city in 1797. Napoleon took Venice's artwork, the four
horses on the basilica, known as *la quadriga*, and burned the floating
symbol of Venice—a ship called the *Bucintoro*, used in the annual marriage-
with-the-sea ceremony—after stripping it of its gold. Napoleon then
ceded the Veneto to Austria; later it was retaken by the French and was
finally bartered back to the Austrians at the Congress of Vienna in 1815.
For the next three decades, Venice remained little more than a province
of Austria, which eliminated its representative government and shut
down its independent press.

Venetian independence reasserted itself in an 1848 revolt led by Daniel
Zanin. Savoia's King Carlo Alberto led his army across northern Italy to
drive the Austrians out of Milan, but he was defeated and exiled. Despite
Giuseppe Garibaldi's efforts, the Austrian military held Venice, and
Zanin's revolt was crushed after a year-long siege. Starvation, disease,
and the humiliation of another surrender ended all hope for a second
Venetian Republic. In 1866 Garibaldi returned to capture the Veneto for
Italy. By 1870 unification had created a fledgling nation-state under a
monarch and a weak constitution that guaranteed few rights. Venice
and the Veneto, once an independent republic and a global power, were
reduced to a minor province of the fledgling Italian state.

The new nation of Italy faced an enormous challenge: it must overcome
regionalism and the power of local identity in the Veneto, which was
rooted in *campanilismo*, the practice of trusting only those from one's
own place of origin. The new Italian government had to build a national
identity, to "make" Italians. Yet Veneti were firmly bound to their culture:

local dialect, patron saints, religious practices, agricultural methods, and food culture. People relied only on friends from their *paese* and on their kinfolk, whereas outsiders who spoke a different dialect were not to be trusted.

When Venetians did emigrate they settled with their own *paesani* wherever they landed. Historians Loretta Baldassar and Ros Pesman observed the persistence of *campanilismo* among the twentieth-century Venetians who settled in Australia. They sought out fellow *paesani*, "who offered emotional and material sustenance, who found them work and accommodation, who spoke their dialect, and shared their customs, values and cultural traditions." There was no self-identification as Italian even though the peninsula had been unified. Historian Donna R. Gabaccia observed that national pride, *civilita italiana* developed within the intellectual elite between 1000 and 1600, but in the nineteenth century powerful regional identity still remained an obstacle to a national one.[3]

Italy, its nascent government based first in Turin and later in Rome, needed to develop the economic power of a modern state in order to survive—surrounded as it was by powerful rivals like Austria, Germany, and France. Regionalism had left the peninsula with no modern transport system or central government for far too long. Before unification, each region on the Italian peninsula had defended its borders, levied customs duties and taxes, and had its own armies and navies. By 1870 Rome had made plans for modern railroad systems and economic development.

One critical focus was the farming sector because foreign imports, especially from the United States, threatened to dominate the Italian market with cheap grain. Rome invested in large-scale *bonifica* (irrigation projects), which channeled investment into extensive lowland estates and monoculture crops. Wealthy investors bought up small farms and hired temporary seasonal labor rather than contracting out small plots of land. Independent farmers found themselves with no alternative but to become day laborers with no job security and low wages. New taxes were assessed to support the creation of a modern society, and some taxes on grain milling hit the poor the hardest. But the onslaught of cheap American agricultural imports, especially of grain, continued to force down farm prices.

Some parts of the Veneto, however, benefited from national investment. Modern port facilities and new rail connections from Venice into the Veneto facilitated the expansion of a modern maritime economy and industrial development in the late nineteenth century. Historian Frederic C. Lane observed, "Venice became again a great port, second only to Genoa among the ports of modern Italy."[4]

The efforts to spur economic development Italy made massive changes to the agricultural sector, rapidly undercutting small-scale farming in the mountains. Ironically, better transport and economic development produced wealth for investors but, again, transformed independent farmers into dependent day laborers with a much lower standard of living. Small farms could not hold out as investors established large estates. Population increases put small farmers' dwindling acreage under more pressure to support larger families. The quality of the daily diet was drastically reduced. As if the economic changes were not destructive enough, in the same decades a variety of diseases and other disasters struck humans, animals, and plants. Malnutrition, pellagra, cholera, and earthquakes ravaged the region. Vines were crippled by fungal diseases, and cattle died. All these changes drove waves of reluctant emigrants from the Veneto. Historians Gherardo Ortalli and Giovanni Scarabello have described "the depressing economic lot" of Venice and the Veneto in the two decades after Italian unification.[5] National and local governments struggled with the most pressing problems of economic underdevelopment and poor housing. The widespread nature of the problem was daunting.

Emigration, regarded by some Italian politicians as a "safety valve" that would carry off the most dissatisfied, did not halt growing labor radicalization. Instead, northern Italy became a center for farm-labor organizers. The young nation had a very narrow electorate and tight restrictions on the vote that amplified political and social unrest. Emigration was for many the only way to survive. In Rome politicians debated whether emigration would mitigate the social tensions that might erupt or whether it would siphon off those who might best build this new Italy. Those who remained in the Veneto often joined the ranks of socialist and even radical parties—not just in the cities but especially in the fields.[6]

Venetians had always been migratory. As early as the eleventh century, they had traveled the world; most famously, Marco Polo traveled across Asia and returned to Venice with tales of China and Japan. The earliest travelers were merchants and traders seeking wealth from spices and silk in the Levant and Asia. Skilled Venetian glassmakers found jobs in the Americas, journeying to the colony of Virginia in the 1600s; other accomplished artisans traveled throughout Europe. Louis XIV summoned Venetian glass specialists to Versailles to create the Hall of Mirrors and then sent for gondoliers to ply the canals of his pleasure palace.

In the 1870s the first waves of postunification Italian migration left from the north. Because this area's population was generally more skilled, more literate, and situated nearer to rail connections than those elsewhere on the Italian peninsula, these individuals had more direct access to central Europe. Some moved down the mountains to work in urban areas and then traveled on foot or by rail over the Alps into Austria, France, Switzerland, Germany, and even England to find work.

The development and expansion of Europe's rail network facilitated this escape, and many sought jobs building railroad lines, digging rail tunnels, and mining coal in Europe. Possession of *il passaporto rosso* (the red passport) of the Italian government made international travel much easier. Steam transport became faster, and transatlantic ticket prices dropped, making it easier to leave from Genoa, on the northwest coast of Italy, for ocean voyages. Many who lacked the red passport, however, slipped from Milan or Turin into Switzerland or France by rail and then headed for Le Havre, France, and from there took transatlantic ships to Brazil, Argentina, Uruguay, and the United States. An American consular officer in Genoa reported in 1886 that "while the Italian government is very strict in regard to its citizens leaving the kingdom by sea without a passport, it is decidedly lax in enforcing this condition on its subjects who cross the frontier into France and Switzerland." Obtaining a passport required a birth certificate issued in one's home village, along with a note called the *nulla ostica* (no obstacle to migration) signifying that there were no unmet military duty obligations or criminal misdemeanors on the records; then the *passaporto rosso* was issued for a fee equivalent to three dollars and fifty cents in today's US dollars.[7] But that relatively small fee was beyond the means of many. Others simply wanted a ticket to "America" and considered any foreign destination as meeting that desire. By 1879 Venetians had begun arriving in Australia.[8]

The pattern of migration from the Veneto differed from the subsequent waves of southern migration in the period 1880–1920. It was shaped by the proximity of the Veneto to European labor markets and to the network of rail and steamer transport. Migration began earlier there, was more individual and less closely managed by labor recruiters (*padroni*), and included more women than migration from southern Italy did. Women migrated seasonally from the Veneto mountains to work first in Italian cities and later in neighboring Austria. Initially, this population movement was much more seasonal than permanent. In the 1920s anthropologist Paul Scheuermeier interviewed Venetians and found a number of *uccelli di passaggio* (lit., "migratory birds"; here, return migrants) resident in the hill towns who had spent years and sometimes decades traveling to find work around the globe.

Migrants held on to the dream of returning to the Veneto, whether by seeking only seasonal work or by laboring abroad only long enough to accumulate enough savings to establish a new, more secure life in the Veneto. In 1901 the Italian government began requiring returned migrants to register with their local governments. The figures for returnees from the United States show that 23 percent of Veneto migrants returned in the period 1906–1908. Yet the percentage of returnees from many other regions was lower, particularly in the south, including Lazio, Marches, Abruzzi, and Calabria; Sardinia had the lowest rate of return, 4 percent. Prior to 1901, return migration to the Veneto may have been higher, as noted in an Italian government report indicating that emigration to the United States in 1902 was "taking on a more permanent character."[9]

These were reluctant migrants. Economic hardship and hunger had broken the will of many people who had been determined to remain in the Veneto. Once on the move, however, they often found ways to return. Migration was a response to the declining quality of life and economic changes that destroyed the traditional agricultural economy of the Veneto. What began as a domestic search for seasonal work soon expanded into European migration and finally into transatlantic migration. Eventually, for many Venetians, life became a transnational existence as temporary jobs and residence overseas gradually became more permanent.

The patterns of migration from the Veneto were shaped foremost by the needs of its people to survive. Their struggle to maintain themselves and their families was undermined by the economic forces that Italy's unification unleashed and by natural forces, especially diseases that struck humans, animals, and crops. The population of the Veneto had steadily expanded over the nineteenth century, but the quality of life just as steadily eroded in the same decades. Only a few years after unification, the Italian government was already struggling to identify the reasons for expanding migration and to deal with its causes, especially the hunger and hardship of life in the mountains. Teams of experts traveled the region to examine the lives of the contadini, and their reports document the gravity of the problem. Politicians in Rome were shocked by the loss of so many young Italians, and landowners feared that the Po River valley would lose most of the inexpensive temporary laborers who had enriched them.

Two qualities marked this migration: its transnational nature and the high level of mobility of the migrants. People whose ancestors had lived for centuries in the same village became "commuters," regularly traveling around Europe or across the Atlantic for seasonal work. Contadini had become what scholars today would call transnational migrants, traveling to foreign nations for work but with the goal of maintaining connections with their original home. Scholar Stefano Luconi has argued that some migrants "retain such strong connections to their fatherlands that they actually end up living in two societies."[10] This view rejects the conception of the assimilationist paradigm of Oscar Handlin. Although not every Veneto migrant pined for home, there is evidence that many returnees were from the mountains. They used the new transport networks to move around Italy, Europe, and the world to find work. Many labored for a season and then returned; others settled abroad for years and then returned. Over time, seasonal migration might be abandoned or give way to permanent settlement, especially given the global disruptions of war.

Internal migration was the first option, and it was often the choice of the young, who might leave their mountain homes for the lower valleys and urban areas seeking wages to supplement family farm income. Daniela Todesco's study of female labor in the Veneto examines the experiences of young women from Belluno, in the northernmost reaches of the Veneto, who migrated into the valleys beginning in the 1850s.[11] Women from Belluno and Feltre migrated seasonally to aid their families, some by working as maids for wealthy Italian families and others as field workers on farms. Early waves of female migration most often comprised movement within Italy and to nearby urban areas. At first these women tended vineyards and mulberries, working in summer and returning to Belluno after the harvest. Todesco described a brief seasonal migration that did not uproot the women or have much impact on society.[12]

Healthy, strong women accustomed to agricultural work traveled to urban Trento and were, in Todesco's words, *umanita mobile* (mobile humanity) who arrived and left on a very specific schedule that was tied to the regional holidays. It was easier to travel and search for work at those particular times. Their migration was referred to as *l'arrivo delle rondini* (the arrival of the swallows). Over time, the work force expanded as younger children joined their older siblings. These women and children were in temporary, often precarious situations because of economic necessity. Public records reveal the darker side of life for them: cases of suicide, sexual molestation, and infanticide, as well as accusations of theft and blacklisting of women on brief evidence. Todesco's study points to the choice between *pauperismo montano* (poverty of the mountains) and *emigrazione di breve raggio* (emigration of a brief period). It soon evolved into chain migration as word passed from early female emigrants to others in Belluno and Feltre.

Though men are often the first to migrate, it was women who led this movement. It may have been difficult, but few had any other choice. Hunger and hardship were endemic in Belluno. A priest recorded one woman's desperate tale, which explained her determination to migrate: "It would be well to remain in our land to work under the eyes of our mothers, but hard necessity pushes us to take passage and leave, because at Belluno, there is a scarcity of agricultural development and other industries, or to die of hunger."[13] Another described the misery in home: her mother constantly wept because she was a widow without sons.[14] Another related that in the mountains "everyone was dead of illness or hunger."[15] Sometimes, however, their new situation was not much better. One Bellunese woman related to the priest that she had returned from a hard day of field labor to find her that employer had provided a bowl of soup as her only sustenance.

One of the most vocal advocates for the northern Italian contadini who emigrated was Giovanni Scalabrini, the new bishop of Piacenza, near Genoa, in 1876. Scalabrini went on a tour of his new parishes and found that twenty-eight thousand of his two hundred thousand parishioners had recently migrated.[16] Scalabrini examined the situation firsthand by visiting Italian communities in Brazil and the United States, and in 1887 he organized the Congregation of the Missionaries of Saint Charles, a seminary to train young northern Italian priests who understood the difficulties faced by migrants living abroad and who spoke their dialects.

The Scalabrinians first established missionary outposts in Providence, Rhode Island, and in Boston, Massachusetts. Among those who arrived there was Reverend Giuseppe Chiminello of Rosá, in the Veneto. He devoted his life to aiding Italian migrants in America. His career began in Providence, continued in Chicago, and ended with his retirement from a parish in California, having followed the Italian migration westward.[17]

By the 1870s the "swallows" numbered in the hundreds, and after 1886 they could take rail passage to Austria to perform agricultural labor there. As past rulers of the Veneto, Austrians looked down upon the rural women while marveling at their robustness, tall aspect, lively eyes, and physical strength. These women arrived in May to begin bundling wood, cutting wheat, tending vineyards and animals, feeding silkworms. They left in hopes of working as servants but were hired to clean stables as often as to clean mansions. By October they were gone, having migrated back to their mountains.[18] Driven by hunger and hardship, these women reluctantly ventured into the valleys and then across borders to help support their families. They were, however, able to return each fall and remain for half the year in their homes with their families. Railroads made their travel easier, but the advent of war with Austria in 1915 ended the swallows' migrations.

Whereas women chose first internal migration then movements to nearby Austria, labor recruiters tempted male contadini to Brazil. One of the first families to abandon the Veneto for Brazil was that of Giacomo Rech Checonét[19], who left behind a collection of letters documenting his experience, beginning in 1876, and how he had made the decision to leave. Life in Seren, a small town near Bassano del Grappa, followed the seasons of traditional mountain agriculture: Checonét cut hay and wood, grew corn and grain, and raised sheep. Polenta, the only food available, was becoming more expensive, and taxes cut into what little income he had. In three years the nearby *comune* (municipality) of Feltre lost six hundred laborers to emigration. This male exodus was very different from the women's emigration: recruiters from Brazil were offering to resettle entire families of contadini, and this meant, in Checonét's words, *partenze senza ritorno*, "leaving without hope of return."[20] The distance was too far for seasonal migration to be practical.

Promised free land and passage to Brazil by agents who traversed the Veneto in search of skilled agricultural labor—much to the resentment of the Italian Ministry of Agriculture, which recorded that "the excitement created by agents of emigration ... [led to] the craving to suddenly get rich"[21]—these men set out for the Americas. Worse yet for those who remained, less-secure farm work yielded less income as competition from large-scale agriculture in the irrigated valley fields undercut the less-productive farm economy of the mountains. The hardships only increased as estate managers hired more temporary day laborers rather than signing contracts with contadini for a year's labor.

Checonét hid money in his clothing and took a train to Genoa and there boarded a ship. As his family waited in Italy, one child impatiently asked when they would cross the ocean to be with their family, to which his mother replied, "When they finish the bridge!"[22] Five years later, in 1881, Checonét sent for his wife and children, and later for his aged parents and other relatives. Checonét's letters describe their struggle in a frontier as a way to maintain some connection with his extended family. As life improved, they were joined by others, and ultimately thirty-one of his kin resettled permanently in Caxias, Brazil. Over the years they wrote home to the Veneto expressing a desire to visit: "We hope yet to return one time to the old country."[23]

But that generation never did. Letters continually passed back and forth across the Atlantic as Caxias became a focal point for Venetian migrants who heard of his success and then followed Checonét. Together they built the Church of Saint Teresa in 1899, and the family prospered as Caxias became a modern, industrialized city. In 1994 the descendants of the Rech Checonét family contacted the Veneto government requesting dual citizenship.[24] The dream of return had passed from one generation to another, and the transnational link had survived.

The example of a successful emigrant and the power of the messages he sent back to a small town could spread the dream to others. In this era, offers of free land and free steamer passage to Brazil were enticing opportunities. Investigators from the Italian government's Jacini Commission recorded a small-town mayor's report from the province of Treviso regarding what local farmers had been told: "Agents of emigration promised the *seas and the mountains* ... great riches in the transatlantic countries ... of *spades, hoes and plows of solid gold, not iron.* You can image the fanaticism!"[25] Dreams of golden tools and free transport to a faraway land seemed, and often were, too good to be true, but the chance to escape hardship and hunger made any destination seem worthwhile. Indeed, contadini from Treviso sang a dialect rhyme that pictured them abandoning their tools and leaving all the work to their landlords: "Andaremeo in Merica, in tel bel Brasil, e qua i nostri siori, lavorara la tera col badil" (We will go to America, to beautiful Brazil, and here our lords will work the earth with shovels).[26] The image of leaving their masters behind to do the labor had a special resonance for the contadini who had suffered so long under their power.

Though they dreamed and sang of "America," that faraway land was not too clearly defined, and even its location remained indistinct. Few migrants cared whether they landed in North or South America, in Brazil, Argentina, Uruguay, or the United States. The word *America* designated a land of opportunity but not necessarily an arrival in New York City. Those who returned from abroad to resettle in Italy were often called "Americani" whether or not they had come from the United States, and their friends and family were eager to hear of their adventures. It was these returnees who began to establish informal migration networks by relaying information about their travel experiences and by dispensing advice about how to emigrate and find work and housing abroad.

The Italian government in Rome was alarmed by the escalating numbers of emigrants and assembled a group of experts that was charged with investigating the condition of the agricultural economy and laborers in Italy to understand why people were emigrating. In 1882 the Jacini Commission delivered its report, a massive multivolume study that covered all of Italy. The fourth volume focused on the Veneto: investigators were stunned by the poor conditions of housing and hygiene, as well as by the prevalence of hunger and malnutrition. Especially alarming was the onslaught of pellagra, which stunts not only growth but also mental development. Pellagra was present throughout the Veneto's mountains. In the province of Treviso, along the Piave River, investigators described *case d'infezione* (houses of infection) where typhoid and cholera were prevalent. The lowland irrigated fields were breeding grounds for mosquitoes, and impoverished laborers often improvised housing from reeds in the marshes. At Povegliano the workers' huts were compared to "burrows for animals and worse." Near Conegliano people were described as being housed "like sardines in a barrel."[27]

In Padova investigators found nearly a quarter of the homes in the worst possible conditions: "a frame of wood and four walls ... covered with reeds, inside and outside coated with clay, covered in straw or hay ... inside this mean environment ... one or two tiny windows and a floor of bare earth. Here is the housing of our contadini." Across the region they saw small villages of cottages "built of cut canes, then covered in hay among the marshes and paddy fields ... better adapted to shelter beasts than as the residence of man."[28] As discussed earlier, the people of the Veneto had, whether they were conscious of it or not, been forced by poverty to live as their ancestors had in *pallefitte*. These hay and reed shelters were covered in mud, resembling the ancient huts built in the lakes beside Revine Lago during the Bronze Age. Similar crude structures were built farther inland. Beaten-earth floors abounded, sanitary facilities did not exist, and their natural situation was in or near marshy areas where diseases like typhoid and cholera were most easily spread.

As for the diet of the workers, the commission measured meat consumption and found that Belluno, Rovigo, and Venice had the lowest meat consumption in the Veneto region. The average yearly consumption for the Veneto as a whole was seven kilograms per person, which averaged about five ounces per week (contadini in Sicily and the southern coast averaged even less, three to four kilograms per year).[29] Ironically, the city of Rovigo is situated between two rivers in a flat plain that was almost entirely covered by irrigated farm fields, yet its people were among the poorest and least well fed in the entire region.

Only in the city of Venice itself were conditions a bit better. The Jacini Commission praised the rich produce grown on the islands of the lagoon, calling them "true marvels of intensive cultivation and where the indefatigable industry of the cultivator obtains rich production," especially on the islands.[30] The investigators also found better living conditions, deeming "the housing ... good or sufficient."[31] But throughout the region, investigators concluded, "the great majority of these hovels are not satisfactory in the most elementary necessities of domestic conveniences."[32] The Jacini investigators did not see these conditions as growing from ignorance and praised the people of Veneto—"The race is originally vigorous"[33]—noting that the Italian military had rejected few for not meeting the height requirement for the draft (at a time when other regions with long histories of hunger produced large numbers of men too stunted in growth to be accepted by the army). But the Jacini Commission concluded it was "contemporary problems" that had much reduced the Venetian people. Reliance on polenta had left children prone to malnutrition and pellagra. Addressing what they termed an epidemic, the group concluded that the Veneto was under "its terrible power."[34] Though the Venetians were hardworking, it was clear that the impact of hunger would eventually reduce the health of those who remained even further. Yet the most pressing question was how to remedy the social problems so that the next generation would not suffer as much—and so that the rate of emigration could be slowed.

Farther up in the northernmost Bellunese mountains, pellagra was endemic, and the magnitude of the problem was even more daunting there. The investigators found landholdings fractioned, and their chief noted the depth of the need: "If you touch the hand of the small proprietor, naked and alone, without other help, it is not enough to improve the social conditions."[35] Near Bassano del Grappa they found farm laborers planning to leave after being swayed by the words of "enthusiastic partisans of emigration." One local official informed them that migration was driven by a number of factors, including "the general discontent, scarcity of products, high cost of living, low wages, and terrible taxes."[36]

The Jacini Report of 1882 made clear to Rome the problems of the Veneto, but an explosion of labor unrest and new waves of emigration in the following years reinforced the message. Known as La Boje, "the boiling over," the Veneto strikes escalated in 1883 then again in 1901 and finally reached a prolonged and sustained peak from 1906 to 1909. The last period coincided with the heaviest waves of Veneto migration to Fitchburg and central Massachusetts. Many of these emigrants intended to remain in America.

There was a substantial audience eager for advice on how to emigrate, and this led to the publication of guides on the subject. Carlo Cerboni wrote of his experiences crossing twenty-four times between Italy and Argentina.[37] He claimed to offer friendly counsel on what to do, key phrases to use when requesting your passport from local officials, and the right type of ship to choose. He promised that emigrants would find a "vast and fertile country [where] you can choose between raising sugar cane or grains."[38] He went on to describe typical crops a contadino would recognize—coffee, tobacco, grapes—and even promised mineral riches. Those Italians who succeeded would become "Americani," a "privileged class" who made fortunes comparable to "hitting the lottery."[39]

Cerboni optimistically described the trip and observed that three regular meals were served on board the ships; then he touched upon the darker side, describing the risks of fire, collision, and sinking. There was advice on selecting the right steamer and how to avoid the *lumaca* (snails) that would only make the arduous journey longer, as well as tips to prevent seasickness.[40] In "perils to avoid" on the journey, he warned against trusting strangers, who were ready to defraud the "naïve, ignorant, and, to express myself clearly, on the imbeciles" careless enough to trust thieves and sharpers.[41] He described the typical emigrant as "the flower of our unhappy people"[42] and warned of the powerful emotions of parting: "Goodbye to Italy ... look well on the last bit you see of your Italy. Who knows if and when you will see it again!"[43]

Many were making that hard choice in even the smallest Veneto towns. Scholars have examined the passport applications and town records from 1876–1905 of Vedelago, a *comune* west of Treviso, to determine the destination, occupation, and the sex of emigrants. The small numbers involved allow a clear picture of emigration from that particular place. These were for the most part permanent emigrants. Despite Cerboni's experience, many of those who left Vedelago and for South America never returned.[44]

A total of 2,500 persons left the town; of those 1,625 went to Brazil, 173 to Argentina, 124 to Austria, and 104 to the United States, and equivalent numbers (more than a hundred each) left for France, Switzerland, and Germany. The timing of their emigration offers insight: the first five emigrants left for Brazil in 1876, as had Checonét; then numbers slowly increased until 1885, when 180 left, and soon nearly 400 were leaving per year. Brazil was the destination of 65 percent who emigrated in this era. In 1884 the first left for Argentina, but no more than a dozen per year set out for this destination. The peak years coincide with periods of labor strife in the Veneto. America was a distant option, and only two emigrants left for the United Stated in 1895; none were recorded in most years. American labor agents in these decades most often sought southern Italian labor for pick-and-shovel work rather than northern laborers. Permanent emigrants to Europe were fewer: Austria rarely received more than six in any year. Small but steady numbers left for France, Switzerland, and Germany, where labor opportunities opened up in railroad and tunnel construction and mining but then rapidly dwindled after 1903. In that year migration to America suddenly rose to twenty-five; it hit sixty-one in 1904 and retreated to sixteen in 1905, as workers pursued better opportunities.

More than twice as many men left Vedelago as women, but this still reflects the fact that women of the Veneto were highly mobile. Southern Italian emigration was overwhelmingly male and young, but Veneto emigrants often left as families or other groups. As discussed earlier, women led the first waves of internal migration down to the northern Italian valleys and then moved seasonally to Austria; they participated in later waves of permanent emigration, too, traveling as families to Brazil or with brothers and husbands to work in America.

The profession most often listed among those leaving was contadini until 1900. After that year, a quarter of emigrants were *braccianti*. In 1901, 1902, and 1903 not a single contadino emigrated from Vedelago, but many day laborers left: 155, 73, and 66, respectively. This most likely reflects not a different class of person leaving but rather the reduced status of contadini over time. In other words, someone who had been a contadino might have been a day laborer by the time he chose to emigrate. Having suffered continuing impoverishment over the decades, the contadini had almost all been transformed into day laborers. The number of emigrants classified as artisans remained in the single digits except during peak migration years for all groups in 1887–1888. Labor historian Emilio Franzina has developed a highly detailed statistical analysis of who left the province of the Veneto in the early decades of emigration, 1876–1901. He has calculated that 1,904,719 people left the Veneto, of which 405,883 (27 percent) were permanent migrants; the remainder were temporary.[45]

In sum, men and women left, more often in family groups, and small farmers left first, but over time day laborers also joined the exiting ranks. Their destination of choice at first was Brazil, and only in the years 1903–1905 did larger numbers leave for America—but in those years emigration to all other European destinations dwindled. It appears that the people of Vedelago chose their destinations based on a common desire to be with others from their home. Once the focus had shifted to a new destination, the new path was selected by subsequent emigrants who communicated their information along an informal network that responded to and adjusted to changes in labor markets around the globe. The evidence from Vedelago corresponds with that from other Veneto *comuni* of the era: seasonal migration shifted to more permanent emigration as the century drew to a close, and though the early destination of choice was Brazil, the United States emerged as a key option in the first decades of the 1900s.

The Polesine, just south of Vedelago, is an area dominated by the town of Rovigo and miles of fields stretching along the Po River valley. Migration from Rovigo, the poorest region and home to the intense labor strife called La Boje, was more permanent and more often transatlantic. The exodus from Rovigo province was much more intense than elsewhere in the Veneto. Rovigo is ideally situated for agriculture, for it dominates a lush plain that is well watered by the rivers and is near to the markets of Venice via railroad. The people of the Polesine are so strongly bound to their home *paese* that the dialects spoken on either side of the valley are considered distinct. In a 1902 study Guido Cavaglieri described Rovigo as "the poorest region of Italy" and its people as living "in squalid misery."[46] Only rarely were they free from hunger. Ironically, Cavaglieri acknowledged that the Polesine was the Veneto's "most fertile and productive province" because its flat plains were easily irrigated for large-scale agriculture. Yet its people were always in search of "labor and bread."[47] He did not fault their personal qualities but praised their general character as hardworking, good, and honest, and observed that they were *facile ai sogni* (lit., "prone to dreaming").[48] But in 1902 they were dreaming of abandoning the Veneto.

Cavaglieri noted that the global labor market required only *braccianti*. These workers first left as temporary migrants seeking construction work on railroads and tunnels in Switzerland, Austria, and Germany. But what began as temporary migration shifted to permanent emigration by the 1880s, and by 1900 the new destination was Brazil. Cavaglieri observed that population density was a problem throughout the Veneto:

even as many emigrated, the number of people in towns often remained steady because family size increased. He identified the turning point when transatlantic emigration had begun as 1886, marked by the arrival of agents offering free land and free transport from the port of Genoa to Brazil. In 1897 there were 155 emigrants, but within four years the total had increased nearly tenfold to 1,472 who chose to resettle across the Atlantic. One key indicator of permanent emigration is gender ratio, and in this case men were journeying not alone but with their families. Cavaglieri found that the ratio of men to women in the period 1897–1899 was nearly one to one among adults: in 1897 there were 1,751 men and 1,467 women who abandoned the province.[49]

The cruel irony was that the people of the Polesine lived in a rich agricultural area where they had once farmed their own land, but those workers had become landless, underpaid, and hungry day laborers. Rome's program of economic incentives for *bonifica* had made the flatlands of the southern Veneto the focus of government and private investment. Historian Luigi Arbizzani noted that the first irrigation machines went into action in 1850 in the lower Polesine near Rovigo. After 1870 large-scale land-reclamation projects were underway on thousands of hectares in what he termed "grand capitalistic plans."[50]

Rice production, once found only to the west near Milan, expanded into the Veneto as paddy fields were established with irrigation systems erected by investment and Rome's support. More often men, women, and children could find only temporary day labor on the extensive farms owned by investors.[51]

The result for the contadini was proletarianization. Small farms were bought out and combined into large estates, *mezzadri* (farm contracts) ended, and security evaporated as the area came to be dominated by these large agricultural concerns that employed only day laborers. During peak periods there was work—at meager wages—for everyone, but once the harvest was in, the laborers were left jobless and landless. Hunger and pellagra ravaged the *braccianti*. Women who had tended small animals on their home farms now worked as temporary field laborers. Arbizzani found that in the eastern regions of the valley, where land was not as easily irrigated, cereal crops and small-market production still dominated. But the social transformation wreaked havoc wherever large-scale investment forced out independent farmers. Worse yet, the massive scale of production soon brought a steady reduction in wages, and the overproduction of a few crops caused the collapse of grain prices. Cheap American grain flooded in, and together these economic factors disrupted the entire Veneto region—but their strongest impact was felt along the banks of the Polesine.

The contadini in the northern Veneto's *prealpi* also suffered as domestic overproduction and American grain imports led to a drastic drop in grain and rice prices in 1880 and 1881. Floods drove the Po and Adige Rivers over their banks in 1872, 1878, and 1882. By 1884 those field workers who remained had begun organizing in what Arbizzani called "the great mobilization."[52] The result was that boiling over of radicalization and protest known as La Boje, mentioned earlier. In May 1890 landowners struck back with the first massacre of laborers at Conselice. Not surprisingly, in the next year the province saw 16,500 workers, most with their families, emigrate from the Polesine. According to Emilio Franzina's calculations, hard-hit Rovigo lost over 71,000 residents in the years up to 1901, and 91 percent of those who left were permanent migrants. Nowhere else in the Veneto did permanent emigration reach such high numbers or arrive so early. On the other end of the scale, Belluno had very high rates of temporary emigration, but the lowest proportion of permanent emigration: 3 percent.[53]

Cavaglieri summed up the personal misery of the typical Polesine day laborer: it was the misery of someone who had seen "enough of the small disasters, the illness, the death of one of the family, high mortality of pigs, chickens and cows ... [and was] in debt to the landowner and taking credit from the little shops in the village."[54] He went on to describe how the cows, cared for with affection, were abandoned by their good masters and taken from their stalls to pay the family's debt. Given the hardships, the desire to emigrate was powerful, and between 1887 and 1901 a stunning 29 percent of the province's people chose permanent migration (64,446 of a total population of 220,000).[55] Whereas other Veneto migrants chose seasonal migration in the hope of holding on to a life in the Veneto, it was the people of Rovigo and its environs who chose to leave and not dream of returning.

Farther north, in Revine Lago, one family's story reveals the constant mobility and transnational nature of the Veneto's emigration. The Grava family first appeared in the town records as the de Gravas, a founding family of the town of Revine in 1426. Throughout its history, they were dominant in the life of the town, and their lands occupied its center. Seven clans of Gravas still live in Revine today; neighboring Revine Lago is home to others. For half a millennium the Revinese cut hay and raised animals and crops. Once agriculture was no longer self-sustaining on the mountain or in the valley, they looked to Switzerland and Austria for work. In the 1880s railroad construction in the Ticino region attracted seasonal migrants, as did the construction of massive tunnels through the Simplon Pass. Then, as throughout the Veneto, eyes turned to Brazil, and finally toward America.

The town's history describes emigration from Revine as beginning with "the mirage of an improbable, easy-living place, 'l'America,' a refuge from grave economic conditions." A trip to Genoa followed by a voyage by ship offered "a miraculous solution" for those armed with the red Italian passport.[56] But for many whose roots lay deep in the mountains, this was a very difficult choice. Often, the solution was temporary relocation, in combination with the dream of returning. Rather than settling in America, Revinese often sought to labor, as they had in Switzerland and Germany, on large-scale public-works projects in the United States, returning when winter reduced paychecks.

Members of the Grava family made numerous Atlantic crossings in search of work and a better life, only to return to Revine and then relaunch their dreams of America. Ermenegildo Grava, one of eleven children, was skilled in stonework and had ambitions to become a sculptor. He left for America on three trips from Le Havre, France, in 1892, 1897, and 1904 and eventually established himself in Connecticut. But on his 1897 return trip, he chose to marry a Revinese woman and left for America with his wife. They had five children, two born in the United States. One son, Giuseppe, followed his father's creative path: born in Waterford, Connecticut, he worked as a sculptor and returned to America (perhaps to Pittsburgh), where he remained for the period 1930–1934. He also returned to Revine to select a bride and completed his military service from 1916 to 1920, a choice that maintained his Italian citizenship. His son, also Giuseppe and also an artist, was born in Revine in 1935 and built a career first in Siena and Milan before resettling in 1977 in Revine, where he is known for carving medals, as well as for his other artwork. Although he was born in Revine, he returned to Connecticut and designed the centennial medal for his father's hometown, and he was made an honorary citizen of Waterford in 2001.[57] Theirs was a transnational life that persisted over generations, as the members of the Grava family lived in both nations and preserved family links to the Veneto rather than marrying in America.

The Gravas held not one but many dreams of America. They left Revine reluctantly and continued to return from America, constructing a transnational life. Other Revinese joined them in America. One group settled in Fitchburg, Massachusetts, and another in Connecticut. They moved across the Atlantic and between these tiny colonies as they worked in quarries, paper and wool mills, and foundries. They remained for a season and returned to Revine, traveling in small groups, living as commuters as they moved between the mountains of the Veneto and the hillsides of Massachusetts.

In 1905 eleven Revinese left the port of Cherbourg, France, for Ellis Island: four Grava men ranging in age from seventeen to thirty-four; five Battistella siblings, including three women between nine and nineteen years old; and two Gandin brothers. The ship's manifest lists their destinations: some were to join a brother in New Haven, Connecticut, and the rest were to meet a cousin in Fitchburg, Massachusetts, along with the Battistellas, who were to meet their brother. The Gandin brothers were on their way to Elkhorn, West Virginia, presumably to work as miners.[58]

The following year another ship from Cherbourg disembarked four Revinese: two Gravas, a Favaro, and a Piccin, all destined for New Haven, Connecticut. Nearly two decades later, they were still commuting: in October 1922 Domenico Grava arrived yet again to meet his cousin Angelo at New Haven, this time accompanied by Angelo's wife and three children. Another Revinese traveled first to Chicago to drive a delivery truck in 1901, and in subsequent years he visited his brother-in-law in Fitchburg, working in the quarry as a derrickman. After seven years of commuting, in 1908 he brought his wife, a Grava, and six children to settle with their relatives in Massachusetts.[59]

During these decades strikes in the Veneto doubled: in 1905 there were 715, and the following year saw 1,641.[60] Years of escalating tensions erupted after years of declining agricultural prices and farm wages into strikes and then migration. Those who left were the healthy, ambitious, and able.

There were a number of advantages to working in Massachusetts: the ports of Boston and New York were much closer to Italy than those of Brazil and Argentina, so migratory workers could sail home as winter shut down construction projects and eliminated jobs. Boston was home to the North End, a substantial Italian colony and resource. Quarries abounded in rocky New England, and in central Massachusetts there were five operating in Fitchburg alone. Mountain laborers who knew stonecutting could readily find work either in the quarries or working on roads and dams. The Monroe Bridge project in western Massachusetts attracted a steady stream of northern Italians, including 2,050 from the province of Trentino.[61]

From the beginning of migration to the United States, Italians in general and northern Italians in particular had established colonies in

Massachusetts and New York. The heavily industrialized economy of Massachusetts, easily accessible via the port of Boston, soon became home to a large Italian-speaking colony. It was easier to maintain transnational links where imported food and compatriots lived. Networks of laborers exchanged information about public-works projects where steady employment might be found; some of the largest projects were centered in Massachusetts and the Northeast. There was also access to Italian markets, as enterprising immigrants established stores and services for newer arrivals. Unregulated immigrant banks flourished not only in Boston's North End but also in central Massachusetts as a whole. The geographic similarities between the mountainous northern Veneto and central Massachusetts may have also struck a chord; they yielded familiar types of labor in quarries, agriculture, and industry.[62] But its geographic situation, as the nearest major port to Europe, made Massachusetts easily accessible and steamer tickets relatively inexpensive, as the Irish had discovered in the 1850s.

In 1894 Italian economist Luigi Einaudi examined and translated US Department of Labor reports and summarized their message in a pamphlet titled *La distribuzione della ricchezza nel Massachusetts* (The distribution of wealth in Massachusetts). His study used economic reports, court filings, and demographic data to examine the distribution of wealth across the commonwealth by social strata. Einaudi concluded that not only were the people in Massachusetts growing wealthier, but men and women at the lowest levels were doing better as well. This was an economy that was expanding, and people at all levels were accumulating greater wealth. Though his main audience was government experts and economists, Einaudi's work shows that Italians at all levels were well aware that Massachusetts was the new land of opportunity.[63] This publication is evidence that the Italian interest in the wealth to be gained in America went beyond the informal network of the laboring classes and was being monitored and discussed by Italian economists; Einaudi's study would have been widely read, and he himself eventually became the Italian prime minister.

For the typical farm laborer, the message that there was wealth to be made in Massachusetts came much less formally. The desperate need to escape economic and social hardship drove the reluctant migrants up a steep learning curve. Less formal publications than Einaudi's appeared in the popular press to offer advice to prospective immigrants, much like Carlo Cerboni's work outlining his movements between Italy and Argentina. But perhaps the most powerful impetus to movement was the information passed by word of mouth along the migration chain. Many *uccelli di passaggio* returned to Italy for the winter and were able to inform other Veneto family members and friends there about work opportunities in Massachusetts. This informal network channeled information about where jobs and housing could be found, which places should be avoided, and how to navigate Ellis Island's inspections. Along with labor strife and low wages in the Veneto fields, all these factors combined to increase the number of Veneto migrants who viewed Massachusetts as their chosen destination.

NOTES

1. Frederic Chapin Lane, *Venice: A Maritime Republic* (Baltimore: Johns Hopkins University Press, 1973), 11, 434–436. Lane observed that in the last days of the republic, "Napoleon plundered Venice systematically: its Mint, its Arsenal, its fleet, its archive and its art treasures" (436). The fabulous treasures that were taken included *la quadriga*, the four horses atop the Basilica San Marco; these were later returned, but arguments continue over artwork, including Veronese's *The Last Supper*.

2. Treviso was captured in 1339, and control over the remainder was solidified between 1404 and 1406 by ousting the Milanese Visconti's power. See Gherardo Ortalli and Giovanni Scarabello, *A Short History of Venice* (Pisa: Pacini Editore, 1999), 67–73.

3. Senator Massimo D'Azeglio, a Sardinian novelist and Italian nationalist, spoke the phrase that defined the postunification challenge of overcoming provincialism: "We have made Italy: now we must make the Italians." Mark F. Gilbert and K. R. Nilsson, *Historical Dictionary of Modern Italy* (Lanham, MD: Scarecrow Press, 2007), 128; Loretta Baldassar and Ros Pesman, *From Paesani to Global Italians: Veneto Migrants in Australia* (Crawley: University of Western Australia Press, 2005), 97. Gabaccia observed, "Nationalists saw the Risorgimento as a modern, political expression of civilita italiana" (35); Donna R. Gabaccia, *Italy's Many Diasporas* (Seattle: University of Washington Press, 2000), 28 and 33–35.

4. Lane, *Venice*, 454.

5. Ortalli and Scarabello, 118.

6. By 1891 industrial development and housing plans were underway, and in 1892 socialists were in power in Venice and building support in the Veneto. See Ortalli and Scarabello, *A Short History of Venice*, 119.

7. Report of Consul James Fletcher, Genoa, Oct. 26, 1886, *Emigration and Immigration Reports of the Consular Officers of the US Bureau of Foreign Commerce* (1854–1903), 257.

8. After the US restricted immigration under the 1920 and 1924 Quota Acts, both Australia and Canada became primary destinations for Venetians. Migration to Australia escalated in the post-1920 era and by 1947 had reached nearly one-third of a million residents; see Loretta Baldassar and Ros Pesman, *From Paesani to Global Italians*, 21, 43.

9. Statistica della Emigrazione Italiana, quoted in Betty Boyd Caroli, *Italian Repatriation from the United States, 1900–1914* (Lincoln, NE: Authors Guild, backprint.com, 2008), 42, 54. Original published by the Center for Migration Studies, 1973 and 2008.

10. Luconi views Italians in America in general as somewhat fitting the category, but I would argue that the distinct Venetian experience fits the model he has portrayed well; see Stefano Luconi, "Italian Americans and Transnationalism Old Wine in New Bottles?" in *Italian Passages Making and Thinking History*, ed. J. P. Russo and T. A. Bengiveno (New York: American Italian Historical Association, 2010), 74–87.

11. Daniella Todesco, D. Berloffa, P. DeBenedet, L. Fontana, *Ciòde e Ciodéti: Un emigrazione stagionale de donne e raggazi dal Bellunese al Trentino* (Feltre: Comunita Montana Feltrina Centro per la documentazione della cultura poplare, 1995). See the chapter by Daniella Todesco, "La Vita della Ciòde in Trentino e l'ufficio del lavoro del comune di Trento.".

12. Casamira Grandi introducing Todesco's research, page 5. Todesco on ciòde, page 9-11. Daniella Todesco, et.al., *Ciòde e Ciodéti: Un emigrazione stagionale de donne e raggazi dal Bellunese al Trentino* (Feltre: Comunita Montana Feltrina Centro per la documentazione della cultura poplare, 1995), 5.

13. "Restare in patria a lavorare sotto gli occhi delle vostre mamme, ma che la dura necessita vi spinge a passare il confine erche a Belluno, mancando lo sviluppo dell'agricoltura e quello di altre industrie di manodopera, si muore di fame." Todesco et al., *Ciòde e Ciodéti*, 9; quoting material in the Belluno bishop's archive dated Apr. 26, 1910.

14. "La miseria a casa ... piangeva perche vedeva i figlia senza," ibid., 82;

15. Desy Berloffa, "Storie di vita raccolte attraverso I documenti d'archivio e la stampa locale," in Todesco, *Ciòde e Ciodéti*, 63–67.

16. Scalabrini established a society of priests, the Missionaries of Saint Charles, known as the Scalabrinians, to carry the church to migrants abroad; see James Robb, "Deep Roots in Italy," *Scalabrinian Fathers* 5, no. 3 (Spring 1995): 184–188.

17. "Giuseppe Chiminello, 1900–1995" (http://www.scalabrini.org/old/index.php?option=com_content&view=article&id=826&catid=120&lang=en).

18. "Queste donne! robustezza, sono brune, alte d'aspettoocchio vivace ... portamento vigoroso." Todesco, "La Vita della Ciode in Trentino e l'ufficio del lavoro del comune di Trento," in Todesco, *Ciòde e Ciodéti*, 16.

19. The family name is Rech and the sopranomme or clan name is Checonét
    – the book alternately uses Rech or Checonét to reference them (i.e., the
    fratelli Rech/Rech brothers or famiglia/family Checonét).
20. Checonét, 5.
21. Italian Ministry of Agriculture, 9.
22. *Quando finiscono il ponte* is known as *la bugia del ponte* (the lie about
    the bridge). Tamara Rech and Marcho Rech, *Scrivere per non dimenti-
    care l'emigrazione di fine '800 in Brasile nelle lettere della famiglia Rech
    Checonét* (Feltre: Libreria Pilotto, 1996), 23.
23. "Speriamo anco di vedervi che una volta o l'altra ritornerete alla vec-
    chia patria"; Tamara Rech and Marco Rech, *Scrivere pe non dimenti-
    care l'emigrazione di finie 800 in Brasile nelle lettere della famiglia Rech
    Checonét* (Feltre: Libreria Pilotto editrice, 1996), 17–23. For an overview
    of Venetian emigration to South America, see Emilio Franzina, *Merica!
    Merica! Emigrazione e colonizzazione delle lettere dei contadini veneti in
    America Latina 1876–1902* (Milan: Feltrinelli Economica, 1979).
24. Rech and Rech, *Scrivere pe non dimenticare*, 152–153.
25. "Agenti di emigrazione promisero *mari e monti* ed I contadini ... grande
    ricchezza dei paesi transatlantici ... come vanghe, zappe ed *aratri d'oro
    massicicco anziche di ferro*. Immaginarsi adunque il fanatismo!" *Jacini
    Commission*, . volume 4, fasc. I, capitolo V, 109.
26. Quoted in Emilio Franzina, *Storia dell'emigrazione veneta dall'unita al
    fascismo* (Verona: Cierre Edizioni, 2005), 85.
27. Volume Quarto, Fasc. I, 4.
28. *Jacini Commission*, 4:3–4.
29. Ibid., 4:149.
30. Volume Quarto, Fasc. I, 6.
31. Ibid.
32. Ibid.
33. Ibid, 7.
34. Ibid.
35. Ibid., 4:7–10.
36. Ibid., 4:110.
37. Carlo Cerboni, *Manuale per l'emigrazione dall'Italia all'Argentina. Pub-
    blicazione approvata dalla Societa di Patronato e Rimpatrio per gli Immi-
    granti Italiani in Buenos Aires* (Buenos Aires: Libreria Italiana "Dante
    Alighieri," 1905), 10, 15–17.
38. Ibid., 15.
39. Ibid., 17.

40. Ibid., 26: "vascello lumaca" (snail ship).

41. Ibid., 39: "Perpetrata a danno degli ingenui, degli ignoranti e per esprimersi piu chiaramente, degli imbecilli, che la pretendono a furbi e sapienti."

42. Ibid., 32: Quoting Luzzatti, "Il fiore di nostre gente infelice."

43. "Addio all' Italia ... guardate bene l'ultimo lembo che vedrete della vostra Italia. Chi sa, se e quando la rivedrete!" Ibid., 24–25.

44. See the chart "Emigrazione all'estero dal comune di Vedelago nel periodo 1876–1905: I paesi di destinazione," in Livio Vanzetto, *Un paese del Veneto rurale nella prima meta del Novecento* (Treviso: Fondazione Benetto Studi Ricerche, 2000), 26–27.

45. See the chart "Emigrazione all'estero dal comune di Vedelago nel periodo 1885–1903: Le famiglie partite e le loro condizioni sociali," in ibid., 28. Franzina, *Storia dell'emigrazione veneta*, 64. For the most detailed statistical analysis, see Emilio Franzina, *La grande emigrazione l'esodo dei rurali dal Veneto durante il secolo XIX* (Venice: Marsilio Editori, 1976), tables I–XV.

46. Cavaglieri, 17.

47. Ibid.

48. "L'emigrazione dal Polesine é specialmente permanente, transatlantica," in Guido Cavaglieri, "La emigrazione dal Polesine," *Riforma sociali,* fasc. 10–11, anno 9, vol. 12 (1902): 16–19.

49. Cavaglieri, "La Emigrazione dal polesine,"17, and chart "Emigrazione permanente 1897–1899," 19.

50. Arbizzani, 127.

51. "Le prime macchine idrovore entrano in azione gia negli anni 1850 nel basso Polesine. Negli anni 1870 ... parte oriental siavvia il prosciugamento artifficiale di decine di miliaia di ettari ... successiva formazione di gradi aziende capitalistiche" in Luigi Arbizzani and Franco Cazzola, *"La Boje!" Moti contadini e societa rurale padana nel secondo Ottocento: Traccia per la ricerca di materiali per una mostra,* in Museo civico San Benedetto Po, *Il lavoro in miniatura* (Rovigo: Istituto Alcide Cervi, 1983), 127–132.

52. Arbizzani, 130.

53. Beginning in 1884 mutual aid societies like Societa di Mutuo Soccorso dei contadini and labor groups like the Associazione Generale dei lavoratori della Terra of Verona, Padova, and Rovigo engaged in protests that lasted into 1885 and led to radicalization; see Arbizzani and Cazzola, *"La Boje!"* 128–132; Franzina, *Storia dell'emigrazione*, 64n14.

54. "Basta la piu piccola disgrazia, la malattia, la morte di uno di famiglia, un cattivo raccolto, la moria nei maiali o nei polli ... i bovari ... abbandonare un buon padrone se non tiene la stalla nel debito onore." Cavaglieri, "La Emigrazione dal polesine," 34.
55. For the population chart, see ibid., 19.
56. "Il miraggio di un improbabile, facile benessere altrove: 'l'America' ... una possibile sanatoria alle gravi condizioni economiche," "una soluzione miracolosa"; Bruna Berti Saccon et al., *Il comune di Revine Lago,* 202–203. On the arrival of the de Grava family, see Tomasi, *Revine: Storia di una comunita,* 176 and 66.
57. Giovanni Tomasi, *Giuseppe Grava 50 anni d'arte, 1957–2007* (Vittorio Veneto: TIPSE, 2008).
58. "List or Manifest of Alien Passengers," SS *Philadelphia,* Mar. 26, 1905 (www.ancestry.com).
59. "List or Manifest of Alien Passengers," SS *Giulio Cesare,* Oct. 1, 1922 (www.ancestry.com). Interview with Ronald F. and US Census Records, Fitchburg, Massachusetts, 1930.
60. Emilio Franzina, *Il Veneto ribelle: Proteste sociali, localismo poplar e sindacalizzazione tra l'unitàm e il fascismo* (Udine: Gaspari, 2001), 159.
61. Renzo Grosselli, *L'emigrazione dal Trentino dal Medioevo alla prima guerra mondiale* (Trentino: Museo degli usi costume della gente Trentina, 1998), 236.
62. In 1908 Italian immigrants established the first Italian-speaking church in north-central Massachusetts, in Fitchburg: Saint Anthony of Padua, honoring the Veneto's most revered saint.
63. Luigi Einaudi, "La distribuzione della ricchezza nel Massachusetts," *Giornale degli economisiti* 14 (Mar. 1897): 1–15. Einaudi, a prominent economist, later became prime minister of the Italian Republic; his original source was *Twenty-Fifth Annual Report of the Bureau of Statistics of Labor,* part 2, *The Distribution of Wealth* (Boston: Bureau of Labor Statistics, 1985), 49–304.

CHAPTER 3

DESTINATION: MASSACHUSETTS

The reluctant emigrants who decided to leave the Veneto often chose Massachusetts as their destination for a number of reasons. Most important, there was a steady demand in the decades after the 1870s for labor on large construction projects in Massachusetts. Contractors needed skilled stonecutters and unskilled laborers to complete massive infrastructure projects that were similar to projects Venetians had worked on in Europe. In addition, there was year-round employment available in the mills and factories of Massachusetts's rapidly growing industrial sector, where textile and paper mills and heavy industrial concerns, especially foundries, created a constant demand for workers.

In time, Boston could be reached more directly from Europe, making the return journey shorter than traveling to New York to board a transatlantic steamer to the Veneto. The burgeoning North End community, with its Italian-owned grocery stores, banking services, and labor agencies, was directly linked to central Massachusetts by rail. By 1896 the migratory flows into the port of Boston led the government to establish District 3 of the Bureau of Immigration in the Italian neighborhood of East Boston; by 1919 a new East Boston station had been built only a short ferry ride from the North End, and by 1924 it had expanded to four stations in the harbor. Immigrants could eliminate transit through New York's Ellis Island altogether, and Massachusetts became even more accessible. The money and the time spent on a transatlantic crossing were greatly reduced, favorable developments for those who made repeated crossings of the Atlantic.[1]

Not only were the impoverished contadini of the Veneto communicating among themselves about the opportunities in Massachusetts, but at the highest levels of the Italian government, economists were discussing this commonwealth in the American Northeast as a place of special opportunity; Luigi Einaudi's *La distribuzione della ricchezza nel Massachusetts*, mentioned in the preceding chapter, found that wealth was expanding at every social level in Massachusetts. Einaudi, later the Italian premier, also observed that industrial expansion in the period 1889–1891 showed the emergence of great factories. The population of the commonwealth had been rising at a rapid rate and had expanded by 25.5 percent between 1880 and 1890. In addition, more renters were becoming landowners, and probate records indicated that women were becoming more independent in this expanding economy.[2]

But for the hungry and underemployed of northeastern Italy it was the quarries, factories, and mills that beckoned, and news of job opportunities was passed from one to another by those who had emigrated to America and returned to Italy. Most often, such migrants first worked seasonally on construction projects, spending winters with family in the Veneto and returning to America the following year. Some settled permanently in Massachusetts, and for them letters and remittances were sent home as evidence of their newly earned wealth.

Whether immigrants arrived at Ellis Island or in East Boston, they had to clear the US government's physical inspection. This was a series of examinations that grew in complexity over time and became progressively more difficult to pass. Ellis Island's inspectors represented the biggest hurdle to entry into America, and this was where many failed. Immigrants were given physical, mental, and even political examinations. These included a painful eye examination for trachoma, an inspection of their hair for a contagious scalp disease called favus, and an estimation of their physical and mental fitness. Then the inspectors interviewed the alien immigrants in detail about their economic and political situations: they probed their ability to support themselves, their level of literacy in their native language, the amount of money they possessed, and their political and social views (anarchists and polygamists were excluded by the Immigration Act of 1891).

Most immigrants who were excluded were those who arrived without any money or who appeared unable to work because of either physical or mental disability. Often, an elderly or disabled person was singled out from a family group to be returned to Italy. If an immigrant passed all the tests but had no money at all, usually having lost it to gambling, theft, or other misfortune on the steamer, they could be designated "liable to become a public charge" and be sent back to Europe at the expense of the steamship company.

In an ironic twist, if immigrants responded positively when asked whether anyone had paid their passage or whether they had signed a labor contract, they were liable to exclusion under the Alien Contract Labor Law, or the Foran Act, passed by Congress in 1885. This law barred the entry of anyone contracted to work in exchange for passage, which Congress deemed a threat to American labor and which drew support from the Knights of Labor as well as immigration restrictionists. Ohio Representative Martin Foran made it clear he aimed to restrict immigration from Italy with this legislation when he argued on the floor of Congress against the admission of "large numbers of degraded, ignorant, brutal Italian and Hungarian laborers."[3] In his 1907 study of the Alien Contract Labor Law, Samuel Orth concluded that the act was passed in order "to sift out from the mass of immigrants the more undesirable individuals and to return them to their native lands."[4] Court testimony in a test case of the legislation revealed the motivation for the law and the deep resentment in Congress toward immigrants, most especially

Italians, who spent as little as possible on housing and food, planning to return to Italy in the fall with their year's savings. Because many of these transnational laborers would readily accept seasonal work for low wages as part of their strategy to return home, they could survive on earnings that no American laborer paying for a tenement would or could accept. Skilled native laborers especially viewed immigrants as a threat to their permanent jobs and to the bargaining power of their unions.

For congressional lawmakers the attitude of the seasonal migrants, the *uccelli di passaggio* was a rejection of the American dream: "Many of them lived when here but little, if any, better than animals ... on nearly nothing ... they only asked, and only received, wages on which an American could not live ... They gave their children no education. They never intended to make this country their home."[5] It was this last aspect of seasonal migration that was most resented by members of Congress and the public because it threatened to undermine skilled laborers who sought higher wages and permanent employment.

The foremost advocates of immigration restriction in Congress were Ohio representative Martin Foran, Massachusetts senator Henry Cabot Lodge, and Vermont senator William Dillingham. Immigration restriction had a small but powerful group of activists who gathered information, wrote articles for the press, lobbied Congress, and waged a decades-long campaign to restrict southern European immigration in general and Italian immigration in particular. Chief in this realm was the Immigration Restriction League (IRL), founded by a group of Harvard alumni and professors based in Boston in 1894. Led by Prescott Farnsworth Hall, Charles Warren, and Robert DeCourcy Ward, members of the IRL were motivated by fear not only that waves of immigrants would overwhelm America's "native" race with large numbers but also that Americans would produce fewer children and lose their economic position. The IRL's legislative success belied its small numbers but was greatly magnified by its politically well-connected leadership. Lodge and Dillingham frequently quoted IRL sources in their reports and heard testimony in Congress from members of the IRL, including the eugenicist Madison Grant.

One of the earliest calls for such legislation was sounded by Harvard College professor Nathaniel Shaler, who wrote "Shall Immigration be Restricted?" for the *Century* in 1887. Shaler argued, "The sober, work-a-day citizen, compelled to stop his work and listen to the ravings of an imported mob, whose natural platform is Drink, Dirt and Disorder, begins to wonder whether he has really been given the providential mission of bearing with this scum." Shaler focused on what he called the "dangerous classes," but not necessarily on Italians.[6]

In 1896, however, IRL president Prescott Farnsworth Hall wrote in the *North American Review* of the threat presented specifically by Italian "birds of passage" who "have been here not once merely, but several times; who came here to live for a time under degraded conditions at a low wage and soon carry their savings back to Italy." What bothered Hall most was that the Italians "migrate back and forth," a practice that he saw as "proof they have no wish to assimilate and to permanently settle here; that they came here not to help build up the country ... they live in a way no American, German or Irishman would live for a day." He argued that most Italians were destined for New England, New York, New Jersey, or Pennsylvania but that "some effective means can be devised for diverting Italian immigration to the west and south, [for] we want no large body of Italian laborers."[7]

Some of the restrictionists distinguished between northern and southern Italians, as did senator Henry Cabot Lodge in an 1891 article in which he argued that Italians emigrated "largely from the southern provinces, Naples and Sicily"; he then quoted an 1886 consular report from Rome stating that "the habits and morals" of those leaving "from northern and central portions of Italy ... are sober and industrious, and as a rule trustworthy and moral. They are generally strong, powerful workers, and capable of enduring great fatigue." The report goes on to describe southern illiteracy and "brigandage."[8] The consul's (and Lodge's) favoritism toward northern migrants, however, quickly disappeared once they had arrived in the United States as all were lumped together as Italian, and together they faced the same prejudice. Racial distinctions drove much of the IRL's ideology, and its input was reflected in the Dillingham Commission report to Congress, which included a *Dictionary of Races or Peoples*, as well as a chart that classified the immigrants of the world into three broad categories: Teutonic, Alpine, and Mediterranean.

According to the commission's dictionary, Italians fell between Alpine and Mediterranean races; Dillingham, Lodge, and the rest of the commission spent five pages struggling to define what they saw as the physical and intellectual differences between north and south. They concluded that Italian immigration was a significant concern for two reasons. First, Italy was "one of the most illiterate countries of Europe," although "the smallest degree of illiteracy is found in the valley of the Po among the North Italians."??? Second, they were concerned by "the immense capacity of the Italian race to populate other parts of the earth."??? Government inspectors at Ellis Island were directed to record under the category "race" whether an Italian was northern or southern.[9]

Thus, Veneto immigrants faced a highly charged atmosphere at Ellis Island and in America with little knowledge of the racial and economic tensions that underlay American society. In 1885 Martin Foran, representative of Ohio, had encouraged the passage of the Alien Contract Labor Law by arguing that Americans were an "advanced and vigorous race" that would be "deteriorated by coming in contact with other races and peoples."[10] Labor scholar Matthew Lindsay termed the restrictionists' argument as "racial nativism" and traced its origins to the extended economic downturn after the Panic of 1873.[11] Repeated boom and bust cycles in the American economy only reinforced the determination to shut what restrictionists called "the unguarded gates" of Ellis Island.

Their first legislative success was the Alien Contract Labor Law, which halted the practice of signing immigrants to a contract overseas and giving them steamship tickets; contractors were not "in any way to prepay or in any way assist or encourage the importation or migration of any alien or aliens"; there were steep penalties of $1,000 per offense. In addition, those immigrants who landed were to be returned at the expense of the steamship company or the contractor.[12]

Restrictionists demanded tighter inspections and expanded the political reasons to exclude immigrants. Statistics regarding the exclusion of immigrants at Ellis Island show that between 1892 and 1900, a total of 22,515 immigrants were excluded; 67 percent (15,070) were classified as likely to become a public charge and another 25.7 percent (5,792) under the Foran Act provisions. Between 1901 and 1910, some 108,211 were excluded, 58 percent (63,311) rejected as liable to public charge and 12 percent (12,991) under the Foran Act. In the period 1911–1920, some 178,109 were returned, of which 50 percent (90,045) were deemed liable to public charge, and 8.6 percent (15,417) were rejected under the Foran Act. Although the percentage sank, the rising totals reflect the massive numbers of immigrants processed at the height of migration, between 1900 and 1914.

Under the Immigration Act of 1917, the categories for denying entry were tightened further: anarchists were first on the blacklist, followed by contract labor (with an exception for artists and singers) and "laborers who come in response to advertisements for laborers published abroad," a provision that extended the exclusion beyond those who had signed a contract to those who admitted they had heard of a job offer. Other categories of exclusion included persons whose passage was paid by any corporation, those likely to become a public charge, and those who believed in the assassination of public officials.[13]

Members of Congress and immigration restrictionists constantly railed about the anarchist threat coming from Europe and feared communists and socialists, as well. Yet inspectors were able to identify and exclude only a very few potential immigrants using the political questions. The fear of anarchism was driven by the tragic assassination of US president William McKinley in 1901. Between 1901 and 1910, only ten anarchists were identified for exclusion (.00009 percent) among the total immigrant population entering the United States. In the following decade, 1911–1920, another twenty-seven immigrants (.00015 percent) were excluded for ideological reasons. McKinley's assassin was a self-proclaimed anarchist, Leon Czolgosz, but he was neither an Italian nor an immigrant. He was the Michigan-born son of Polish immigrants. But the two branches of the government that dealt with immigration and its impact, the Treasury Department and the United States Labor Department, were studying the effects of the waves of immigration on the American economy and labor market. Labor Department analyst John Koren focused his research on Italians in particular and wrote an 1897 report titled *The Padrone System and Padrone Banks.*

Italian immigrants were the particular focus of contract labor questions owing to the prominent role of the padroni. Italians were often sent to Italy to recruit laborers, who would get a ticket in exchange for a promise to work off the debt, but this led to widespread abuses. Upon arrival, each immigrant had to give the name and address of someone at his or her chosen destination. Those who arrived with a specific destination with a relative or friend to help them could easily navigate past the immigration inspectors. These restrictions made it critical that the new immigrants, or greenhorns, learn from the worldlier *Americani*, who had literally been in their position before. Thus, the exchange of information and the construction of a web of contacts on both sides of the Atlantic became vital for the Veneto migrants.

Koren argued that most Italians arrived under the control of the padroni and "were already bound out to service."[14] Although "more stringent enforcement of the contract-labor law" since 1882 had its effects, Koren pointed out that the "common laborer, or *cafone* as he is vulgarly called"[15] was afraid to act for himself and readily paid his padrone the *bossatura* (fee) for a job. Moreover, in Boston padrone bosses supplied "nearly all there is of unskilled Italian labor to the railroads and for the multitude of contract jobs carried on in the cities and towns of

Massachusetts."[16] But Koren viewed favorably the efforts by Boston's Italian Workmen's Aid Association to counter the padroni, as "in no other city in the country have efforts led by people outside the colony been made to dislodge the bosses and improve the condition of their victims."[17] He warned against "the peculiar system of banking in vogue among the Italians"[18] and the "multifarious occupations of the Italian banker."[19] In particular, he warned that Italians who sent remittances home to support their families were often victims of the padrone bankers they had trusted. The remittances of Italian laborers were of massive proportions. Koren quoted a Senate committee's calculation that Italian banks, in New York alone, had transferred anywhere from $25,000,000 to $30,000,000 per year to Italy.[20] Koren's research on the fate of Italians in the American economy was translated into Italian and reprinted in the journal *La Riforma Sociale* later in 1897, the same year that Luigi Einaudi also translated and reprinted a US Department of Labor study on wealth in Massachusetts.[21]

Padroni operated even in small towns as local bankers and job agencies and on a more massive scale as subcontractors on public-works projects. The Italian term *padrone* was originally associated with estate managers who hired and managed farm labor, but in America the word was applied to Italian labor contractors and subcontractors, as well as to bankers. Eventually, the American usage of the term encompassed labor subcontractors from other ethnic groups. Historian Gunther Peck, in an exploration of the padrone's power over Italian, Greek, and other ethnic groups, noted that "although immigrant workers rebelled against the padrone's exactions, they did not reject the language of contracts that sanctioned his authority."[22] In other words, even though a padrone exploited them, greenhorns desperately needed someone to guide them into the labor market and preferred to trust one of their own. Seasonal migrants quickly learned how to avoid the pitfalls and work for those they could trust, but they still had to carefully answer the questions at Ellis Island regarding contract labor.

There was a delicate balance to answering the immigration officials' questions correctly, assuring the inspectors at Ellis Island that newcomers would work and support themselves. Most often they responded that they were headed for a specific destination where they had friends to help them establish themselves but that they had no padrone connection. Once past the gates, they then had to find their way to their destination, rent lodgings, maneuver into the labor market, and earn enough to survive. Therefore, having a network of friends or kin from one's home *paese* removed the greatest risks facing the new immigrant.

Once beyond this daunting gantlet, immigrants bought rail tickets or took the ferry. Once they had arrived at the North End, successful Veneto migrants would find one of the largest colonies of Italians in America, stores stocked with Italian imported food products, people who might speak their dialect, and Italian-speaking priests and church communities, as well as padrone banks. Rail transport was only a short walk away: the Haymarket Square station opened travel on the Boston and Maine railroad and to Causeway Street, where the Fitchburg Railroad Depot served all points west across central Massachusetts.[23] Fitchburg was a rail crossroads with connections north into Vermont (another destination for northern Italian migrants, especially marble workers, was Barre), south to Connecticut, and west through Albany, New York, to Chicago, Illinois.

The Fitchburg Railroad had been built as a fifty-mile link to Boston by Alvah Crocker, the owner of a large paper mill in Fitchburg and opened in 1845, but this was only the first stage of a massive plan that focused on central Massachusetts. All along this industrial belt were factories, mills, and public-works projects in need of cheap labor. For the skilled and the unskilled alike there was tremendous opportunity, and economic growth was taking place throughout the state, especially across this northern tier. Fitchburg's population was 2,604 in 1840, but after the rail line opened it nearly doubled, reaching 5,120 in 1850, and its growth continued steadily over the following decades.[24]

Fitchburg's six quarries provided granite for railroad bridges, building projects, and road construction. Stone from the quarries in Fitchburg was used to construct the rail depot in Boston, and Crocker later established a northern Vermont and Massachusetts railroad from the town. His dreams of railroad construction farther westward, beyond the means of local investors, would open commerce from Boston to the western territories which attracted support from the Commonwealth of Massachusetts.

In addition, Fitchburg became a center of development for related industries: steam-engine equipment manufacturing, tool and die making, and iron foundries. Mills and factories based in Massachusetts dominated the production of wool and cotton cloth, paper, saws, and farm machinery. After 1874 raw materials and finished products could cross through the region to every point on the compass via rail, and Fitchburg's population rose again to 12,429. This economic engine drove commercial expansion and opened up western Massachusetts public-works projects.

Once the railroad project started, Crocker appealed to the Commonwealth of Massachusetts for financial support. Boston's legislators agreed to the massive project, which cut a rail connection to New York State that opened a direct line to the west. The biggest obstacle to success was the need to dig, blast, and cut a five-mile-long tunnel under Hoosac Mountain. By 1862 the drilling and digging required massive amounts of labor, and the project appeared to stall. Fitchburg inventor Charles Burleigh designed a rock drill that was able to shatter the rock and bore through the Hoosac range, opening the way to New York. The use of black powder gave way to that of more powerful but less stable liquid nitroglycerine, which took many workers' lives. But even with these advances, construction crept on for a quarter of a century and cost the Massachusetts legislature an alarming twenty million dollars. The project was lampooned as "the great bore" for its financial and human cost, as well as its seemingly endless delays. Skeptics included Oliver Wendell Holmes, who poetically mocked the hope that trains would one day "Roll through the Hoosac Tunnel bore" and pessimistically concluded, "when you see that blessed day, then order your ascension robes."[25]

But the project made Fitchburg a booming railroad and industrial center. Burleigh's drill was adapted for use in building the Brooklyn Bridge and in western mining operations, and his company made a fortune producing the drills in Fitchburg and shipping them across the country by rail. The railroad opened up a convenient path for a new generation of immigrants to find work in central Massachusetts and farther west.[26] Fitchburg's industrial base expanded as factories and mills found markets for their products. Proud city fathers called Fitchburg "Machine City" as steam engine companies, foundries, boiler works, and bicycle, saw, and scythe factories expanded and as numerous paper and textile mills shipped their goods across the nation.

By the 1890s a new crisis had emerged in Boston that affected central Massachusetts and created even more demand for labor. The rapid population influx to metropolitan Boston resulted in a water-consumption rate that promised to soon outstrip the water supply. The only way to provide enough water to Boston and its environs was via a massive dam, reservoir, and aqueduct project that would drain the watershed of central Massachusetts for delivery eastward. This project would require massive amounts of labor to clear the land and build both the dam and its network of delivery tunnels.

By the early 1900s laborers from the Veneto and northern Italy arrived to work on the massive Wachusett Dam and Reservoir project in Clinton, Massachusetts. The plan was to clear a valley of all its trees, buildings, and topsoil and then to build a massive dam; this became the largest hand-dug reservoir project in the world. The undertaking attracted many skilled stonecutters and quarry workers from Italy, as well as masses of unskilled pick-and-shovel laborers. Work began in 1896 and lasted for a decade, just as the worst economic and social misery was striking the Veneto region.

The Wachusett Dam was described as similar in design (but not scale) to New York State's Croton Dam, a project that also used large number of Italian laborers working under padroni. *Scientific American* magazine described the massive amounts of stone required to construct a barrier capable of holding back sixty-three billion gallons of water: "It is 19 feet in thickness at the water level and at 145 feet below the waterline the thickness increases to 120 feet. It is built of first-class masonry laid in cement. The maximum depth ... is 158 feet."[27] The dam's vast scale attracted national interest even as it attracted international labor.

Scientific American ran a series of features describing the immense venture and compared it to the Periyar project in India. No American undertaking equaled its ambitious scope. It would drain 118 square miles of watershed to provide water to the entire Boston metropolitan region. Nearly four thousand acres of topsoil had to be removed and four hundred buildings destroyed, as well as more than 1,700 persons relocated—all to clear eight miles of valley. It was necessary to strip the topsoil to reduce the potential for organic contaminants in the reservoir, and the work was to be done using the least expensive means: hand labor. Removing nearly a foot of loam, along with groundcover and trees, from so vast an area was described as "the heroic task of scraping the surface soil from the whole of the six and a half square miles." The burgeoning population of Boston was promised the project would provide "an abundant supply (of water) for the future, presumably for all time, but in fact for nearly a century."[28]

The work force was almost entirely composed of two groups: Italian stonecutters and laborers and African American laborers. The first workers to arrive from Italy were largely northerners experienced in working with stone. Throughout the Veneto, as mentioned earlier, a variety of stone was cut from quarries for the construction of homes, barns, other buildings, and memorials. Decorative stone carving and sculpture were well-respected arts, and the Veneto's native tufa stone is soft and easily cut and worked. To the west of the Veneto were marble quarries, as well. Northern Italian stonecutters and unskilled workers soon began the voyage to the staging area of the massive project in Clinton, Sterling, and West Boylston, Massachusetts.

One of the earliest arrivals was Pietro Cassinari. *Pietro*, the equivalent of the name Peter, is similar to the Italian word for "rock," *pietra*. Cassinari was part of a large web of workers whose network enabled them to safely navigate the immigration restrictions in the United States and to construct a transnational life between northern Italy and central Massachusetts. He left from Rivergaro, near Piacenza in northwest Italy; he could read and write, and his most marketable skill was that he knew how to cut stone. Cassinari continued to make transatlantic trips to work on the Wachusett Dam project for over a decade, while he left behind his wife and a son, Giuseppe, born in Italy while his father was away working.

Why leave wife and son in Italy? Seasonal work could provide substantial savings, leaving enough to pay for a return ticket to the Veneto. Much of the project shut down during the harsh New England winters, and most workers found it better to spend the money on a return trip rather than on rent during idle times. The work camps were unappealing. The sites were isolated and populated almost entirely by men. They had been organized by the Metropolitan Water Works and had two commissary buildings, but no permanent housing had been constructed. Workers lived in flat areas in nearby Sterling and West Boylston, where they constructed crude huts.

The United States Census Bureau visited the workers in 1900 and recorded forty-one Italians as residents, including Pietro Cassinari, at the "Italian Colony in Metropolitan Water Works" and described each as a "boarder" and a "day laborer." Of nearly fifty Italians resident at the site, twelve could not read and write. Hebert Bazoli was listed as manager of the camp. Only one of the men was residing with a wife and a nine-year-old son, who was listed as "at school," along with a four-year-old daughter.[29] All the other workers, whether single or married, lived with other men.

These work camps were no place for young women or children. Period photographs reveal a dusty hillside, with small, square huts built of branches rather than sawn wood sprouting up amid a tangle of broken wagons, wagon wheels, and dirt. Other images show closely packed rows of huts with tree-limb frames and patchwork roofs. Men in rough clothing and work vests peer back at the photographer, and a dog stares at the camera, but there are no visible water taps or sanitary facilities. The only conventional buildings, farther afield, were two long, narrow commissary buildings that served food and beer.

The Veneto migrants had constructed from scavenged wood and reeds dwellings that closely resembled the ancient *pallefitte* of the Bronze Age settlers in the Veneto. In the 1880s, before they left Italy, the poorest farmers of the Veneto had resorted to building similar huts during the worst economic hardships, as discovered by the Italian government's Jacini Commission. Those who had escaped the starvation and disease-ridden Veneto now found themselves huddled in similar unsanitary conditions, working hard every day yet desperate for shelter. Without water or sanitary services and home to a population composed almost entirely of men in their twenties and thirties, these camps were primitive settlements. Italians were criticized by American immigration restrictionists for not permanently settling in America, especially for spending as little and saving as much cash as possible.

But workers like Cassinari and his fellows pursued a different American dream. They aimed to earn money in America but to return to northern Italy, carrying their wealth with them. The harsh winters of Massachusetts led many to return home armed with the savings of a summer's harsh labor. Each spring they returned, the *uccelli di passagiati*, crossing the Atlantic. Often, Cassinari returned with a relative or a friend and continued working, even after the dam project was completed in 1905. In 1909 he was still commuting, and in 1919 his nineteen-year-old son, not Giuseppe but Joseph Cassinari, left Rivergaro, joining him in the quarries of central Massachusetts.

Allessandro Bottazzi arrived in 1897 to work on the dam. Described by officials at Ellis Island on the ship's manifest as a "peasant," he was thirty-one years old and had left his wife in Italy. In 1909 his daughter, Teresa, joined him, but they did not lodge in the camp. They lived in the town of Clinton, where rooms could be rented. A skilled stonecutter, he worked until an accident crushed a leg and left him in failing health; Bottazzi decided to return to his wife across the Atlantic. But he journeyed back to Piacenza alone after his teenage daughter refused to accompany him. Bottazzi's last act before leaving was to entrust his daughter to the care of Pietro Cassinari's son and daughter in Fitchburg. In her late teens, Teresa Bottazzi lived on Pine Street and found work with many other young northern Italian women as a spinner in a mill. A few years later, she met and married another immigrant from Rosà, in the Veneto, and remained in America.

In 1909 Pietro Cassinari made yet another transatlantic journey, and on his return to America he took with him Giovanni Bottazzi, another relative, to join Teresa.[30] They were children of the same *paese*, and their fathers were friends. They had begun to organize regular voyages to expand the network of kin working together. Although the journeys had begun as seasonal migrations, their transnational network began to establish roots in America and to take the place of the family from which they were separated. In dialect, an older woman might be called, *comare*, which could mean she had been your godmother at your baptism, a blood relative like an aunt, or simply someone like the Cassinari, you had come to trust and treat as kin. In the isolation of the steamship voyage, the construction camps, and urban tenements, it was vital to forge these bonds, even among friends or the friends of friends. In this way the Veneti constructed new bonds among their *paesani* in order to establish some desperately needed security far from home. In this way social networks emerged in America. People bound by these informal relationships often played important roles in their lives as people married and had children. They might work together, board together, and eventually when they married these persons might serve as a best man, maid of honor or a real godparent in religious ceremonies. They took responsibility for looking after each other and their children. Over time they appeared to be part of each other's family. In this way they created a new social network in America to replace the family network they had left behind in the Veneto. These networks were especially important because illness or injury might leave them isolated and vulnerable in America. Italians in Massachusetts often undertook dangerous work in factories, quarries, or construction.

Workers remained largely isolated and nameless, however, as they labored on the Wachusett Dam. Newspaper accounts of death and injury on the job rarely identified the person involved. Work was dangerous, and they were considered quite literally in terms of numbers; their treatment by their employers was impersonal. A Massachusetts Department of Conservation and Recreation historian of the Wachusett project, Kelley Freda, described their anonymity: "All Italian laborers were given a number upon arrival in the camps and work sites, after which they were rarely referred to by name."[31] Throughout the process of immigration, these workers had already suffered the misspelling of their names and the mangled pronunciation of their home *comuni*, but now they were reduced to nameless numbers for the convenience of their employers. The Metropolitan Water Works was not alone in this practice of using numbers to identify foreign-named workers. It was common in Massachusetts and perhaps reflected an American impatience in dealing with the foreign. Under the padrone system, employers could use a middleman to find the workers, and they often remained in that role, so there was a complete disconnect between employers and Italian laborers.

The massive dam project's Italian labor bosses provided another more important degree of separation between government funding and the disbursement of pay to workers. Under this system a padrone contracted with the state to provide a set number of workers, who were described as day laborers and were paid only for the time during which their labor was required. There was no job security. If they were not needed owing to weather conditions or a shift in the project's requirements, they went unpaid. The system was very similar to that in the Veneto, where *braccianti* were hired as farm labor, paid for the days they worked, then released. Moreover, not all their wages went to them. Under the *bossatura* system, the padrone subtracted a fee from his workers' wages for having provided them with the job. Payment for their labor was remitted by the Commonwealth of Massachusetts to the padrone, who in turn paid the workers after subtracting his fee and the cost of food, board, and so on, from the total. As boarders in the camps, workers were paying a percentage of their wages for board though they were living in self-constructed reed huts that lacked sanitary facilities.

Thus, the padroni could easily profit at the workers' expense, as one local newspaper reported: "in September 1896, all but one of over 200 Italian laborers working under a single contractor refused work because they had not received their pay for over two and a half months."[32] Once the state had paid the labor contractor, any question about payment was between the padrone and the workers. There was ample room for corruption. Once the state had paid the padrone, it was his duty to pay the workers the rate he had promised them and had billed the Commonwealth of Massachusetts. Only the padroni knew whether the amounts were the same.

Relations between the residents of the camps and the town were strained. Clinton had remained "wet," while neighboring towns went "dry," forbidding the sale of alcohol. But the presence of large numbers of workers in the camps and the sale of beer in the commissaries caused trouble. Police raided the camps and in 1904 banned the sale of liquor in commissaries.[33] When the Wachusett project was completed in 1905, the workers were compelled to leave when the Sterling area camp was closed. On the New York Croton Dam project and the Ashokan Dam, built between 1905 and 1907, as well as other massive public-works projects, it was common for local governments to specify before work began that no permanent housing was to be built by contractors. Communities in New York State and the Commonwealth of Massachusetts wanted the projects completed but did not want the workers to take up residence there or to compete for other local jobs afterward. Thus, the work camps, purposely temporary in nature, were to be so unpleasant that laborers would leave the area once the project was completed.

Fitchburg's population swelled with Italians from both the north and south after the conclusion of the Wachusett Dam project. Numerous stonecutters found work in Fitchburg, home to quarries and heavy industry. In addition, in the period 1892–1912 the local trolley system, the Fitchburg and Leominster Street Railway, was dramatically expanded, requiring gangs of laborers to lay thirty miles of rail lines. Throughout central Massachusetts, the early railroad lines were being expanded as new industries connected to the system. The demand for construction labor and factory workers continued to expand. A seasonal job on a construction site might disappear after a few years, but a migrant might become a mill worker and decide to settle more permanently with a steady paycheck.

A historian of Fitchburg's industrial development observed "industry rushing ahead in a frenzy of expansion sounded the cry for cheap and unskilled immigrant labor. Agents [were] sent to Europe recruited labor with stories of rosy prospects." But the influx was not welcomed by the general population. In the same paragraph, the historian termed the immigrants "the incoming hoard" that arrived only to find "low wages and wretched homes in crowded city slums."[34] The city was ideally situated to boom, and those investors who established foundries, boiler works, and engineering and steam works became known as the Machine City tycoons.

The key to the boom was the position of Fitchburg in north central Massachusetts as a rail crossroads. As discussed earlier, the completion of the Hoosac Tunnel in western Massachusetts opened up an east-west corridor from Boston to Chicago, and there was also a north-south axis running from Worcester to Canada. Eino Wiita, a railroad worker, recalled the Fitchburg's central role as a freight crossroads and its key role in moving the production of its heavy industry: rolls of paper for newsprint could weigh tons, so moving heavy freight out of the granite quarries, machine shops, and the Dillon Boiler Works necessitated rail transport. To Wiita, Crocker's railroad benefited all of the region's industrialists: "They needed the railroads for transporting most of their goods ... there was no other way to get it out."[35]

Among these industrial entrepreneurs were Hiram Maxim, who settled in Fitchburg as a machinist and apprentice before leaving for England, where he patented his design for the Maxim machine gun; and Charles Burleigh, who made his fortune when his steam drill that tunneled through Hoosac Mountain later was used in silver and gold mines out west. Heavy industry, especially iron and brass foundries, were established next to the rail yards at the end of Water Street, where they could supply the repair sheds in the yards. In addition, the city of Fitchburg, from east to west, was home to textile mills, including the Parkhill Mills and the Wachusett, Orwell, Cleghorn, and Duck Mills, which manufactured everything from delicate cotton gingham to heavy wool, as well as rugged duck cloth for soldier's clothing. The Fosdick brothers established the Fitchburg Steam Engine Company and built machines to replace the old water-powered systems throughout Massachusetts. The Crocker, Wallace, Lowe, and Burbank families established a number of paper mills. Many of these "tycoons" employed hundreds of workers and steadily expanded their work forces, and although they also set an example as philanthropists in the city, that did not insulate them from labor unrest.

In the 1890s a series of strikes in the machine shops brought labor violence into the city. It returned in 1907 with a vengeance: even the Fosdicks' steam-engine works was struck. The Fosdick brothers had prided themselves on treating their workers well but eventually resorted to importing machinists from New York. The identity of the replacement workers is unknown, but there were two Italians (Peter and Michele Cielo) among the thirty-seven apprentices who went on strike. The machinists' union invited all union men to join them in a labor parade that was led by the Fitchburg band and the Italian Roma Band.[36]

The influx of foreign labor not only more than doubled the population of the city but also changed its demographic composition. By 1895 the population had reached 26,409, of which 9,060 (34 percent) were foreign born. As they settled and established families, the foreign born grew to 36 percent of Fitchburg's population, and their children represented another 38 percent, totaling 74 percent of Fitchburg's population. Within a few decades, Fitchburg had been transformed from a small town of a few thousand Yankee families into an industrial center where three out of four residents were either foreign born or the children of foreign born.[37]

Housing these new workers in the community was a challenge. The Rollstone Hill quarries crown the hilltop in west Fitchburg, and wound around the hill's slopes were dozens of triple-decker tenements, a uniquely New England form of dense urban housing. Small, cold flats—apartments lacking hot water and central heating—usually in three-story buildings, often had shared bathrooms accessed in the hall but were a vast improvement over life in the Metropolitan Water Works camps. Such buildings often had two or even three apartments per floor and were constructed cheaply of wood in a balloon-frame design that took up very little acreage. Tenements were built on lots so small and were packed so densely along Leighton Street that a daring person could jump from the roof of one triple-decker to the next. Originating in Worcester, Massachusetts, such housing offered a path to home ownership for an ambitious worker who could secure a mortgage on the tenement, occupy one floor, and use rents from the other apartments to pay off his debt. But the vast majority of workers lived in rented tenements or boarded with others as they pooled their earnings to survive. They were highly mobile; many still arrived in spring and left in late fall, but others who remained in residence year round also moved from tenement to tenement, either seeking improved conditions or escaping rental debt.[38]

The improved living conditions in Massachusetts opened the way for wives, sisters, and children to leave the Veneto and join family in America. This expanded multigenerational migration led to apartments housing a blend of family members and extended networks of kin and friends sharing expenses. A single boarder without friends to contribute to a shared rental might pay weekly for a room in someone else's rented apartment. Larger families with eight or nine children often squeezed into a three-bedroom apartment where everyone shared beds, but it was not uncommon to find even a small family with several boarders all sharing a single bedroom. Among those who arrived for the first time, most often a group of kin or village friends pooled their earnings to pay the rent in a boardinghouse for a season.

Life in the tenements was hard but better than in the mountains of the Veneto. A wood or coal stove in the kitchen allowed for cooking and was often the only source of heat. Apartments were so cold that frost formed on the inside of windows in the winter. As in the Veneto, cornmeal provided enough polenta to fill hungry mouths but did not supply all the nutrients that were needed. In America it was cheap and easy to buy a box of cornmeal, but that required cash; workers had access to a broader variety of foods, especially fresh vegetables and meat, but they had to pay for them. Italian stores sprouted in immigrant neighborhoods to provide imported foods and wine.

Even in the heart of the city, tiny *orti* (vegetable gardens) supplemented the diet. Veneto migrants reverted to their favorite foods, sometimes to the consternation of Massachusetts natives, who did not understand why foreigners were harvesting dandelions along the roadside or eating fried zucchini flowers. Small caged areas of tenement yards were populated with rabbits, chickens, and even pigs raised for slaughter. Homemade sausage and salami were preserved every fall to last the family through the winter.

One resident of Beech Street recalled that her father, a widower, had raised nine children in an apartment above their store. He slaughtered a pig in fall, ground the meat, and hung the sausages and salami to dry from poles mounted around the kitchen ceiling. He bought baskets of grapes in the same season, crushed them in a wine press, and buried the wine bottles in the dirt cellar of his tenement. Nothing was wasted: the remnants in the press were used to make grappa.[39] Veneto migrants followed the foodways of their homeland as closely as they could and managed with what was available in Massachusetts. *Radici* were gathered, most often dandelions, and cooked and served in spring. Tomato, squash, and zucchini plants were cultivated in the smallest corners of tenement yards. The Veneto migrants harvested the flowers when zucchini plants were less than three inches long and breaded and fried them as a delicacy. American neighbors found "fried flowers" difficult to imagine. The Crocker family, wealthy industrialists, allowed local Italian children to harvest dandelions on the broad lawn of their home in spring. The massive estate had stables, as well as gardens designed by Frederick Law Olmstead, and dominated a hilltop overlooking the town. For the children it was one of the few rural spots they could walk to in such an industrialized area. In the fall the last carrots from the garden were buried in the sandy cellar. The traditional economizers, pasta and polenta, filled empty stomachs, but the Italian stores offered more affordable foods and a more varied diet. The scourge of pellagra was left behind in the Veneto, although a variety of communicable diseases were rampant in Fitchburg's crowded tenements.

The influx from the Veneto followed a distinct path: new arrivals landed in one of the town's poorest neighborhoods, once mainly Irish, called the Patch. The neighborhood ran along Water and Middle Streets near the largest Roman Catholic church, Saint Bernard's, which had served an Irish American congregation since 1845—a group that had helped build Alvah Crocker's railroad. By 1880 the parish had constructed a large church, but the Irish priests found that their new Italian congregants practiced a very different Catholicism. Veneration of saints, especially Saint Anthony of Padua for the Veneti and the Madonna della Cava for the Avellinese, was foreign to the Irish parishioners and priests. Italians clashed with Irish priests because the Irish strongly opposed Italian ceremonies which venerated saints with processions and festivals in parishes serving both ethnicities. Italians were often relegated to separate Masses in church cellars. They were strongly motivated to establish their own parishes with Italian-speaking priests.[40] Southern Italian festivities were much more intense than northern Italian festas, and alien to the Irish. In Newark, New Jersey such events were described as "pagan and irreligious" and civil authorities to attempt to ban them.[41] Some southern Italian processions included "pentinents" walking barefoot behind saintly processions and some crawling on their knees.[42] Although the Latin mass was easily understood by people with roots in Italian, other communication remained a challenge, and Saint Bernard's Irish priests needed help. The Scalabrinian brothers, the missionary order from Piacenza in northwest Italy mentioned earlier, dispatched Father Pasquale M. Russomanno to minister to the four hundred Italians of Saint Bernard's in 1907, and by 1908 he had begun a fund-raising movement to build a church for the Italian newcomers. In the 1930s and 1940s, Rev. Giuseppe Chiminello, a Scalbrinian from Rosà in the Veneto, periodically visited St. Anthony's from his post in Providence, Rhode Island, to visit with Veneto families.

In the Patch Italian migrants settled where they found corner markets stocked with familiar foods, where padroni offered jobs and other services tailored to their needs. When they arrived at Ellis Island, the Veneto migrants almost universally identified Middle Street or Middle Street Lane as their first destination to the immigration inspectors. Once established there, they sought work in the foundries at the end of Water Street and in the developing Italian businesses along that artery. Usually within a year or two, the Veneti moved westward to the Cleghorn area; particularly, those working in quarrying settled in the Rollstone Hill area. Like Water Street, Cleghorn was a business district outside the Main Street of Fitchburg but with numerous groceries, shops, and factories. Men worked the quarries, and their wives, sisters, and children found work as spinners, doffers, and bobbin boys in the cotton and wool mills throughout west Fitchburg. Nevertheless, the Patch remained the first destination for newcomers.

One of the padroni and a leader of the Patch's Italian community was Angelo Seretto, a native of Avellino east of Naples, who had lived in Clinton and ran a boardinghouse near the Wachusett Dam. After the project ended he followed the Italian laborers, arriving in Fitchburg to establish a business importing Italian food and wine, as well as a labor agency. Over the decades, Seretto expanded his labor exchange into a small empire of real estate investments, a bank, a steamship ticket office, and a currency exchange. He advertised as an "employment agency for Italian laborers for excavating, grading and Railroad Construction Work," among many other things.[43] Seretto's storefront was a center for Italians in the Patch who needed a labor agent, banker, travel agent, food and wine supplier, or landlord.

One Veneto migrant found his way to Fitchburg after a long journey through Europe, working as a miner and crossing the Atlantic in search of a living wage. Albino Canale arrived from Tonezza, east of Cortina d'Ampezzo in the province of Belluno, in 1903. When he was interviewed in the 1960s by a historian about his immigration experiences, he told the interviewer that he spent his youth tending cows high in the mountains near Austria but had been reduced to smuggling Austrian goods into his home village to survive. He left for Germany at age sixteen and then decided he could do better in America. He made his way to Le Havre, France, in 1903 with two Belluno friends, and went first to Pennsylvania then to Ohio but found no decent wages. He was told by a friend he could nearly double his earnings in Fitchburg's quarries. In his narrative the journey is a direct one to Fitchburg, where he worked at the McCauliff quarry running a stone saw.

But Canale's story is perhaps more complex, in terms of both the path he traveled and the variety of jobs he undertook. Ship's manifest records show that in 1913 he arrived in America—again—from Antwerp, Belgium (possibly having worked as a miner there), and during the First World

War he left the quarry for a job as a blacksmith's assistant in Fitchburg at Simonds Saw and Steel. He eventually did settle permanently near the quarry, and by 1924 he was a naturalized US citizen with a wife and four children. But his story, like those of many transnational migrants, is far more complex than it first appears, characterized by multiple transatlantic journeys searching for better wages and greater security.

The rounded top of Rollstone Hill, in geological terms a monadnock, was fringed with tall steel derricks used to hoist the granite out of the pit. The largest pit was owned by the Rollstone Quarry, but the Shea, McCauliff, Godbeer, Litchfield, and other quarries ringed the hilltop. Ninety tons of granite a day were processed and shipped out, and the stone chips were ground into dust for concrete. This resilient stone was used for buildings, railroad bridges, curbstones, and cobblestones for paving streets. At the quarry Albino Canale's friend Giovanni Fava, a derrickman from Revine Lago, oversaw the lifting of the stone, while Canale supervised its cutting. Some men worked cutting cobblestones, and a skilled laborer could cut one thousand in a week.[44] This was hard and dangerous work that exposed men to stone dust and hazardous explosives. The hilltop was covered with blasting caps and explosives used to split the stones in the pit. One stonecutter's child was killed near the pit while playing with a discarded blasting cap. The Shea quarry kept its explosives carefully locked inside the powder house, but the owners found that despite the lock and a key described as "weighing two pounds" used to secure the storage area, local youths managed to get inside. Shipments of explosive powder arrived by rail on flatbed cars and required so much care in unloading that workers spent half a day at the task.[45]

In a memoir of the Shea quarry on Rollstone Hill, the former owner's son, Dick Shea, recalled that "40 carloads [of granite] a day went out of the quarry to Boston."[46] First oxen then teams of horses dragged wagons up Beech Street to the quarry and brought the stone down to the railroad for shipment. Granite was used on bridge construction jobs as far away as the Hudson River and in Pittsburgh. Stones were split by the "plug and feather" method: a row of long, narrow holes was drilled along the seam then packed with explosive powder.

Once more, the names and identities of the Italians were erased. Shea recalled that their foreman "could not spell or pronounce these Italian names, so the men all got Irish names." He went on to describe how "Mike Salerno became Sullivan, Vito Pasco became Peter Rome, Maffeo became Murphy." This arbitrary change was demeaning enough, but it was perhaps not as harsh as the Wachusett project managers' use of numbers instead of names. Shea recalled that the practice did not last, but this was not because the company grew to know workers better: "When the Social Security Act came along [in 1935] they got their right names back. [They] had to send to Italy for birth certificates and [had the] names changed back on work slips."[47] But the precise recording of names, whether at work or by census and Ellis Island officials, had long been problematic. Michele Cielo arrived in 1899 to work in the quarries and raised eight children, his eldest named Pietro. In the quarry his foreman changed his name to Mike Celli, and the 1900 census further mangled it to Sielo.[48] Cielo regained his proper name only when he left to work for the Fosdicks.

United States Census reporters must have been daunted entering the Fitchburg tenements. In 1910 the US Census recorded the national origins of Middle Street residents: Italian (no specific dialect), Austrian-Polish, Irish-English, Russian-Polish, Russian-Lithuanian, and Canadian-French, as well as a few Massachusetts natives. It must have been a challenge to complete the interviews, but the record was obscured as well. Cursive handwriting only further complicated the result. In the census the name Bizzotto appears as Bissotto, Ferraro as Feraro, Cecchin as Chickin, Boscardin as Boscavelin, Battistella as Bartistella, and common first names were likewise changed: Ricardo to Richardo, Bianca to Biancha. When the Battistella family applied for a passport to return to Revine Lago, the government recorded their home as Ravina. Very often, immigrants on their way to Fitchburg, Massachusetts, on ship's manifest records were first listed as headed to "Pittsburg"[49]; this appears crossed out, with *Fitchburg* written over it. The confusion over the names continued on both sides of the Atlantic: one Grava family memoir written in Italian records an ancestor's immigration to Pittsburgh, although their namesake Giuseppe Grava spent years working in Fitchburg.[50]

A stream of migrants arrived from the small Veneto *paese* of Revine Lago. The Grava family, which had dominated the town and landownership there since the fourteenth century, arrived in Fitchburg, and some settled in southern Connecticut. Over the years generations arrived, worked, and moved on. In 1904 Giuseppe Grava arrived and with the help of an uncle found work at the F. H. Goodnow Iron Foundry on the edge of the Patch; he roomed with two friends from Rosà, Italy: Tony Ferraro and B. Bernardo. Ferraro and Bernardo had journeyed together across the Atlantic in 1907 on the *S. S. Barbarossa* from Genoa. The ship's manifest recorded so many northern Italian immigrants that it took two days to process them all.

In April 1907 six of those processed at Ellis Island from Rosà were all headed to Antonio Boscardin's residence on Middle Street Lane in the Patch. All in their twenties, some married and others single, they were a mix of unskilled laborers and farm laborers. Along with them were *braccianti*, masons, carpenters, and farmers from the Veneto: Bassano, Rosà, and San Zenone were represented, as well as Pavia, a rice-growing area farther west. A few days later another group of northern Italian arrivals included two young men from Rosà: Giovanni Moretto, headed for the Boscardin residence on Middle Street Lane, and his friend, Domenico Rubbo, who headed out west.[51]

What might have happened to them in the short term? An examination of the 1910 census shows that many of the Wachusett Dam workers and their Veneto compatriots had settled and resettled throughout Fitchburg. Pietro Andreatta's son Joseph settled on Pine Street and moved from quarrying to work as a machinist at the Union Foundry; Pietro's daughter,

Giovanna, married Mario Bizzotto, a foundry worker who had emigrated from Rosà a few years earlier. His friend Giovanni Moretto first worked at F. H. Goodnow's Foundry and then moved closer to the quarry, where he opened a grocery store. Antonio Boscardin left Fitchburg, perhaps for western Massachusetts, but his brother remained and established a home and family.

The 1910 census found one group of northern Italians living at 11 Railroad Street in Fitchburg. A few years earlier, they had been a disconnected group of individuals, and all thirteen individuals living at that address had arrived between 1903 and 1909. Giovanni Boscardin had stopped boarding with his brother; he now had an apartment with a wife and two small children and worked as a laborer in the iron foundry. Living at the same address was Giuseppe Grava of Revine Lago and the two friends Ferraro and Bernardo. Grava worked at the foundry, Ferraro had a substantial job at one of the paper mills, and Bernardo worked for the railroad. The Andreatta family, headed by Pietro's oldest son, also Pietro, included a wife who did not work and his brother Joseph and sister Giovanna, along with a sister-in-law, Nella Batistella, and Michael Bizzotto, who boarded with them.

Although the men all listed themselves as farm laborers or simply laborers upon arrival, none sought farm labor. For most men who arrived in the city, a job in one of the iron foundries was the first step into the economy. Working in the mills meant advancement into less hazardous work. A short walk from the Patch there were at least two foundries and a number of machine shops. Many of the Goodnow Foundry's sixty laborers were Italian. For women, the mills in west Fitchburg offered the best opportunity; Nella and Giovanna both worked as spinners in the cotton mill—almost the only acceptable option. Northern Italian women rarely worked as housekeepers or in other occupations in their first years after arrival. They could walk down the hill from the quarry area and over a steel stairway that spanned the railroad line, then cross River Street, where nearly a dozen cotton and wool mills were in constant need of new workers. The emigration of more women and younger members of established families signaled the beginning of a more permanent settlement.

The 1920 census reveals some significant changes: none of those early Veneti who had lived at 11 Railroad Street remained there a decade later. By then the Andreattas had moved out of the city, and Giuseppe Grava had become Joseph Grava,[52] with a wife and son and two stepchildren, as well as continued employment as a machinist—a well-paying job. Giovanni Boscardin was now John; his wife, who had been listed in the 1910 US Census as Terravino (not the correct spelling of an Italian feminine name), was now listed as Antonia, their daughter Louisa was now Louise, and their son Ricardo was listed as Richard. Two younger daughters, Mary and Philomena, were born in Massachusetts. John still worked in the foundry, but their residence was a rented home on Albee Street, a quiet neighborhood of single-family homes and duplexes. They were now a short walk from a public school for their children and two blocks from Saint Anthony of Padua Church.

The anglicized names represent a decided trend. Within a decade of immigration, many newcomers abandoned Italian spellings for their first names, either under pressure from employers or simply as a reflection of their own assimilation. The 1920 United States census listed the names of one family as Giovanni, Angelina, Rosa, Giacomo, Amerigo, and John, but by 1930 the changes were remarkable: John, Angelina, Rose, George, Amerigo, and John Jr. The shift parallels the experience of many of these Italians, who began as bird of passage but eventually put down deeper roots in the United States: the Veneto migrants struggled to cross the ocean, to navigate through Ellis Island, to find a place to live and work, and then to advance themselves. In order to succeed, they had to learn how to live in America, where jobs and housing could be found, and the most important part of this endeavor was their network of friends from their home *paese*, relatives, and other individuals they came to regard as family. Once established, the newcomers relocated within the city as jobs changed and as they moved from being boarders to renters; some became homeowners. Others moved across the country in pursuit of better jobs and housing.

Over the years, the reluctant migrants began to establish the foundations of a permanent colony in Fitchburg that blended people from the entire Italian peninsula. Those who gave up transnational migration and settled in Massachusetts wanted the foods of home, creating business for Italian-food importers. Many still wanted to travel visit their original homes, which supported padroni's steamship and banking interests. Although their particular village origins and identities were important to these immigrants, their employers and the larger American community around them viewed them not as migrants from the Veneto or Treviso or Piacenza or Avellino. Anyone from the Italian peninsula was identified by the rest of the population not even by the rough northern/southern division recorded on Ellis Island but as an "Eye-talian," in Yankee pronunciation.

The Patch, which had once been French Canadian and Irish, had blossomed under the next wave of immigrants. Italian entrepreneurs soon dominated the businesses along Water Street: Secino the tailor, Carbone's Market, Barone's Pharmacy, Addante's Shoe Repair, Ciufetti's Market, Santora's Barber Shop, Padula's Bakery, Romano's Market, Zarrella's Market, and nearly fifty other businesses—including a taxi service, a print shop, fruit and vegetable stores, and an insurance company.[53] For decades, this remained a center for Italians. At the same time, those who had moved to areas near the quarries also established businesses serving the residents of the Cleghorn neighborhood.

The first real industrial entrepreneur to emerge from the community of Italian immigrants was Francesco Mastrangelo, who had arrived from Avellino in 1913. Blessed with a talent for woodworking, he renamed himself Frank Angel and established the Angel Novelty Company. Although his firm was relatively small, Angel made it his business to hire many of his fellow Italian immigrants and their children. The company produced small toys and gifts at first, but when the Italian community began to build homes in the 1930 and 1940s, he expanded into more sophisticated wooden products for home construction. The Angel Novelty Company hosted a yearly company picnic, just as the big paper mills in Fitchburg did for their employees. In the post–World War II building boom, Angel Novelty became a regional brand supplying kitchen cabinets and interior finished shelving. Its lasting contribution was to provide an alternative to the harsh life in the foundries and quarries—and an example of Italian success in a city dominated by American-owned heavy-industry concerns.[54]

The area that northern and southern Italians first cooperated on was the need for an Italian-speaking church. By 1906 there was a substantial population of over four hundred Italian-speaking immigrants living in the Patch; and newcomers wanted to attend church and be counseled by priests who spoke their language and understood their religious traditions. They all attended Saint Bernard's Church, a largely Irish parish organized by Irish railroad laborers in 1845 that had expanded in 1888 into a large brick edifice that anchored one end of Water Street. But it had no Italian-speaking priests until the arrival of Father Russomanno, a Scalabrinian missionary who became known as the church-building priest. He encouraged his parishioners to raise funds for the construction of an Italian parish, which would become the first in the entire region.

A small group of a dozen Water Street businessmen led by Giuseppe Gallo and Giuseppe Provenzani[55] began raising funds in October 1906. They canvassed not only the Patch but across the city and Cleghorn every Sunday, and by 1907 they had raised nearly two thousand dollars— a substantial sum drawn from the community of nearly as many Italian-speaking residents. One woman, whose name is lost to the historical record, labored for four dollars and fifty cents a week in a cotton mill but managed to contribute fifteen dollars to the building fund. After the founders met with the bishop in Worcester, the construction plan was approved, and Father Russomanno[56] helped to establish the parish.

The local Vittorio Emanuele Society, organized in 1903, provided further support, and Russomanno contributed some of his own savings.[57]

Construction began in 1907 and was completed the following spring. The Church of Saint Anthony of Padua (Padova) honored the patron saint of the Veneto. When the building was dedicated in April 1908, the first baptism held was for Giuseppina Carmela Passinnato.[58] Her parents were typical of those who populated the church: Giuseppe Passinnato had left Rosà for America in 1903 at twenty-three years old and as an experienced miner, probably from working in Belgium, Germany, or Switzerland. After his arrival at Ellis Island, he went to Fitchburg seeking work. In 1907 he returned, a bit older and with a friend, M. Bizzotto, to stay at 37 Middle Street Lane. Within a few months Elena Lorenzato and her cousin Rosa journeyed together across the Atlantic to join Elena's husband in Fitchburg. The following year their daughter was baptized; Carmela Romano stood as *comare*, and Giuseppe Grava from Revine Lago was her *compare*.

The members of this group were linked by a variety of connections that they had constructed: friends who had journeyed together from Revine Lago, friends who had roomed or worked together, multigenerational relations, and friends from neighboring Rosà. Few would have known each other before they arrived in the United States, although they lived in towns about twenty miles apart in the Veneto; even so, in their new home they had taken on the role of kin to one another and become family. They were linked by the need to form a network that would replace those relatives they had left behind. Family was the most important bond in Italian culture. Ultimately, Saint Anthony of Padua Church gave them another connection as parishioners and neighbors in a growing Italian colony. In 1919 four Venerini nuns arrived to establish an elementary school. By the 1930s Saint Anthony's had purchased a defunct Methodist church building to serve Italian laborers who had settled farther afield, in the Cleghorn section of west Fitchburg. Prior to this, many Veneti had made the four-and-a-half-mile round trip to Saint Anthony's in the Patch every Sunday on foot.[59]

The decision to shift from an existence as *uccelli di passaggio* was driven by the continued unraveling of the labor economy in the Veneto, as discussed in earlier chapters. As living standards declined, malnutrition bred pellagra and other diseases. Labor unrest had boiled over in strikes during 1883 and continued to escalate into the 1900s. Consequently, the peak years of Veneto labor strife (1907–1908) were the peak years of migration. Historian Emilio Franzina recorded the rising strife of these years in *Il Veneto ribelle* (The rebellious Veneto), noting that socialist labor organizers found it easy to organize in a region where major protests and discontent had begun in the 1880s. Strikes (*scioperi*) escalated in these years, and Franzina charted their dramatic rise in the Veneto: in 1905 there were 715 strikes, in 1906 there were 1,641, and in 1907 they peaked at 2,258; and the following year the number was 1,745. From 1910 to 1920 there were at least a thousand strikes each year—even as laborers left to seek work elsewhere. Labor discontent in the Veneto reflected the continuing economic and social hardships suffered by those who had remained.[60]

Immigration to central Massachusetts expanded as better ship and rail connections developed through the port facility in East Boston. The booming industrial economy continued to expand as long as the influx of fresh labor arrived willing to accept any wage to survive. United States census records for Fitchburg indicate that many of the young workers and their families from the Veneto arrived in the first two decades of the twentieth century, with the peak years being 1907-08, after which the Great War severely reduced migration.

The Dillingham Commission's congressional report distinguished between northern and southern Italian immigrants and found that for the twelve-year period ending in 1910, some 1,911,933 southern Italians had arrived in America, even as 372,668 northern Italians had immigrated. Of these, 22,062 arrived in Massachusetts—an average of 1,838 per year. The

Dillingham Commission reported that most of the northern migration was "of a temporary character" and that the average stay was eight years. By this time southern Italian immigration had grown dramatically; with a rate of 3 per 1,000 residents in the north but 12 per 1,000 in the south.[61]

For the Veneti the option of earning money in America, saving it up, and then planning a return to the Veneto grew more difficult with time. Both labor unrest and political complications made it less likely that the migrants could continue their transatlantic passages: by 1914 Europe was at war, and in 1915 Italy took the precipitous plunge that led to another Austrian military occupation of the Veneto. Those who had not emigrated were trapped under a deadly military dominance by the conflict, and many starved or were killed in the fighting.

But in Massachusetts the reluctant migrants had found their destination. They began to move out of the unskilled jobs; they established small businesses, founded social organizations, and built the first Italian church in the region. At the same time, their community moved from being populated by workers at the bottom of the wage scale to the beginnings small-business ownership. As wives, sisters, and children made the journey to Massachusetts, they also revealed their desire to settle permanently in what had become a substantial northern Italian colony in central Massachusetts.

NOTES

1. The East Boston facility was opened in 1892 and staffed with sixty-four personnel, including two dozen inspectors and four interpreters. It was smaller than the Bureau of Immigration's Ellis Island Station (1892–1954) and the San Francisco facility at Angel Island (1910–1940). See Barry Moreno, *The Illustrated Encyclopedia of Ellis Island* (New York: Fall River Press, 2004), 10, 26, and 124.
2. Einaudi, "La distribuzione," 1–9. Special thanks to Alessandro Paglia for making me aware of this source.
3. Patrick Ettinger, *Imaginary Lines: Border Enforcement and the Origins of Undocumented Immigration, 1882–1930,* (Austin: University of Texas Press, 2009, 33.)
4. Samuel P. Orth, "The Alien Contract Labor Law," *Political Science Quarterly* 22, no. 1 (Mar. 1907): 49.
5. Testimony United States v. Morrison, 109 Fed. Rep. 891. Quoted in Orth, "Alien Contract Labor Law," 50.
6. Nathaniel Shaler, "Shall Immigration Be Restricted?" *Century,* no. 6 (October 1887): 954–955.
7. Prescott Hall, "Italian Immigration," *North American Review* 16 (Aug. 1896): 252–254.
8. Henry Cabot Lodge, "The Restriction of Immigration," *North American Review* 152 (Jan. 1891): 31.
9. Ibid. William Paul Dillingham, *Report of the Immigration Commission: Dictionary of Races or Peoples,* US Immigration Commission, Dec. 5, 1910 (Washington, DC: Government Printing Office, 1911), 83–84, and "Comparative Classification of Immigrant Races or Peoples," 5. (Comparative Classification of Immigrant Races or Peoples is a section of *Report of the Immigration Commission: Dictionary of Races or Peoples.*)
10. Foran quoted in Lindsay, "Preserving the Exceptional Republic."
11. Matthew J. Lindsay, "Preserving the Exceptional Republic: Political Economy, Race and the Federalization of American Immigration Law," *Yale Journal of Law and the Humanities* 17, no. 2 (2005): 181–251.
12. For the text, see Orth, "Alien Contract Labor Law," 51.
13. The immigration exclusion statistics are from Barry Moreno, *Illustrated Encyclopedia of Ellis Island,* 75 and 124.

14. John Koren, *The Padrone System and Padrone Banks*, US Department of Labor report (Washington, DC: Government Printing Office, Mar. 1897), 9: 114.
15. Ibid., 117.
16. Ibid., 123.
17. Ibid., 124.
18. Ibid., 125.
19. Ibid., 126.
20. Ibid., 113–129.
21. John Koren, "Lo sfruttamento degli Italiani a New-York. Le frodi dei bosses e dei banchieri," *La Riforma Sociale*, Anno IV, volume VII, (Torino: Roux Frassati, 1897), 697–711. "New-York" is hyphenated per the source.
22. Gunther Peck, *Reinventing Free Labor* (Cambridge: Cambridge University Press, 2000), 11.
23. Anthony Mitchell Sammarco, *Boston's North End* (Charleston, SC: Arcadia Press, 1997), 6, 96–99.
24. US census figures.
25. Doris Kirkpatrick, *The City and the River*, (Fitchburg, MA: Fitchburg Historical Society, 1971), 185.
26. Ibid., 178 and 185.
27. "The Wachusett Reservoir for Boston Water Supply," *Scientific American*, July 1, 1905, 11–12.
28. It took only forty years for Boston's demands to outstrip the Wachusett Reservoir's capacity; then the new Quabbin Reservoir project farther west inundated five towns; see Thomas Conuel, *Quabbin The Accidental Wilderness*, (Brattleboro, VT: The Stephen Greene Press) 1981. Also see J. Stewart, "Building of the Great Wachusett Dam," *Scientific American*, supp. 1302, Dec. 15, 1900, 20863–20864.]; "The Wachusett Reservoir," *Scientific American*, supp. 1518, Feb. 4, 1905, 24318–24319.
29. Jim Taylor, "Building Wachusett Dam," *Downstream* 12 (Spring 2005): 3. The Department of Conservation and Recreation archive contains photographs of the camps and plans to digitize them. For camp settlement, see Twelfth Census of the US, Schedule no. 1 Population Sterling Town, Worcester County, Massachusetts, Enumeration District no. 1686, Sheet no. 12, From 1 to 50 Italian Colony in Metropolitan Water Works section, June 23, 1900 (www.ancestry.com).
30. "List or Manifest of Alien Passengers," SS *La Provence*; departed from Le Havre, arrived in New York on May 1, 1909. Confidential interview

with Bianca M. (daughter of Carlo Alberto Society member), Fitchburg, Massachusetts, 2012.

31. "Wachusett Dam and Reservoir Past and Present," Kelley Freda, Massachusetts Department of Conservation and Recreation Environmental Analyst, Powerpoint, undated.

32. Kelley Freda, "Wachusett Dam and Reservoir Past and Present," *Downstream* 12 (Spring 2005): 1–8; in the same issue, also see Jim Taylor, "Building Wachusett Dam," and "Wachusett Dam: 100 Years Old." Dave Greenslit, "Wachusett Reservoir Work Upset Central Massachusetts Towns: The Sacrifices Were Many," *Telegram & Gazette* (Worcester, MA), July 9, 2000.

33. Clinton town historian Terrence Ingano has reported, "Clinton went dry for two years, [because] they were so afraid of this immigrant element," and one West Boylston resident commented that the reservoir would be "the death of Boylston"; both quoted in Greenslit, "Wachusett Reservoir Work," n.p.

34. Doris Kirkpatrick, *The City and the River*, (Fitchburg: Fitchburg Historical Society, 1971), 303.

35. Oral history interview with Eino Wiita, *Oral History of Fitchburg Railroads*, interviews by Fitchburg Bicentennial Commission, manuscript, Fitchburg Public Library, 1979.

36. "Bondsmen Sued. Putnam Machine and Fitchburg Steam Engine Companies Attach Property of Twenty Involved by Apprentice Strike," *Sentinel* (Fitchburg, MA), July 18, 1907.

37. US census figures show that the population of Fitchburg had begun to decline by 1930 without the steady influx of immigrants. Mike Prescott, "Trolley Towns in Worcester County" (www.transitmemory.org). Doris Kirkpatrick, *Around the World in Fitchburg* (Fitchburg, MA: Fitchburg Historical Society, 1975), 208, 303–307, 351. On the foreign born in 1895, see Kirkpatrick, *Around the World*, 389; and on Fitchburg's foreign born in 1910, see George William Tupper, *Foreign-Born Neighbors* (Boston: Taylor Press, 1914), 24. By 1910 the population had reached 37,826, and it rose steadily up to the 1920s, but when Italian immigration was limited by the Emergency Quota Act of 1920, the population began to shrink.

38. On construction in Worcester, see Roy Rosenzweig, *Eight Hours for What We Will: Workers and Leisure in an Industrial City, 1870–1920* (Cambridge: Cambridge University Press, 1983); and Worcester Preservation's digital photo exhibit *Three Deckers* (www.preservationworcester.org).

39. The combination of wine making and residential mobility created a problem when her father abruptly moved and only later realized that the wine bottles had been left behind in the cellar of their former home. Confidential interview with Bianca M., 2012.

40. Stephen Puelo described the clash in the North End in *The Boston Italians*, (Boston: Beacon Press, 2007), 14–15.

41. See Michael Immerso, *Newark's Little Italy*, (New Brunswick: Rutgers University Press, 1999), 81–82.

42. See *The Madonna of 115th Street Faith and Community in Italian Harlem, 1880–1950*, (New Haven: Yale University Press, 6.

43. Kirkpatrick, *Around the World* (Fitchburg: Fitchburg Historical Society, 1975), 209.

44. Unsigned typescript, "Stone Crusher," "Albino Canale," and "Patsy Roma" in the "Italians Biography" file, Fitchburg Historical Society, Fitchburg, Massachusetts. Probably interviewed by Doris Kirkpatrick for *Around the World in Fitchburg*. "Ship's Manifest of Alien Passengers," of the SS *La Gascogne* from Le Havre, Nov. 9, 1903; and "Ship's Manifest," of the SS *Lapland* from Antwerp, Belgium, June 23, 1913. 1930 Federal Census, Plymouth Street, Fitchburg, MA (www.ancestry.com).

45. Unsigned typescript, interview with Dick Shea, "Quarry," probably by Doris Kirkpatrick for *Around the World in Fitchburg*, on page 3 of the "Rollstone Hill—Quarry" file, Fitchburg Historical Society.

46. Ibid., 1.

47. Ibid., 2–3.

48. US census 1900 and 1910.

49. Between 1890–1911, when many of these persons were passing through Ellis Island, the proper spelling was without the "h," the US Board on Geographic Names altered the spelling; see Carnegie Library of Pittsburgh reference http://www.clpgh.org/exhibit/apology1.html

50. US census 1910 records, Middle Street and Middle Street Lane, Fitchburg, Massachusetts. "Ship's Manifest" listing Antonio Boscardin, Pittsburg/Fitchburg, SS *Buenos Aires* from Genoa, May 1906.

51. "Ship's Manifest of Alien Passengers," of the SS *Barbarossa*, from Genoa, Italy, Apr. 26, 1907, and Apr. 28, 1907. These are the processing dates. The ship sailed landed April 26 but a number of the manifest sheets have April 26 stamped on them but are overwritten by hand with April 28.

52. The alteration of names might be a personal decision to fit into their new home or forced by an employer or fellow workers. Evidence of the personal decision is that often children born in America had anglicized

birth names—one Grava mother named her first son born in Fitchburg as Amerigo and the next John. Census officials did not, to my knowledge, purposely alter names (although Ellis Island officials did); but Census recorders often made serious mistakes; for example, here listing Pietra Andreatta as a male and Nella Battistella as Nella Bartisttela.

53. Map of Italian American businesses, *History of Saint Anthony of Padua Parish* (n.p., 2009), 74–76. For records of the first baptism, see 8–11 and 16.

54. Theresa Mastrangelo, Sogni d'Oro Oral History Collection, Center for Italian Culture Records, MS 11, Fitchburg State University archives, Fitchburg, Massachusetts (hereafter, Sogni d'Oro Oral History).

55. Listings in 1950s City Directories show it was spelled Provenzani, as in St Anthony's church history.

56. St Anthony's church history consistently spells it Russomano in text but reproduces two baptismal documents he signed Russomanno. Fitchburg *Sentinel* article in 1907 spelled it Russomanno. City Directories of 1908 and 1909 spelled with two n's.

57. Father Russomano was so successful that he was transferred only four months after the church dedication to Illinois, where he continued his church-building career; see *Sentinel* (Fitchburg), Aug. 5, 1907; and *History of St. Anthony of Padua Parish*, 10–11.

58. "Passinato" is recorded in city directories but "Passinnato" on baptismal certificate. I would assume they were most careful of spelling on baptisimal form.

59. In the 1920s growing numbers of southern Italian parishioners formed a Madonna della Cava Society. By 1935 in neighboring Leominster, a number of innovative women, mainly immigrants from Avellino, had organized Saint Anna's parish.

60. Emilio Franzina, *Il Veneto ribelle*, 159.

61. Wiilliam Paul Dillingham, *Report of the Immigration Commission: Dictionary of Races or Peoples*, US Immigration Commission 1907-1910, (Washington; Government Printing Office, 1911), 85.

CHAPTER 4

ARRESTING THE PADRONI

THE ITALIAN BUREAU, 1881–1901

Over two decades, from 1881 to 1901, as the Veneto migrants established themselves in Massachusetts, a conflict grew between the Italian Foreign Ministry and the American government regarding the protection of Italian nationals living and working in America. The battle over Italian immigration was waged on a national and an international level. It magnified the tensions already brewing over the increasing waves of immigration from both the north and the south of Italy. The fight also displayed the political power of the immigration restrictionists, who opposed southern European immigration in general and Italian immigration in particular.

There are two perspectives to examine in this story. First, there was the crusader Celso Cesare Moreno, who sought to end the *padrone* system of contract labor agents and wanted to rescue those he called *schiavi bianchi* (white slaves). But his campaign to protect Italian immigrants devolved into exaggerated and destructive attacks on the Italian ambassador and his staff. The second perspective is that of the Italian ambassador, Baron Francesco Saverio Fava, who worked to stem the influence of the padroni and to establish the Italian Bureau[1] at Ellis Island to protect

Italian immigrants.[2] Ironically, the ferocity of Moreno's attacks on Italian diplomats only served immigration restrictionists like Terrence Powderly and Henry Cabot Lodge, who wanted to eliminate the Italian Bureau in order to restrict and eventually halt Italian immigration.

Scholar Joseph Cosco has shown in *Imagining Italians* that Americans in the 1890s at first regarded Italian culture as a reflection of their interest in the art and music of Italy, but they discarded this romantic view of Italians in the tumult of labor strife in a shift to what he called Italophobia. John Zucci, in *The Little Slaves of the Harp*, described the scandalous abuse of Italian children who worked as street musicians—after padroni masters had literally bought control of them from their parents—that created deep-seated hostility toward Italians, especially the padroni. This image was inflated in the popular press by contemporary writers like Horatio Alger Jr., who authored *Phil the Fiddler* about an abused Italian child. Luciano Iorizzo briefly examined the battle surrounding the Italian Bureau in an article titled "The Padrone and Immigrant Distribution," and Italian historian Laura Pilotti has examined these events from the perspective of the Italian Foreign Ministry.[3]

But little has been written about the complex nature of the clash between the shadowy figure of Moreno and the Italian ambassador to the United States Francesco Fava. Moreno's relentless campaign to rescue Italian children from the padroni and what he claimed was an international web controlling Italian labor degenerated into attacks on Italian diplomats who were fighting the same evils. His language became so malicious that he was jailed for libel in 1895; he then wrote a book, *History of a Great Wrong*, launching even more virulent attacks on the Italian Foreign Ministry.[4] Rome also wanted to stem the padrone problem in America, but efforts were damaged by Moreno's campaign. Moreno increasingly drew his support from nativists and immigration restrictionists, thus aiding those whose goal was not to protect Italians in America but to halt Italian immigration altogether.

The Terrence Powderly Papers and the records of the US Industrial Commission reveal the central role Moreno played in destroying the Italian Bureau on Ellis Island. Materials in the Charles Sumner Papers evidence his persuasive ability to draw support from politicians and to advance his own legislative agenda. Moreno corresponded with presidents, kings, and politicians, and *History of a Great Wrong* reveals much about him and his crusade. He testified before American congressional committees; drafted legislation on contract labor, Pacific fisheries, and a transpacific cable scheme; and had contacts in the Harrison and McKinley administrations. On the other side of the debate, the Italian diplomatic records in the Archivio d'Stato in Venezia, the *Bolletino d'emigrazione*, *Documenti diplomatici*, and Italian Bureau Reports reveal the Italian Foreign Ministry's battle to protect Italians in America against the padroni and lynching. The Italian Bureau operated for a brief five years between 1895 and 1900, but the titanic struggle between Moreno and the Italian diplomats spanned more than two decades. In the end, his crusade helped American immigration restrictionists more than it did Italian immigrants.

In order to understand these events, it is important to examine the origins of Moreno's campaign to rescue the *schiavi bianchi* in post–Civil War America. Celso Cesare Moreno, born in Dogliani, Italy in 1839 or 1841, was already a global adventurer and soldier of fortune when he arrived in America (after sojourns in Sumatra, China, Vietnam, and Hawaii) in about 1868. He later claimed that the sight of Italian children working as street musicians one cold February night began his quest for anti-padrone legislation. He wrote dramatic letters to senator Charles Sumner appealing for a campaign to free the white slaves. Then in 1873 Moreno turned to the Associazione Donnarumma, an Italian American group, speaking at its picnic in New York City about "the Italian slaves." He made a dramatic plea to "bring about the abolition of this new system of slavery" and received coverage in the New York papers.[5]

Understanding the issue as a struggle against white slavery, a powerful argument immediately after the American Civil War, the Donnarumma

group pledged its support in what appeared to be a humanitarian cause—
Moreno's campaign to rescue fellow Italian immigrants. Less prominent
in the resolutions was a wholesale attack on the Italian consul for not
promoting Moreno's agenda. Moreno also continued to write to Senator
Sumner and to Frederick Douglass, echoing the rhetoric of their crusade.
He called upon Americans to "assist us in the deliverance of the whites"
and to "see crowned with success our efforts in delivering from the most
abject slavery thousands of Italian children."[6] Moreno helped Sumner
draft and pass the Padrone Act in 1874.

Anti-padrone legislation was enacted at the federal (and state) level
in three phases: first, protecting children from apprenticeship contracts;
next, halting adult labor contracting; and finally, shutting down the
padrone-operated banks. The key piece of legislation, passed in 1885
as the Alien Contract Labor Law, or the Foran Act, attempted to halt
these abuses by giving US immigration inspectors the power to deport
immigrants suspected of having signed labor contracts.

The Italian government also passed legislation, crafted by two consuls
in New York City, to halt the padroni's ability to transport children out
of Italy on labor contracts. From the Italian ambassador's perspective,
the best safeguard for adult immigrants was to separate them from the
padroni at the gates of Ellis Island. Ambassador Fava lobbied US secretary
of the treasury John G. Carlisle for permission to open an Italian Bureau
on Ellis Island that would enable the consulate to assist and guide Italian
immigrants once they were ready to leave Ellis Island and to move them
past the padrone waiting at the gates. Ambassador Fava also worked with
developers to establish two farming communities in Arkansas. Neither
succeeded because Italians perceived that the American south bore
marked similarities to the Italian south: disease-prone lowlands rife with
malaria and characterized by a problematic land-tenure system (southern
landowners required a delay of twenty years before immigrants could
purchase the land they worked). Increased lynching attacks on Italians,
most often southern Italians, (and others) in the south worsened the

situation. The final stage of the ambassador's campaign was legislation in Italy that would establish a government-sponsored labor agency within the Italian Bureau and cut out entirely the web of labor agents preying on immigrants. He then planned to charter a Banca d'Italia branch to safeguard financial transactions for those both arriving in the United States and returning to Italy.

The Italian Bureau on Ellis Island was thus intended to deal with the most fundamental needs of immigrants and to provide the services that the padroni had used to gain power over newcomers. But obtaining approval from both the American and the Italian government took time. In 1894 the ambassador received permission from treasury secretary John Carlisle to establish the Italian Bureau to protect immigrants and to cooperate with the US immigration inspection staff. Maintaining the trust of the US government was critical to this plan, for no other nation had such an office on Ellis Island.

The two main actors in the drama, Moreno and Fava, although they shared an interest in protecting Italian immigrants, constantly clashed regarding how that might be done and who was responsible for the problem. The Italian ambassador, Francesco Saverio Fava, had first served the Bourbon regime in the Kingdom of Two Sicilies. After the Risorgimento he served the new Italian government, and his long tenure in Washington spanned twenty critical years in Italian-American relations, 1881–1901. He was appointed the first Italian ambassador to the United States and later the dean of Washington's diplomatic corps. During the 1891 New Orleans lynching controversy, he was recalled for more than a year when diplomatic relations were broken and war threatened, but in 1893 he returned to Washington raised to the status of ambassador plenipotentiary, and he reestablished good relations with the Harrison administration. It was at this point that he received approval to establish the Italian Bureau in New York and in a decade of rising racial tensions fought to have those who lynched Italians tried in federal courts. But during these years Moreno's attacks on Fava intensified, ultimately destroying much of the legacy Fava had worked so long to build.[7]

The legendary, almost mythic figure who battled the ambassador was Moreno, that Italian adventurer, freebooter, and world traveler. He claimed to speak fourteen languages, to have married the daughter of the king of Sumatra, and to have inspired a revolt against the Dutch to turn Sumatra into an Italian colony. In Hawaii he obtained both a diplomatic title and was appointed prime minister for five days before American planters forced the king to oust him. He was secretly an officer of two companies planning to lay a transpacific cable to Asia, but they failed to find enough willing investors. He claimed that the French government had decorated him for service in Tonkin. He traveled to America, resided in New York in the 1860s and early 1870; then he resettled in Italy and ran for Parliament from Genoa. After being defeated in his Italian political quest, Moreno returned to the United States. Elsewhere, he claimed to have been invited to reside in America via a letter of introduction to the secretary of state.[8]

All this would have been merely laughable (and barely believable), except that Moreno was a persuasive public speaker and adroit in his dealings with the press and politicians. He readily found an audience anywhere he went; moreover, he did testify before Congress, he did draft legislation, and he did receive a charter to lay a cable to China. It was when he turned his outrage against the Italian Bureau that he became truly a destructive figure. This quest had a deleterious impact on Italian immigrants, whose cause he always espoused. Long aware of Moreno's dislike of him, Ambassador Fava dismissed his staff's concerns about Moreno in 1892, saying, "Oh, it keeps him employed, and it does not hurt me." [9] But the ambassador underestimated his nemesis and the lengths to which he would go to destroy him.

Moreno always presented himself as the protector of Italians and enemy of the padroni, but his motives were never clear. Driven by extreme ambition and what might be termed "status anxiety," he had traveled to Hawaii and Sumatra in search of a diplomatic title for himself and retained an intense hatred of the former Bourbon rulers of Italy, as well as of the Italian nobility. In 1870 Moreno headed a committee to celebrate the unification of Italy, which marked the defeat of the Bourbons. Perhaps his intense dislike for the Italian embassy staff was linked to its titled diplomats, who had once served the Bourbons and now filled the Foreign Ministry's ranks: Baron Fava, Count Oldrini, Marquis Romano, Chevalier Rossi, among others. Moreno had traveled the globe in a desperate search for power and position but never really achieved any rank; he often styled himself Capitano Moreno (a title he had earned as an Italian naval cadet).

Over time, journalists grew wary of Moreno. The *New York Times* reported in 1892 that Moreno had leaked a phony diplomatic dispatch from Rome summoning Baron Fava to Italy for stealing money from embassy accounts and living lavishly. Members of Washington's diplomatic corps came to the ambassador's defense, and the *New York Times* concluded that Moreno had "one absorbing object in life ... the political destruction of the Italian minister,"[10] for "his hatred of Baron Fava amount[ed] almost to monomania."[11]

But the ambassador had much more serious matters to deal with in America. Lynching, once a crime committed almost exclusively against African Americans, was increasingly targeting Italians.[12] The first Italian lynching took place in 1874, but occurrences intensified in the 1890s. A study of mob violence against Italians in the United States in the years 1874–1915 identified fourteen major incidents of lynching and murder, totaling forty-two dead, many injured, and over fifty thousand dollars of indemnities paid by Congress. The worst anti-Italian lynching, which took place in New Orleans in 1891, took eleven Italian lives and remains the largest mass lynching in American history.[13]

During the New Orleans incident, in which crowds were invited to gather, police did nothing to halt the tragedy, and afterward the perpetrators were not punished. In a string of incidents in Louisiana, Mississippi, and Colorado, violence against Italians went unpunished by both local and state courts. Ambassador Fava, recalled by his government in 1891, could gain nothing save monetary compensation for those immigrants who remained Italian nationals. He campaigned for federal jurisdiction over lynching, arguing that since "state courts are absolutely ineffective" in protecting foreign citizens, Congress should move jurisdiction to the federal courts. This effort ran into congressional opposition because any antilynching law that protected aliens resident in the United States raised questions about equal protection for African American citizens.[14] Fava's principled stand was unsuccessful. Strong southern political opposition to federal antilynching legislation prevented such action. America was unique in the prevalence of lynching in these decades, and after African Americans, Italians were the primary target of southern lynchers. The last lynching of an Italian in America occurred in 1944.[15]

The way that race played into the New Orleans incident became clear when London's *Punch* magazine published an insulting satirical poem, "A Fair Exchange," which took aim at Ambassador Fava and the Italian protests over the New Orleans tragedy. The *Punch* satirist complained of those "who shriek in Hitalian, across the waves," minimized the military threat posed by the Italian navy (then the fourth-largest naval force in the world), and dismissed the recall of Fava: "Let Fava stay, Take the *Mafia* away, and we'll call it a right square deal!" Finally, *Punch* inserted a small squib: "What the Italians seem to want in Louisiana.—An *unfair* field or no FAVA!"[16] This was a pun on the demands of American traders in China: a fair field and no favor.

Fava's recall occurred after secretary of state James Blaine informed the embassy that despite an 1871 bilateral US-Italian treaty that specifically offered protection to foreign nationals resident abroad, he had no power to right the injustices.[17] Yet when two US sailors were killed in a knife fight outside a Valaparaiso saloon, US president Benjamin Harrison demanded an indemnity, and a US Navy commander threatened to "shoot any and every man who insulted me or my men or my flag in any way."[18] The key problem for Washington was, again, that if lynching of foreigners was made a federal crime, stricter laws would have to be set in place regarding the murder of African Americans.

After Fava was recalled, Senator Preston B. Plumb of Kansas announced: "Who cares? His departure is of no more consequence ... than if the banana-vender [sic] who presides over a pushcart at 15th & F Streets ... decided to go home."[19] Senator Henry Cabot Lodge of Massachusetts, a leading immigration restrictionist, defended the New Orleans mob, arguing that the lynching had "no race feeling whatever" and advising that the "intelligent restriction" of immigration was the solution.[20] The southern response was different. Former Confederate soldiers pledged themselves willing to defend America if war with Italy came. One historian of the South wrote in 1942 that southerners viewed the threat of war with Italy in this era as a key event in the reconciliation of North and South after the Civil War.[21]

American bluster quickly evaporated when Washington realized that the Italian navy was a powerful opponent. The secretary of the navy told the press the American fleet was "in no shape for war" and concluded that enemy naval forces could shut down New York City. He lamented that the United States had only one battleship, and this, ironically, was in dry dock to have new guns installed. The United States considered "buying and building a fleet" but determined that this would take six months.[22] Washington paid an indemnity once war with Italy was on the horizon, but that was all. Nearly a decade later, Fava still continued his protests, terming another lynching "effectual grounds for pressing the Louisiana authorities to fulfill the contractual obligations of the confederation to which they belong and ... the general principles of universal justice."[23] The Italian government, and Fava in particular, were continually concerned about the threat to Italians resident in America and with good reason. Washington's payment of the indemnity revealed a reluctance to avoid war with Italy but to avoid any federal action against lynching. This was reflected in Massachusetts senator Henry Cabot Lodge's article defending the lynchings as the byproduct of "unrestricted immigration." The lynching of Italians continued for another decade in the south and west. Three were killed in Colorado in 1896 and another three in Lousiana in 1898. In 1899 and 1901 there were two more incidents in Mississippi resulting in ten deaths. The ambassador continued his anti-lynching campaign into his retirement and later wrote an article outlining the judicial questions in 1902.[24]

Race remained a key element in the 1890s for the opponents of immigration and for Moreno, as well. He chose to launch his most blatant attack against the Italian ambassador in a Washington paper, the *Colored American*. This time the target was not just the ambassador but the entire Italian embassy staff. He wrote an article that claimed they worked with padroni and operated a "nefarious traffic in human flesh,"[25] including "Italian slaves of both sexes."[26] Moreno also charged Fava, Count Oldrini, and the Italian consuls with having "received millions in money from the Italian padroni as their share of the spoils derived from this traffic of Italian slaves."[27] He turned to anti-Semitism, saying that Fava was "a Hebrew, [possessing to a] superlative degree all their faults, such as meanness, greediness, profit and niggardliness."[28] This attack may have been prompted by Fava's renown for having rescued Romanian Jews decades earlier when ambassador in that country.[29]

In addition, Moreno accused the ambassador of enriching himself through the padrone system in the United States, claiming that Count Oldrini was his go-between with the padroni. Moreno also named the consuls in every US city, as well as the Italian foreign minister, as members of the gang. But the most dangerous accusation was aimed at the Italian Bureau: Moreno claimed that its staff worked to "delude, deceive and mislead policemen"[30] and had deceived the Commissioners of Immigration. This was the most dangerous charge because it undercut the one reason the Italian Bureau had been permitted special access to Ellis Island: Fava had personally promised to staff it with *onesti agenti* (honest agents) and had affirmed that the Italian diplomats would work *with* US immigration inspectors—not assist Italians in evading them.

Because these charges appeared in print rather than having been spoken, Moreno was open to a charge of libel, but Fava refused to press charges. Instead, in an unprecedented action, the US attorney won a grand jury indictment against Moreno for libel in July 1895. As evidence of Fava's innocence, he cited the ambassador's 1884 correspondence with treasury secretary John Carlisle seeking a means to "effectively suppress" the padroni, and his appointment of Alessandro Oldrini as chief of the Italian Bureau with the charge "to interview and advise" immigrants and to "promote their welfare and give information to the officials of the [US] Government of any violation of the immigration or contract labor laws."[31]

The ambassador was subpoenaed but could not be located by the court officers. His reluctance proved wise. Moreno enthusiastically informed the *New York Times* that he "rejoice[d] in the opportunity ... he long ha[d] been waiting for ... he [would] be his own attorney, and [would] put Baron Fava upon the stand and cross-examine him for a week, if necessary."[32] It was not necessary.

The US attorney concluded his case against Moreno by charging that that latter was "a person of evil and wicked mind, and of a most malicious disposition" whose actions had "wickedly, maliciously and unlawfully [contrived] ... to aggrieve, vilify and defame" the ambassador and the Italian Foreign Ministry's staff. The jury returned a guilty verdict, and the court jailed Moreno for ninety days and fined him. After his conviction, the *Washington Post* reported an ironic twist: Moreno "denied having any malice toward Baron Fava and admitted that he did not know him"[33]; in addition, Moreno claimed to have earlier made similar allegations before a congressional committee with no response from the ambassador. Interviewed later, during his incarceration, Moreno announced to the press his willingness to sell an island off Sumatra to the US Congress for $750,000.[34] This statement was prompted by his discovery during his incarceration that Russia was attempting to "appropriate" the island which he told reporters he had earlier "offered to sell" to the United States. Moreno was again attempting to demonstrate to reporters his self-styled importance in world affairs. He reiterated the story in *History of a Great Wrong*, noting that Italy had failed to take control of what he termed the "Island of Pulo Way (known in the Malayan Archipelago as the Moreno Island)" in 1866–1867 and America had failed in 1868, while he was "the projector of the trans-Pacific cable" project and presumably control of the island was critical to that effort.[35]

Sometime after the court issued its verdict in the libel trial, Moreno took up his pen yet again and wrote a book that summarized his battle against the padroni, *History of a Great Wrong*.[36] The full title reveals his thesis: *Italian Slavery in America (Schiavitù Italiana in America): The Italian Representatives, Ambassador Fava, Corti and Blanc, the Italian Padroni, Their Accomplices and Go-Betweens. Its Horrors, Its Miseries, Its Cruelties, Its Atrocities, Its Robberies, Its Delusions, Its Tears, Its Desolation, Its Sorrows, Its Crimes, Its Demoralization, Its Torments, and Its Tormentors. Homo Homini Lupus. A Deplorable Mistake.*

Moreno's book describes how he had fought first to protect Italian street children and then Italian laborers. He reprinted in full the article that had led to his trial and then moved beyond his violent antipathy against one Italian diplomat, expanding it to take in the entire Foreign Ministry and the Italian prime minister, Francesco Crispi, for good measure. Gradually, his book becomes a scream of outrage at a world that first listened to him and then turned away. Pages are filled with reprinted newspaper articles from the United States and Italy, open letters to King Umberto, and what Moreno claimed were excerpts from his testimony to various congressional committees and the Italian Parliament, as well as letters to American presidents, secretaries of state and treasury, and Italian politicians. He included letters of praise from Frederick Douglass, as well as from the office of the mayor of New Orleans, missives penned shortly after the mass lynching thanking him for his statements to a Senate committee. Although Moreno denounced lynching, he garnered praise from mayor Joseph Shakspeare, who helped shield the lynchers.

Moreno's book condemns Ambassador Fava and every Italian diplomat in America, along with the Foreign Ministry and Foreign Minister Blanc, who are berated as "the two most immoral, most corrupt, most mercenary, and most despised mountebanks..." as well as being "loaded with crimes; both are low and degenerate morally and politically, both are bribe takers ..." and then he cited that for 50,000 lira they had sold "one of the highest decorations of Italy to the swindler Jew Cornelius Herz of Panama Canal fame." Under their leadership, "with their wives," these men made the "principal factors in the Italian government" the qualities of "ignorance, immorality, servilism, shame, corruption, cowardice, thievery, oppression, bribery, intrigues, absolute want of dignity and of honor...the government of the *demi-monde* and of rascals."[37] All of this was written *after* he had been jailed for libel and he accused Blanc's wife of selling state secrets.[38] Moreno wrote a series of letters to King Umberto including ones which made a series of accusations against the wives of Blanc and Crispi, including a statement that baronessa Blanc and her husband were capable of "delitto a danno della patria" or crimes against the country.[39] Moreno's text pleads with King Umberto to sweep them all out of office and then shifts back to condemning the Italian Parliament and the Italian Geographic Society (referred to as the "Italian Society Ignorant of Geography") for refusing to back his attempt to persuade Italy to seize the island of Sumatra from the Dutch.[40] The author saved particular venom for Prime Minister Francesco Crispi, whom he called "a trigamist, a perjurer and an extortioner...and a blackmailer"[41] and "without backbone, without honor and without shame," in the original Italian "uomo senza vertebra, senza onore e senza vergogna," in an open letter to King Umberto I.[42] The book also predicts that the following March, "Cabinet Ministers will find their downfall" and "Italian representatives abroad will fall, according to Moreno."[43] "Italian representatives abroad" would suffer as well, according to Moreno.

The volume encapsulates Moreno's lifelong quest for power and influence and illustrates his failings. At first his charges almost sound credible, but seeing them repeated over and over is like listening to Joseph

McCarthy rant about communists. The charges initially attract attention, but the lack of evidence undercuts his wild claims. And Moreno resembles McCarthy in another way: the numbers never add up. First there are seventeen thousand Italian slaves[44] and elsewhere eighty thousand[45] and thousands and tens of thousands.[46] He variously claimed that his anti-padrone crusade began in 1871[47] and 1869. Moreno's jealousy of Italian diplomats as anti-padrone activists comes across clearly in an 1875 letter denouncing King Victor Emanuel's decoration of Consuls Ferdinando Deluca and Luigi Corti for drafting legislation to protect Italian children from the padroni ("abolizione del traffico dei piccoli schiavi Italiani"). Corti and DeLuca's work was credited at the time with giving the Italian government power to act against padroni before they took children out of Italy. It was a major advance, but Moreno protested.

His accounts of walking the streets of New York at night in search of the *schiavi bianchi* are fascinating, but having traced the children back to their padroni, he was unable to give evidence of their link to the diplomats. Instead, in dramatic prose Moreno blamed it all on a massive plot whereby Italian diplomats "continue to blind the American police and continue to mislead the US Commissioners of Emigration at Ellis Island ... violate the American laws ... like giving lambs unto the custody of wolves."[48] On page 23 he offers his core accusations: Italian diplomats masterminded the system and profited from it, and the means of profit were certificates they gave the padroni—"The Italian consuls furnished the padroni with certificates stating that the slaves were their sons and daughters, or relatives." Thus, immense profits, "the division of the spoils," from the white-slave trade were to be earned by Fava and his consuls. In an exchange of letters with the Superintendent of Immigration, Herman Stump, in 1894 Moreno could claim only that "this traffic could not have lasted ... without the complicity of Italian representatives." He condemned these "bad Italians in America" and pleaded with US commissioner of immigration Herman Stump and secretary of the treasury John Carlisle to "demand their recall" to Italy.[49]

The focus of Moreno's anger, Ambassador Fava, is relentlessly referred to throughout the book as "Don Basilio Fava," after a character in the *Barber of Seville*. Moreno apparently drafted a congressional resolution attacking Fava in August of 1894 that was most likely ignored but may have ultimately led to the libelous article in the *Colored American*. During the trial, he argued that he had already made those charges in testimony before Congress, but only printed accusations can be prosecuted as libel.[50]

Moreno also included an ominous 1894 exchange of correspondence with commissioner of immigration Herman Stump on "the Italian slave trade" in which he claimed that the Italian Bureau "recently established at Ellis Island by Baron Fava" had been created to "keep the matter more secret and to blind the American people." He concluded that Fava and Oldrini take the "lion's share of the spoils derived from this traffic in human flesh."[51] Stump responded by requesting specifics on August 14, 1894, and his secretary wrote in October acknowledging the receipt of a letter. Moreno did not reprint that text, and Stump had generally maintained a good relationship with the Italian Bureau, even praising its staff in one of his Washington reports.

What evidence could Moreno present? He accused Fava and Giovanni Branchi (Italian Consul General at New York) of involvement in a plot to mistreat Italian laborers connected to a railroad project in Jamaica, comparing their treatment of the laborers as "tortures by vampires," but the wild charge appears without specifics as to how Fava might have profited from it.[52] Moreno claimed that the planned Arkansas farming community, Sunnyside, was part of the plot, but that was never more than a failed charitable plan to put Italian contadini on a large tract of farmland. Sunnyside lost money from the very beginning, and although Fava had supported the plan in the hope that Italians would move out of the New York slums, Sunnyside never appealed to immigrants. Most Italians were unwilling to live in the south as lynching intensified in the 1890s.[53]

Moreno's personal charges against Fava are revealed here in a way that rarely appeared in the American press. Ironically, Moreno's only rationale against the ambassador in a letter to King Umberto was to describe the ambassador's poverty. He claimed that Fava resorted to moving his diplomatic residence from one "garret"[54] to another in Washington— and then listed every flat and described the neighborhood that was, he claimed, so low and shameful that the Italian flag could not be displayed. Here the details appear: every house number, descriptions of a flat situated between a small store and a barbershop on Connecticut Avenue. Moreno claimed to know the name of Fava's Irish cook, Brigid, who lived in the attic. Moreno contended that the king was paying Fava sixteen thousand dollars a year but being badly represented and discredited.[55]

It particularly annoyed Moreno that the ambassador visited with other diplomats over lunch; he claimed that Fava cadged meals. Moreno ignored the fact that one of the chief activities and expenses of diplomatic representatives is entertaining. In fact, Fava traveled to visit the Italian communities in New York and in Massachusetts to escape the heat and tropical disease then rampant in the city of Washington, DC. Perhaps the ambassador had incurred personal expenses owing to the continuing ill health of his wife, Nicoletta. At one time Fava took a leave of absence to personally escort her back to Italy to convalesce. It was at this moment, when the ambassador was out of the country, that Moreno informed the American press that Fava had been recalled for "malversation of funds" and that photographs of his "palatial residence" had been supplied to the Italian Foreign Ministry (conversely condemning the ambassador's apparent poverty while accusing him of profligate spending).[56] The rumor was immediately squelched by members of the Washington diplomatic corps, who rose to Fava's defense, and by his son, Frank R. Fava Jr., who explained that the ambassador was unwilling to let his wife sail back to Italy alone and had not been recalled by Rome.[57]

Moreno had obviously taken a great deal of interest in tracking (one might term it stalking) the movements of the ambassador and the members of his household, and he used the ambassador's trip with his ailing wife as an opportunity to attack. Moreno proved to be a determined nemesis whose antipathy for the ambassador never abated. Taken as a whole, his book *History of a Great Wrong* reveals the mentality and the modus operandi behind the earlier attacks. In retrospect, it can be read as an explication of the great wrong perpetrated by Moreno against the ambassador, his staff, and their anti-padrone creation, the Italian Bureau.

Ambassador Fava had not defended himself against Moreno's charges in the courtroom, but afterward he publicly defended the Italian Bureau, arguing that it was "the only means to protect the Italian immigrants against the rapacity of the *padroni*."[58] He concluded that unless immigrants were "directed," they would inevitably fall into the hands of the padroni. He was well aware that in 1894 he had won Treasury Department approval by pledging to staff the Italian Bureau with those he called "honest Italian agents" who would be trusted to work inside Ellis Island in close contact with US inspectors.

If Moreno's charges could gain traction with the new McKinley administration, the ambassador must have known that the expansion of the Italian Bureau was in jeopardy, as well as its very existence. By 1898 Fava was near to realizing the last two stages of his plan: legislation was moving through the Italian Parliament to establish a labor agency and to charter a branch of the Italian National Bank in New York to serve Italian immigrants. Both were to be linked to the Italian Bureau.

This effort aimed to address the two reasons Italian immigrants were most often rejected by US immigration inspectors: when immigrants entered the United States, under the Foran Act of 1885 the inspectors were required to ask whether newcomers had jobs promised or awaiting them. If an immigrant in any way implied that a labor contract existed, written or oral, he or she could be immediately sent back to Europe. Immigrants were also asked the amount of money they carried, so as to ensure that they would not fall into the category inspectors termed "liable to public charge"—in other words, persons unable to support themselves or who had arrived on Ellis Island without funds. Some greenhorns had been robbed on shipboard or fleeced by con men and faced being shipped back to Italy without having set foot in New York. If unable to show evidence of self-support then they very well could be deported. The judgment lay with the inspector and the immigrant's ability to make a case, often through a translator.

These rules put Italian immigrants in a double bind: evidence of a guaranteed job or a signed a labor contract was illegal and grounds for rejection, as was a lack of sufficient funds to support oneself. Most immigrants were coached by the more worldly birds of passage on shipboard to learn answers that would satisfy the inspectors, but fear of answering incorrectly at the very gate of America put many at risk. With the planned expansion of the Italian Bureau, both of these risks would be eliminated and more Italians admitted to the United States. Fava intended to have new immigrants deal directly with Italian Bureau staff to secure jobs without being signed to labor contracts and to receive funds sent by their friends and family.

Ambassador Fava argued, "The only means to protect the Italian immigrants against the rapacity of the *padroni* [will be] an office of Work-Labor." He believed that immigrants required direction from the consuls in order to avoid the padroni waiting beyond Ellis Island. The Italian Bureau would, he said, "cut out" the padroni and answer the Immigration Restriction League's critique by producing what Fava termed "a better class of immigrant." The key was *agenti Italiani onesti* (honest Italian agents) to channel immigrants to safer places than New York's slums or the volatile southern states and the western mining camps where Italian lynching raged in the 1890s.[59] The ambassador saw this as the Italian Bureau's role.

Following the Spanish-American War in 1898, Americans viewed the world differently. Issues of race, military power, and America's role on the global stage were seen from a new angle. Industrialists wanted an endless supply of cheap labor, and American labor leaders resented immigrants as competition. The rise of the Immigration Restriction League (IRL) in

1894 signaled a more organized opposition that joined American labor to work against the Italian Bureau.

The drive for immigration restriction linked the interests of labor leaders like Terence Powderly with that of imperialists like senator Henry Cabot Lodge. President William McKinley was elected in 1896 with the support of Knights of Labor grand master Terence Powderly, who then sought and obtained the post of chief of immigration at Ellis Island. From an exploration of his personal papers, as well as his two memoirs, *The Path I Trod* and *Thirty Years at Labor*, it is clear that Powderly held two deep fears: that the growing wave of immigration from southern Europe was a threat to American labor and that Italian anarchists were among these newcomers. Newspapers increasingly focused on the activities of Italian anarchists in a string of political assassinations in Europe, which created a highly negative image of Italians in the American mind. In response, senator Henry Cabot Lodge and the IRL championed literacy tests, health inspections, and additional inspections prior to boarding in Italy to stem the tide.[60] The conflict regarding Italian immigration to the United States played out in this volatile mix of American expansion in the war with Spain, US entry into an increasingly globalized commercial market, a highly mobile foreign unskilled labor force competing with nativist skilled labor, an expansionist administration in Washington, and a small but highly visible international anarchist movement.

Powderly, as chief of immigration, was the key witness when the US Industrial Commission examined the status of American labor in 1899.[61] Powderly focused his testimony on the threat of Italians and claimed that they evaded the Alien Contract Labor Law. His testimony was particularly anti-Italian, but even he did not go as far as some of his questioners did: one referred to immigrants as "a lower race." Powderly's response was "I would hate to say they were a lower race ... Put it this way: Less desirable."[62] Powderly said he had once abolished the Italian Bureau, in 1898, (but the ambassador succeeded in getting the order reversed by appealing to Powderly's superior in Washington) because of "reports made to me from inspectors there that agents of this Italian Bureau would prompt [immigrants] to evade our laws." Asked whether he suspected that the padrone system had been linked to the bureau, he noted, "I have been told that it was." These claims echoed Moreno's libels. In fact, Powderly went on to identify Moreno as his informant, but his testimony took a strange twist when he first admitted that Moreno had been wrong about some things but argued nonetheless that he had been right about the issue of padroni: "From him I have heard that that Bureau is simply an agency of the *padroni,* and many of the things he told me, I know, were not borne out by the facts or by the circumstances as they transpired under my own observation at New York; others, I have reason to believe, he is pretty well informed on."

Powderly's accusations against the Italian Bureau reached Rome, where the American ambassador, William Draper, reported that attacks on the embassy staff were unfounded and offensive. Powderly's assertion that Italian Bureau staff had sought to aid immigrants "to evade our laws" was very serious. If sustained it could become a criminal charge. In addition, Powderly, as a defender of native skilled labor and former head of the Knights of Labor, saw unskilled immigrants as a threat. The padroni were regarded as a criminal element by Moreno and made it clear he believed they operated a massive underground labor system that was slavery. In the United States only three decades after the Civil War his arguments resonated. He relayed the Italian government's "sense of wonder" that evidence from Moreno had been accepted as congressional testimony *after* he had been convicted in Washington for libel.

In addition to Powderly's testimony, the Industrial Commission also heard from the IRL's Prescott Hall, who argued that immigrants depressed wages and were undesirable; he complained that Ellis Island "shut out the skilled mechanic with $100 in his pocket and let in the Italian peasant with 52 cents."[63] Hall linked illiteracy and the high percentage of unskilled workers arriving from southern Italy, 85.8% of workers were unskilled, he argued that skilled workers could shift to unskilled work in times of unemployment or underemployment, 54. This paralleled Terence Powderly's testimony that the unskilled worked for lower wages and were "less desirable," 34. [64] Stump, chief of immigration under Harrison from 1885 to 1889, took a softer line as he explained that the padroni agents kept "the poor Italian ... a debtor and slave for years." More recently, padroni had begun to "call themselves bankers."[65] A few years earlier Stump had praised the Italian Bureau's cooperation with Ellis Island staff. The Industrial Commission later reported that Italians were used by the padroni as strikebreakers and that they "[took] the places of the union men." Conversely, a few became skilled workers, but then "as an artisan he comes into conflict with American workmen." The commission concluded that Italian labor, whether skilled or unskilled, represented a threat to American labor.[66]

The chief of the Italian Bureau at Ellis Island and an Italian national, Egisto Rossi, also testified before the Industrial Commission. The commissioners appeared in New York to hear his testimony, but their tone was hostile. Indeed, Rossi's testimony was gathered *after* Powderly's 1898 initial effort to close the Italian Bureau and during a brief reprieve.

Rossi was under oath as he explained the Italian Bureau had been created to protect Italian immigrants from "the padrone system and its evils, and to warn them." Rossi denied that special privileges were being granted to the diplomats of the Italian Bureau: "We have only the right to mingle with the immigrants as soon as they are discharged." He reiterated that the Italian staff had "no access" to immigrants before they met with US inspectors.[67] Powderly had accused the Italian Bureau of coaching immigrants, but Rossi demanded proof, arguing that the Italian Bureau had "done much to reduce the evils of the padrone system ... we have prevented our immigrants from coming into contact with the padrone."[68]

The commissioners told Rossi, "We do not see why you have any right to do any business in the Barge Office." They argued that no other nation had such an office on Ellis Island—to which Rossi responded, "No other nation has it, but no other nation has an immigration of our kind."[69] Then, asked whether he had been engaged in the padrone labor and banking system or "had friends in it," Rossi testified (again, under oath), "No, I have been engaged in no business whatever except this of the bureau." The commissioners pointedly asked, "What good has your Bureau accomplished?"[70] It became apparent that the Industrial Commission was gathering evidence to close the bureau.

The circumstances of Rossi's testimony led to an explosion in the Italian embassy. Ambassador Fava waited a month for a transcript, which never arrived, before requesting the text directly from the secretary of state. A week later, transcript in hand, the ambassador protested the way in which Rossi had been questioned and refuted the charges leveled against the Italian Bureau, noting that the bureau's goal was to "eradicate the padrone weed" and that it had worked against "self-styled bankers, lodging-house keepers and saloon keepers."[71] Fava dramatically described the vulnerability of immigrants: "Wherever there are lambs to be eaten, there are always wolves ready to eat them up. It is true, not only of New York, but the world over."[72] Despite these charges, Fava contended, the Italian Bureau "still succeeds in neutralizing ... the pernicious influence which the padrone system freely exerted in the past under the very eyes of the Federal authorities." He requested that the commissioners "be called upon to furnish proof of their charges."[73]

The US Industrial Commission hearings gave Powderly the material he needed to convince the secretary of the treasury to close it. The Industrial Commission, especially in the questioning by Chairman Smyth, asked questions from the standpoint that the Italian Bureau had special privileges and were gathering information from other witnesses as to the undesirable qualities of Italian immigration. Fava stated the Italian Bureau could not defend Italians before the Ellis Island board of inquiry but that "benevolent socieites and the shipping companies" were allowed to do so. The ambassador argued the controversy over the Rossi testimony and these facts regarding the limited access of the Italian Bureau to aid immigrant appeals "implies an unwarranted distrust of the Italian

Bureau."[74] He had tried to shut the Italian Bureau two years earlier. The Industrial Commission's questioning of Egisto Rossi reveals a design to elicit evidence that could be used against the Italian Bureau which Powderly, and his allies senator Henry Cabot Lodge and the IRL's Prescott Farnsworth, could use against it, but protests from the Italian embassy staff and the American ambassador to Rome reversed the decision, albeit only briefly.

While the battle raged on, assistant commissioner of immigration Thomas Fitchie wrote to his friend Powderly. In an 1898 letter preserved in Powderly's personal papers, Fitchie laid out his objections to the employment of an Italian American at Ellis Island: "I am sorry to learn there is even the remotest intention of appointing of Jas E March [or Marchetti]—to any position ... I am afraid the large numbers of public charges would not be discovered, much less the murderers & thieves."[75] Here was a US immigration official telling Powderly that March would abet the entry of Italian criminals into the United States.[76] But there was an ironic coda for Fitchie. In 1901 newspapers revealed that US immigration inspectors at Ellis Island had sold forged immigration papers to an estimated ten thousand illegal aliens. Fitchie ordered an investigation, but his own staff was implicated in the scandal, which received broad press coverage. President Theodore Roosevelt ousted Fitchie and his staff.

These events occurred in the midst of a chaotic, violent era both in America and Italy. In 1900 an Italian American anarchist assassinated King Umberto. President McKinley offered his condolences. Less than a year later the Italians sent condolences to the White House after a Polish anarchist shot McKinley. Immigration restrictionists feared anarchists and stereotyped Italians as knife-wielding, quick to anger, and a threat to the jobs of American workers.

But was there another reason why the Italian Bureau was shut down as the twentieth century dawned? Powderly's papers contain an English-language report written by Egisto Rossi heralding the achievements of the Italian Bureau. In it Rossi touted the bureau's success in aiding the growing number of Italian immigrants—citing a 35 percent increase over the numbers in 1898.[77] From Powderly's perspective, such success signaled that Italians would arrive in ever greater numbers—and create still more competition for American laborers. He had long expressed a fear of anarchists, and Italians were more prominent in this movement after a series of assassinations in Europe.[78] The report also discusses the bureau's plans to establish a labor office and charter a branch of the Italian National Bank. Powderly knew well which methods could legally be used to restrict Italian immigration: labor contracts and the "liable to become a public charge" question were the keys. Rossi's report made clear the Italian Foreign Ministry's strategy to eliminate these issues, and the Foreign Ministry were close to achieving their aims. The Italian Bureau was ready to facilitate the renewed, and probably expanded, entry of Italians to the United States after the Spanish-American War ended in 1898. Therefore, Powderly attacked the Italian Bureau, using Moreno's information, and convinced the treasury secretary to eliminate the Italian Bureau just when Italian immigration promised to increase.

The twin threads of Moreno's anti-padroni crusade and the Italian ambassador's career ended together in 1901. Moreno collapsed on a Washington street, alone and impoverished, and died a few days later. Upon his death the *New York Times* wrote of Moreno's nature that he had been "relentless in opposition ... once aroused [he] would fight all the world."[79] Ambassador Fava retired a few months later and returned to Italy, where he wrote *I linciaggi agli Stati Uniti: La questione giuridica* (Lynching in the United States: The legal questions), arguing that the lynching of foreigners in America should be the jurisdiction of federal courts. He observed that two presidents had called for such legislation and that "our countrymen labor to increase the riches and wealth of the Great Republic."[80]

In retrospect, the outcome of the dramatic battle over the protection of Italian immigrants reflected the deep-seated Italophobia that had developed in America during the 1890s. Only in such an atmosphere could charges as wild and unsustainable as Moreno's were be used so effectively to close the one agency that might have eliminated the padrone problem altogether and rescued the *schiavi bianchi*. The twentieth century dawned on January 1, 1900, with all safeguards for Italian immigrants removed from Ellis Island. On that morning, the Italian Bureau was closed.

NOTES

1. This was established in the Barge Office by an Italian diplomatic team under Dr. Egisto Rossi, with the permission of American immigration authorities as negotiated by the Italian ambassador in Washington. The Italian diplomats aided their countrymen while they were under American authority on Ellis Island. But when Terence Powderly was put in charge of Ellis Island, he ordered the Italian Bureau closed and the ambassador briefly succeeded in having his superiors order it remain open. The Society for the Protection of Italian Immigrants later took up its role but could only operate outside the gates of Ellis Island. SPII volunteers did the work, with private donations from American citizens and some Italian government financial support.

2. Francesco Saverio Fava, often referred to as Baron Fava—a title he held before becoming ambassador—is no relation to the author. Much key material regarding Cesar Celso Moreno can be found in the Boston Public Library's special collections; regarding Ambassador Fava's family, especially his son Francesco's life in Washington and his role in defending his father, see the University Archives at the Gelman Library of George Washington University.

3. Cosco, *Imagining Italians*, 8; John E. Zucchi, *The Little Slaves of the Harp: Italian Child Street Musicians in Nineteenth-Century Paris, London, and New York* (Montreal: McGill-Queen's University Press, 1992); Horatio Alger Jr., *Phil, the Fiddler* (Philadelphia: Porter and Coates, 1872); Luciano Iorizzo, "The Padrone and Immigrant Distribution," in Silvano Tomasi and Madeline Engel, *The Italian Experience in the United States* (New York: Center for Migration Studies, 1970), 50–52; and Laura Pilotti, *L'ufficio di informazione e protezione dell'emigrazione italiana di Ellis Island* (Rome: Istituto poligrafico e zecca dello stato, 1993), 31–36.

4. Celso Cesare Moreno, *History of a Great Wrong*, in Boston Public Library special collection, labeled Gift of the Immigration Restriction League in 1900. Undated internal evidence suggests that it was originally published circa 1895 or 1896.

5. For Moreno's letters, see *The Papers of Charles Sumner*, Houghton Library, Harvard University, Boston, Massachusetts. Sumner must have followed Moreno's career, for in 1869 he also donated a book by Moreno about the Hawaii controversy to the Harvard College Library. Immigra-

tion scholar Rudolph Vecoli was working on a biography of Moreno at the time of his passing. The University of Minnesota holds Vecoli's academic materials, and another scholar has, as of this writing, begun an effort to complete this much anticipated work.

6. Unsigned, "The Italian Slaves: The Question Discussed at a Picnic – Resolutions Adopted," New York *Times*, July 1, 1873.

7. For a short biography, see Francesca Loverici, *Il primo ambasciatore Italiano a Washington: Saverio Fava*, Clio: Rivista trimestrale di Studi Storici 13 (Naples: Edizioni scientifiche Italiane, 1977), 239–276.

8. "I came to America in the month of May, 1868, at the request of the Hon. William H. Seward, then Secretary of State..." in Moreno, *History of a Great Wrong*, 28.

9. Unsigned, "Baron Fava's Trip Home," *New York Times*, September 19, 1892, 1.

10. See "Baron Fava's Trip Home."

11. "Baron Fava's Trip Home: Reports of His Recall Not Credited," *New York Times*, Sept. 19, 1892. "Baron Fava Forced to Act ... Annoyed for Years by Moreno," *New York Times*, July 13, 1895.

12. On prevalence of Italian lynchings and indemnities paid, see Luciano Iorizzo, "The Padrone and Immigrant Distribution," in Tomasi and Engel, *The Italian Experience*, 50–52. On New Orleans, see Richard Gambino, *Vendetta: The True Story of the Largest Lynching in US History* (Toronto:: Guernica Press, 2000).

13. *Lynching* is defined in a US source as "to execute without due process of law; especially to hang"; *American Heritage Dictionary of the English Language*, 1969 (4th printing), s.v. "lynch." English sources define it as a uniquely American crime: "The practice of inflicting summary punishment upon an offender, by a self-constituted court without legal authority ... summary execution of one charged with a flagrant offense ... shocking [though] it may seem to Europeans"; *Oxford Universal Dictionary*, 3rd editon, s.v. "lynch."

14. Over 100 African-Americans were lynched in the year 1890; the preceding decade had seen 1,400 such executions, and the next decade saw nearly 1,000.

15. In Aug. 1944 an Italian POW, Private Guglielmo Olivotto, was lynched in Seattle by a white army policeman; see "Italian POW and Rumors Put to Rest," *Seattle Times*, July 22, 2008; and Jack Hamann, *On American Soil: How Justice Became a Casualty of World War II* (Seattle: University of Washington Press, 2007).

16. Emphasis and spelling as in original. *Punch, or the London Charivari*, Apr. 11, 1891, 173–174. The rhyme was based on a mispronunciation of Fava's name.
17. Marco Rimanelli and Sheryl L. Postman, eds., *The 1891 New Orleans Lynching and US-Italian Relations: A Look Back* (New York: Lang, 1992).
18. This event occurred in October 1891 U.S. Navy Commander Robley Evans quoted by Harry Thurston Peck, in "Twenty Years of the Republic," *The Bookman*, volume 21, (New York: Dodd and Mead, 1905), 373.
19. Plumb quoted in the unsigned article "The Week," *The Nation*, Apr. 23, 1891: 337–339.
20. Henry Cabot Lodge, "Lynch Law and Unrestricted Immigration," *North American Review*, May 1891, 602, 604.
21. Alexander Karlin, "The Italo-American Incident of 1891 and the Road to Reunion," *Journal of Southern History* 8, no. 2 (May 1942): 242–246.
22. "In No Shape for War, Defenseless Condition of American Coasts," *Washington Post*, Apr. 2, 1891; "America in the Right," *Washington Post*, Apr. 4, 1891.
23. Fava to Secretary of State Hay, *Foreign Relations of the US* (Washington, DC: : Government Printing Office, 1900), 715.
24. Henry Cabot Lodge, "Lynch Law and Unrestricted Immigration," *The North American Review*, Boston, volume CLII, May 1891, 602–612. Saverio Fava, "I linciaggi agli stati uniti la questione giuridica 1900–1902," *La Nuova antologia*, Roma, February 16, 1902, 644–649.
25. *Colored American* article, quoted in court document page 9. Quotes from the statement of Arthur A. Birney, Attorney of the United States in and for the District of Columbia. Text of the article was "offered in evidence" during the trial, see statement in court document manuscript appendix "US v Moreno Judges notes" (spelling and punctuation as in original) and Washington *Post* report.
26. Ibid., 10.
27. Ibid., 12.
28. Regarding the assertion that the ambassador is "a Hebrew" included by Moreno in *History of a Great Wrong*, page 5, reprint of his Washington *Herald* article of Sunday, May 3, 1891.
29. United States v. Moreno, Record Group 21, District Court of the US, DC, file 20399; and "Libeled Baron Fava" in *Washington Post*, Oct. 30, 1895. In text individual quotes have been marked with page numbers in court documents including unpaginated, handwritten notes in an appendix. The Washington Post article reports that the Colored American article

was read to the jury. Regarding asseration the ambassador "is a Hebrew" included by Moreno in *History of a Great Wrong*, page 5, reprint of his Washington *Herald* article of Sunday, May 3, 1891.

30. Quote in court document, 8, and *History of a Great Wrong*, 9.
31. Attorney Arthur Birney's statement in court document, 4.
32. "At the National Capital," *New York Times*, July 20, 1895.
33. Unsigned, "Libeled Baron Fava," Washington *Post*, October 30, 1895.
34. "Has an Island for Sale," *Washington Post*, Dec. 16, 1895.
35. *History of a Great Wrong*, 28.
36. Moreno, *History of a Great Wrong*.
37. *History of a Great Wrong*, 6, quoting from his own article in the Washington *Herald*, Sunday May 3, 1891.
38. "ha fatti millioni colla vendita dei segreti di stato" or she made millions with the sale of secrets of state, in *History of a Great Wrong*, 50. Moreno claimed to have published these charge in page 50.
39. "Lettera aperta a Umberto I," *History of a Great Wrong*, 44.
40. Moreno letter "dal giornale il cristoro Colombo," October 5, 1895, *History of a Great Wrong*, 50.
41. *History of a Great Wrong*, 6.
42. "lettera aperata a umberto I." *History of a Great Wrong*, 42.
43. *History of a Great Wrong*, 7.
44. Moreno, 11.
45. Ibid., 16.
46. Ibid., 17.
47. Ibid., 2.
48. *History of a Great Wrong*, 9.
49. Ibid., 27.
50. Moreno reprinted letters, the *Colored American* article, and other materials in *History of a Great Wrong*.
51. *History of a Great Wrong*, 27.
52. Moreno, *History of a Great Wrong*, 41 and 42 ("torturati da vampire").
53. The communities of Sunnyside and Tonitown were both begun with good intentions but failed. Ambassador Fava encouraged both developments, but the combination of malaria and financial losses destroyed them. Lynching of Italians also made immigrants wary of settling in Arkansas. For the ambassador's view, see Francesco Saverio Fava, "Le colonie agricole italiane nell'America del Nord," in *Nuova antologia* (Oct. 1904): 466; and Amoreno Martellini, *Fra Sunny Side e La Nueva Marca:*

Materiali e modelli per una storia dell'emigrazione marchigiana fino alla grande guerra (Milan: FrancoAngeli Storia, 1999), chapter 6.

54. Moreno, 9.
55. The *New York Times* reported in Sept. 1892 that Moreno had leaked a phony diplomatic dispatch from Rome that supposedly summoned Fava to return in disgrace. See Moreno's letters in his *History of a Great Wrong.* See "Baron Fava's Trip Home," NY Times, Sept 19, 1892; on pay and flags, Moreno, 5.
56. Unsigned, "Baron Fava's Trip Home," New York *Times,* September 19, 1892.
57. "Baron Fava's Trip Home," *New York Times,* Sept. 19, 1892.
58. Original "the only way to protect" letter Fava to Walter Q. Gresham, Secretary of State, April 19,1894 in *Executive Documents of the Senate of the United States 1893–1894,* 104–105.
59. My translation of "Memorandum," annesso A and B, "Le precarie condizioni" in *Camera dei deputati: Documenti diplomatici,* 7 July 1894, 21; and *Camera dei deputati Documenti Diplomatici presentati al parlamento Italiano,* dal ministro degli affair esteri (Blanc) Seduate del 7 luglio 1894, (Roma: Tipografia della camera dei deputati, 1894). This is a printed, published set of documents which is analogous to the Foreign Relations of the United States series, and available in libraries.
60. These inspections were held in the port before a person was allowed to emigrate from Italy. The steamship companies grew increasingly particular about the conduct of these inspections since a rejected person would be returned to Italy from New York at the company's expense.
61. Terence Powderly, *Thirty Years at Labor, 1859–1889* (New York: A. M. Kelly, 1967), 227; also see his other memoir, *The Path I Trod: The Autobiography of Terence V. Powderly* (New York: Columbia University Press, 1940).
62. "Testimony of Hon. T. V. Powderly, Commissioner-General of Immigration, Feb. 10, 1899," in *Reports of the Industrial Commission on Immigration: Including Testimony, with Review and Digest and Special Reports; and on Education, Including Testimony, with Review and Digest* (Washington, DC: Government Printing Office, 1901), 15:32–46.
63. Testimony of Prescott Hall, "Hearings before the Industrial Commission," *Reports of the Industrial Commission on Immigration,* volume XV, (Washington: Government Printing Office, 1901), 65.

64. "Testimony of Mr. Prescott F. Hall, Secretary, Immigration Restriction League, Apr. 8, 1899, and Appendix Submitted Thereafter," *Reports of the Industrial Commission on Immigration*, 15:46–67.

65. President Benjamin Harrison,Testimony of Herman Stump, 8.

66. "The Padrone System and Common Labor," undated and unsigned report in *Reports of the Industrial Commission on Immigration*, 15:430–432, 435.

67. "Testimony of Dr. Egisto Rossi, Chief of Italian Bureau, Port of New York, July 26, 1899," *Reports of the Industrial Commission on Immigration*, 15:154–155.

68. Ibid., In testimony Congressmen and some witnesses shifted between: the padrone, padrones, padroni. Rossi referred to it as the padrone system.

69. Rossi, 157.

70. Ibid., 154–160.

71. *Foreign Relations of the United States*, Transmitted to Congress, volume December 5, 1899 (Washington: Government Printing Office, 1901), 116.

72. Fava statement quoting Egisto Rossi, *FRUS*, volume December 5, 1899, 116.

73. Fava, *FRUS*, 419.

74. Fava, *FRUS*, 418.

75. See Fitchie to Powderly, July 14, 1898, in *Terence Powderly Papers*, Catholic University of America (libraries.cua.edu). March—his original name was Marchetti—was a prominent Italian American in New York City.

76. See also Wilton Tifft, *Ellis Island* (Chicago: Contemporary Books, 1990), 65. Tifft noted that Powderly, along with his aides Fitchie and McSweeney, was vulnerable when "new scandals broke in 1901, and charges of fraud and ineptitude once again erupted against the Fitchie administration." (69).

77. Egisto Rossi, *Italian Immigration to the US*, Fifth Annual Report, fiscal year June 30, 1899, 3.

78. Italian anarchists murdered a French official in 1894, the Spanish prime minister in 1897, an Austrian empress in 1898, and King Umberto of Italy in 1900. The king's assassin was an Italian who had emigrated to work in Paterson, New Jersey.

79. "Five Days a Premier: Once Headed Revolt in Sumatra," *Washington Post*, Mar. 13, 1901.

80. Francesco Saverio Fava, "I linciaggi agli Stati Uniti," *Nuova antologia*, Feb. 16, 1902, 644–649; and "Ex-Ambassador Fava Dies," *New York Times*, Oct. 4, 1913.

CHAPTER 5

THE SECOND GENERATION

AT HOME IN AMERICA

Tenements and the factories became the center of life in central Massachusetts for the people who had migrated from the Veneto. But by the 1910s many Venetians began to settle in central Massachusetts, and seasonal migration waned. In 1900 an estimated sixty Italian families had settled in Fitchburg, but within a decade there were about three hundred families resident in the city.

Even as more people left the Veneto between 1905 and 1910, fewer remained transnationals, and fewer returned each winter to the Veneto. The Italian government passed a law in 1901 requiring a returning migrant to register in his or her home *comune* within a month of repatriation. Even as immigration from the Veneto to America escalated, a steep decline occurred in the number of those who returned to the Veneto: repatriates represented 35.6 percent of total emigrants in 1901–1902, but only four years later repatriates dropped to just 8.8 percent of total emigrants. In 1911 the Italian government reported that the Veneto had one of the lowest percentages of return immigration, with only 11 percent of emigrants applying for repatriation (only the island of Sardinia reported significantly lower rates, at 6 percent).[1]

Why did seasonal migration decline? The transnational life was demanding, and over time employment became more permanent, personal relationships deepened, and migrants built a church and social organizations in central Massachusetts. Some Veneti referred to their settlements as colonies, and they formed small but significant clusters of *paesani* in their new home. Migrants who had journeyed each year from the mountains of Italy's northeast began to settle into new lives centered in urban central Massachusetts. Moreover, in the mills and factories there was a constant demand for labor as the region's economy expanded, along with new protections for laborers as Massachusetts became the first state to institute a minimum wage in 1912.

In addition, the economic situation in Italy declined as labor strife and continuing agricultural depression left workers in the Veneto with little hope for a better life. Even those who returned from America with substantial savings found themselves in a chaotic situation. A number of events tested the government in Rome: in 1900 the king was assassinated by an anarchist; a 1908 earthquake killed two hundred thousand people in Sicily, leaving Rome an insurmountable human crisis; and labor conflict led to numerous strikes. War loomed, accompanied by the possibility that conscription might entangle returned migrants and their children, for the Italian military could require terms of service as long as seven years. In 1911 Italy launched a new colonial war to wrest Libya from the Ottoman Empire in the hopes that it would become a new destination for Italian immigrants within Italy's control.[2] In 1912 and 1913 two wars erupted in the Balkans, portending the larger conflict in 1914 that would threaten transatlantic travel and separate families. In April 1912 the passenger liner *Titanic* sank, taking with it more than fifty Italians and publicizing the risks involved in seasonal migration.

Rome was concerned that the informal Italian colonies signified a population lost to the Italian state, and the birth of the second generation of emigrants far from their parents' homeland marked a new challenge. In the United States members of this generation were born as American citizens, spoke English in public schools, and learned American ways. The second generation was caught between the traditions and language of Venetian parents and the American world outside the tenements. They grew up with no direct knowledge of the Veneto and were often torn between the disparate demands of these two forces.

In an 1897 study of Boston Italians, settlement-house worker Frederick Bushee found that "nearly all the children [of immigrants went] to public schools" and quickly became "interpreters for the family."[3] The Italian government wanted to hold on to those living abroad, and political arguments favoring colonialism were framed in terms of providing a new destination for Italians that would remain part of an Italian empire. Landowners were concerned by the massive work force lost to emigration.

The American process of naturalization was problematic for some older Italians who were unwilling to take the final oath, which required that they disavow loyalty to any monarch and to any nation other than the United States. Those migrants who could not complete the naturalization process by learning English, passing a citizenship test, and taking the oath of loyalty remained aliens in America.

But the advent of the Mussolini regime in 1922 magnified these issues; Il Duce was determined to expand Italian power and to create a new Roman empire, stating that it was "better for Italians to work their own lands rather than those of others."[4] Numbers for Italy's military constituted a deep concern, and if an American-born son returned to Italy, he could be conscripted. The Fascists sentenced political opponents to confinement, and historian Martin Clark has observed that they also "withdrew all passports and imposed severe penalties for clandestine emigration."[5] Rome's 1926 Decree on Public Safety required everyone to carry identification cards and aimed to control "persons dangerous to public order" by forbidding them "to leave the country for political reasons" without proper documentation and by authorizing "the use of weapons" against escapees.[6]

Two factors defined the status of Veneti in America: the quality of their English-language skills and whether they pursued naturalization as a path to American citizenship. Developing facility in English made it easier to negotiate life in America and made it possible to begin the process of naturalization. Younger immigrants could adapt more easily, and some filed what were called "first papers" for citizenship. Older family members who struggled with English often remained in unskilled jobs and were less likely to attempt naturalization. But for all migrants, the golden age of unfettered transatlantic travel was ended by the advent of war in Europe. Those Italian nationals living in America were classified by the government as *aliens* until the Smith Act of 1940 termed them *enemy aliens.*

The community in Fitchburg was divided into two neighborhoods. The starting point for Italian immigrants, whether from the north or south of the homeland, was an area known as the Patch, discussed earlier—rows of tenements and foundries lining Water and Middle Streets. Jobs were easy to find in the iron and brass foundries clustered at the end of Water Street that supplied equipment for the nearby railroad yards. Industrial concerns there included a railroad-repair yard, a sawmill, and factories that produced heavy machinery, boilers, saws and scythes, bicycles, and tools.

But the Veneto migrants usually moved to the Cleghorn neighborhood in west Fitchburg because Veneto men were often skilled in quarrying, so they were drawn to the quarries on Rollstone Hill, and Veneto women were apt to have experience in silk spinning, so the textile mills along River Street offered opportunity. Tenements lined Leighton, Kimball, and River Street in the neighborhood that ringed the Rollstone Hill quarries. Cleghorn's Parkhill Mills were part of a dense cluster of factories that produced textiles, shoes, locks, stoves, pianos, and other products with in a single square mile. It was a commercial, residential, and industrial area and home to the Florence Stove Works, the Magee Stove Company, and the Independent Lock—all of which included brass foundries as part of their operations.

Cleghorn grew into a city unto itself. Originally home to French Canadian immigrants, its hills were lined with rows of small businesses surrounded by a dense landscape of tenements and its own post office. The Nashua River wound through west Fitchburg and provided a half-dozen paper mills along its banks with the water needed to produce anything from rolls of newsprint to sheets of fine writing paper. The paper mills included the Crocker, Burbank and Company complex, which was spread along a half-mile of the river; Fitchburg Paper, with its massive Number Four Mill; and the Dejonge paper mills, further downstream. These operations required enormous amounts of water to power machinery and to produce the slurry of pulp that became paper. The untreated wastewater was discharged into the Nashua River, turning it an opaque white at the start of the week that bloomed into vibrant colors by Saturday. On Sundays, the paper mills shut down to clean out their machinery, and the cycle began anew. The Nashua River became one of the most polluted rivers in America.

Closer to Rollstone Hill were rows of massive brick textile mills that expanded over acres and stood as high as five stories. Textile and shoe factories boomed in Massachusetts until the 1920s. They processed raw cotton and wool into yarns and fabrics and were key employers of unskilled labor, especially women and young men. Children of foreign-born immigrants often left school at fourteen or fifteen to work in the textile mills and gave their earnings to their parents. But the viability of the textile industry in Massachusetts was threatened in the 1920s by the dramatically lower labor costs in the southern United States. Massachusetts mill owners struggled to compete with southern mills, whose workers accepted wages 20 percent less than those found in New England.

Young Veneto men hoped to escape the heat and fumes of molten metal in the foundries to find a better-paying job in the extremely humid paper mills, where the wages were better. Young Veneto women almost universally sought work in the cotton mills, where their knowledge of spinning was valued, and their families viewed this as an acceptable occupation because many had already worked in Italy's silk mills. Most other employers, especially paper mills, did not hire women for work that was physically demanding. Italian-speaking women could not find work in households in a state where Irish American women dominated that sector of the job market.

Cotton and wool mills hired many young women, men, and children to spin, weave, and dye yarn, gingham fabric, cotton duck, khaki, and worsted woolens. But high-speed spinning machinery and looms posed physical risks and had few safety features. Cotton dust filled the air and made breathing difficult. Workers emerged at the end of the workday coated with fine particles of white dust that clogged their nostrils. Clothing factories like the Asher Pants Company required women to know how to sew, a skill most young Veneto women possessed, but this formerly leisurely art of the home was accelerated under the pressure of the piecework system. Women were transformed into sweatshop workers running electric industrial sewing machines in an atmosphere filled with cutting and sewing machines, as well as with cotton dust. Asthma plagued many. The infamous 1912 Triangle Shirtwaist Factory fire in New York City was an example of the dangers that mill work posed for young immigrant women.

The quarries clustered atop Rollstone Hill were also dangerous places to work. Quarrying required the use of explosives and drills to split the stone, heavy steel derricks to haul chunks of granite up from the depths of the quarry, giant stone saws to slice the granite, and grinding machines to make stone dust from the remaining chips. Work continued even as storms blew across the hilltop. Teamsters used horses and later trucks to haul the stone to the rail yards and to bring new supplies of explosives up to the quarry. But perhaps the most hazardous places of employment were the brass and iron foundries, where workers labored surrounded by molten metal, toxic fumes, and the hammering of drop forges.

Imagining the atmosphere of Cleghorn in the 1910s requires envisioning an unregulated industrial environment: steam locomotives swept through the city burning coal and belching smoke and steam; foundries released toxic gases from molten iron and zinc; heavy trucks and horse-drawn wagons wheeled through the streets, where animals left behind manure; water-powered machinery had given way to noisier coal-burning factories. Steam-powered saws milled lumber, and rolling mills shaped tools as spinning frames and looms rattled in massive textile factories. Explosions punctuated the day in the six quarries on Rollstone Hill as tons of stone was hauled down Beech Street, and wagons rattled back up the hill for another load. Everywhere people were surrounded by the sounds, noises, and impact of heavy industry. The Nashua River was the color of the paper that the mills produced on any given day.

Trolleys rattled through the streets to deliver workers to factories that ran three shifts, twenty-four hours a day. And returning home at day's end offered little respite. Tenements were packed tightly with families and boarders who came and went at all hours, used coal or wood stoves to cook, and heated with kerosene stoves in winter. Everywhere smoke, dust, and dirt spewed from factories, mills, and chimneys.

Despite Massachusetts's reputation as an early adopter of worker protections, such as child-labor laws and a minimum wage, there was little recourse for a worker who was injured on the job. Mills had only to look outside their gates for a ready supply of replacement workers. Immigrants realized their vulnerability and organized their own system of self-insurance to provide some small security in case of injury or death in the workplace. *Mutuo soccorso* (mutual benefit) societies were among the first social groups that many Veneto and other Italian immigrants organized. The Carlo Alberto Society, the Venetian Club, the Societá Italiana Vittorio Emanuele III di Mutuo Soccorso, and the Loggia Cristoforo Colombo Order of Sons of Italy in America pooled regular contributions of small amounts to provide a cash payment in case they were injured or killed at work. In addition, the larger groups offered inexpensive doctor visits at a set fee. The societies began as small groups of immigrant workers who met to talk, play bocce or cards, and network. Most clubs gathered in tenements or boardinghouses but over time took on more formal trappings and eventually rented halls for large meetings.

The Commonwealth of Massachusetts insisted on regulating any group offering insurance and required these societies to register with the state as insurers. The Loggia Cristoforo Colombo began as group of Italians gathering to "sip on a glass of wine and enjoy many leisure moments in folk dances and music" around 1890, but by 1910 its members had established "with great enthusiasm" the Societá Italiana di Mutuo Soccorso e Beneficienza Cristoforo Colombo.[7] In 1926 four women of the group organized the Regina Elena Lodge as an auxiliary.

A similar group, the Societá Italiana Vittorio Emanuele III di Mutuo Soccorso, grew so rapidly that by 1912 it boasted an enrollment of four thousand members, many of whom were Italian constructions workers on large public-works projects, including the Fifth Street Bridge and Fitchburg's sewage system, and mill employees. The president was Angelo Seretto, a padrone who operated Seretto Brothers General Contracting, the Inter-City Express, and the Employment Agency for Italian Laborers, as well as a real estate agency, steamship ticket and banking operation, and importing business. The vice president, Giuseppe Provenzano, had been a key fundraiser for Saint Anthony's Church. The local paper termed the Vittorio Emanuele group "one of the strongest Italian societies in the country" with more than a dozen administrators and a physician, Dr. C. E. Geary, on call for its members.[8]

Over time these groups became more sophisticated in terms of the benefits they offered to workers and the social programs they organized. In 1913 there were only three Sons of Italy branches in Massachusetts: in Worcester, Fitchburg, and neighboring Leominster.[9] Italian settlement was concentrated in the state's most industrialized areas. Other Massachusetts cities were larger, but Fitchburg became home to the first Italian-speaking parish north of Worcester and a number of Italian social organizations.

Italian-owned businesses emerged in Cleghorn and in the Patch, as well. In the latter the demographic—an Irish neighborhood with an Italian presence—was reversed as a number of Italians established specialty stores and small businesses to serve the expanding population. Entrepreneurs put their children to work to help staff their markets and shoe shops. Water Street was lined on both sides for nearly a mile with businesses that offered Italian groceries, wine, fruit, and vegetables, along with a pharmacy, two rival padrone banks, steamship ticket offices, shoe repair shops, and barbershops. The Patch was an Italian colony where differences in dialect might complicate the transactions, but imported Italian products and services were available for all. Saint Anthony's Church was established in 1908, a few blocks above Water Street, and as discussed earlier was the central parish for Italian-speaking Catholics in Fitchburg—but within a decade, it needed to extend its services to parishioners who had settled miles away in Cleghorn. Although Cleghorn was also home to Saint Joseph's, a French Canadian parish, the Holy Rosary Mission was established to reach out to Italians in the neighborhood. Prior to the establishment of the mission church in 1935, St. Anthony's occasionally sponsored a bus to bring parishioners to the church so they did not have to walk the four-mile roundtrip.

Older women's lives were bounded by the tenement, the church, and the mills. The neighborhood was where women shopped for food, socialized, and raised their children, most of whom were sent to public schools. Those who could afford the fees sent their children to Saint Bernard's Elementary School, established by the Irish parish, but Saint Bernard's required students as young as ten years old to take a temperance pledge. Italians often made and consumed wine at home, so their children found themselves outsiders at Saint Bernard's. Other parents chose to send their children to Saint Francis Elementary School, where classes were conducted in French. Pity the Italian children, freshly arrived in America and struggling to cope in English, who found themselves being instructed in yet another language.

In 1919 Reverend Angelo Carpinella of Saint Anthony's parish invited the Venerini Sisters from Viterbo, Italy, to establish a convent in Fitchburg. The first four nuns arrived to find that the parish had nowhere to house them and no money to pay them. The pioneering sisters struggled without compensation or financial support, and according to the church's history "relied mostly on generous parishioners for food and donations."[10] They managed to establish an *asilo*, or nursery school, and later an elementary school. The Venerini Sisters focused their outreach on the women of the parish and offered evening social activities that included classes in the Italian language, embroidery, and needlework, including lace making. On Sundays they supervised the children's mass in the church basement.[11] One student recalled that the sisters had insisted that their elementary school students speak the northern dialect of Italian.[12]

But the second generation of Italians was living in an English-speaking world, and language was a source of conflict in some homes, as well as in the schools. Some parents encouraged English in the home, whereas others never learned English themselves and relied upon their children to act as translators. Dialect further divided the Italian community because Venetians, Neapolitans, and Sicilians could not understand one another and tended to cluster together with their own *paesani* when it came time to socialize in clubs and organizations.

Public schools functioned as vehicles of assimilation in a city where so many residents were either foreign born or the children of the foreign born. One of the biggest challenges for Fitchburg's educators was to keep immigrant children in the schools. Italian parents often withdrew children from the schools at age fourteen and encouraged them to help support the family. Italians expected their children to arrive home with an unopened pay envelope, which was to be and turned over to the parents; only a small amount, if anything, was returned to the child. The struggle to survive shortened the educational careers of many second-generation Veneti.

This was not entirely an Italian practice. In the first decades of the twentieth century, young children were expected to enter the workplace at a young age. In 1915 the United States Bureau of Labor Statistics examined the causes of children's leaving school. The investigation revealed that 30 percent left because of real economic need, another 27 percent left because a child's help was "desired though not necessary," 26 percent left owing to the child's "dissatisfaction with school," and only 9.8 percent left because of the child's "preference for work."[13] The report notes that many of those who left had repeated grades; some were as far as three years behind. The assimilation of children from homes where a foreign language was dominant must have played a part. Leonard Covello, an educator and Italian immigrant in New York, argued that assimilation could not be forced and that a gentler model of educating the second generation must be found. Covello was reacting to the pervasive negative view of young Italian children in the New York school system. The stigmatization in Boston schools was to such an extent that a settlement house worker wrote "Their dread of appearing strange before their playmates stimulates them to imitate American ways....Even their euphonious names become distasteful to them, and a Marondotti wishes he were a Smith or a Brown."[14] Covello fought the system of testing immigrant children that was pioneered by America's leading educational psychologists, including Dr. Arthur Sweeney, who described Italians as "imbeciles" whose intelligence "was scarcely superior to that of an ox." Sweeney testified before the House Committee on Immigration and Naturalization that such groups should have "no place in this country and no voice in its affairs."[15] Despite these challenges, in 1903 Mary Cosentino, the daughter of Italian restaurant owners, became the first Italian graduate of Fitchburg High School and went on to attend Becker College, a business school.[16] By the late 1920s Italian youth were regularly a part of the FHS graduating classes, but a small percentage.[17]

But in Fitchburg, with its plethora of mills constantly in need of unskilled labor, it was very easy for a young person to abandon school and never return. The city established an Americanization Office, headed by Margaret Kielty, to organize basic English-language training and citizenship classes. Kielty, who spoke Italian, worked in the public school system to help children transition to English and established the Water Street Clinic, where Italian women could learn about managing a home in America and prepare for naturalization.

Tenement life was vastly different from the alpine mountain existence of the Veneti. As discussed earlier, many had abandoned the Veneto for Massachusetts because of the prevalence of pellagra. The disease struck farmers and their children, stunting growth and delaying the mental development of the young. In 1912 Stewart Roberts identified the "triple causes" of pellagra as "peasant life, poverty and polenta" after examining victims in the Veneto.[18] In 1909 pellagra began spreading in the American south, where doctors named it "Italian leprosy," believing (incorrectly) that it was contagious. Rural southerners consumed large amounts of processed cornmeal called grits, and Roberts traced the outbreak to a change in the milling process that removed the niacin from grain.[19] Most of the diseases that plagued the Veneti did not follow them to America; however, in a 1904 study of emigration, the Italian government identified 278 cases of tuberculosis among migrants who had returned to Italy from America. Not a single case of tuberculosis was detected among migrants leaving Italy the same year. The new plague was being bred in the crowded American tenements and factories.[20]

In America immigrants were felled by diseases that originated in the tenements and factories, and obtaining medical care was expensive. Tenements were designed to pack as many people as possible into the smallest amount of space; the triple-decker was developed in New England as cheap housing for workers. In Fitchburg such housing might be three or even five stories high, with two or more apartments per level. A tenement might produce income from as many as sixteen apartments. The goal of investors was to minimize costs, and they often installed shared toilets on each floor. Bath tubs and showers were luxuries. Tenements were heated with wood or coal stoves, which contributed to poor air quality. In winter heavy storm windows were hung over the sashes and bolted on. Storm windows doubled the insulation, but in spring landlords often left them on the building, thus limiting ventilation.

Whether occupied by a family or a group of workers, these units were crowded. A flat with two or three bedrooms might house up to a dozen people in close quarters, and in large families children slept two or three to a bed. Families that could not afford their own rent took in boarders (essentially subletting a room). Crowded rooms, little fresh air, and cold New England winters without central heating promoted illness. Influenza and pneumonia always lurked among their human hosts. Similar problems are recorded in historian Donna Gabaccia's account of tenement life on New York's Elizabeth Street and in Anthony V. Riccio's study of Boston's North End Italian community.[21]

In the daytime, tenements were the world of women. They cooked and washed for their families and for their boarders as well, chopped wood or hauled coal for their stoves, and hung laundry as they struggled to adjust to urban life. Traditional Italian foodways were maintained if the family could afford imported products, or polenta, pasta, salami, and homemade wine were served. Home gardens yielded vegetables and were established in any corner of dirt that could be cleared for a garden. Women gathered *radici* wherever they could be found in the city, just as they had in the mountains. Veneto migrants sought to replicate their diet in the mountains by setting up backyard chicken coops, a pen with rabbits, even shelter for a pig. In Fitchburg , the local Armour and Swift packinghouses would sell half a pig to those ambitious enough to make their own sausage, salami, and prosciutto at home. Dirt cellars were ideal places for storing root vegetables buried in the sand. Wine was made from grapes bought downtown rather than from one's own vines. The wine bottles were stored in cellars after the grapes had been pressed, and the leftover skins and seeds from the press were converted into powerful grappa and then stored for the winter.

One central stove in the kitchen was usually the only source of heat in a tenement flat. Sometimes a free-standing coal or wood stove in the parlor provided additional heat, and space heaters, three-legged kerosene stoves, could be set up in a bedroom or parlor. Unvented kerosene space heaters were outlawed in Massachusetts decades later, after they were implicated in a number of deadly fires, but in the 1910s they were a cheap source of extra heat. Kitchen ranges often had double burners that also served to heat the tenement. Wood had to be chopped in the backyard or kerosene hauled up three flights of stairs. A kerosene barrel in the yard was considered a modern convenience. A strong member of the family would remove the kerosene can from the back of the kitchen range, haul it down three flights of stairs to the kerosene barrel, refill it, and then lug it back upstairs to fuel the stove.

The cold flat, with no hot water or central heating, was emblematic of tenement life. The lack of hot water also complicated personal hygiene given that a kettle had to be heated in order to provide enough hot water for a bath or a shave. Unheated bedrooms had ice on inside of the windows on winter mornings, bathrooms were down the hall, and there were no bathtubs in the apartments. It was difficult for a person to keep clean when hot water was so difficult to produce.

Some tenements still had privies as the city debated the expense of a sewage system. Fitchburg had struggled for decades with what was called "the sewage dilemma," the conflict between enforcing an expensive cleanup that might drive mills out of the city and risking the health of residents. So much sewage flushed into the Nashua River that the Wheelwright Paper Mill's boilers were fouled. One crusader calculated that there were thirteen paper mills, twelve textile mills, and numerous industrial shops, as well as homes, draining waste into the Nashua. After the failure of his crusade, the town history recorded that "the Nashua flowed on its odoriferous way."[22]

The city provided reservoir water to homes in most residential areas, but factories used city water for drinking and river water for manufacturing processes. City water was piped in from reservoirs and metered; hence it was more expensive and was used only for drinking. Nashua River water was also piped directly into the factories for toilets and sinks. River water did not cost anything as it fed the mills, but as it flowed through the city, it grew increasingly polluted. Factories labeled separate water sources for washing up and for drinking.

Almost all of the diseases that plagued immigrants were bacterial in nature and spread easily in the workplace. People worked on long shifts in close quarters where sanitation was a challenge. Some factories had toilet and washing facilities, but older factories did not; outdoor privies were still used by some. Foremen often resisted employees' pleas for access to toilets outside of scheduled break times, and this was a particular problem for women in the mills.

Of the 209 foundries in the state, more than a half-dozen were located in Fitchburg, most in the Water Street neighborhood.[23] Work areas were unventilated, and hot particles of fine sand swirled around workers' faces during the molding process. Foundries were unheated in winter and unventilated in summer. The William Hardy Foundry was the largest brass foundry in Fitchburg, but the Magee Stove Works, Florence Stove, and Independent Lock Company all did brass casting as well, a type of work far more dangerous than ironworking.[24]

During the production of brass casting, molten zinc released fumes into the air. Under ideal conditions, these would be drawn off by ventilation, but in many Massachusetts foundries, poor factory design left few avenues for the fumes to escape, and foundry workers inhaled the zinc fumes. If the fumes reached toxic levels, workers might experience trembling, shivering, vomiting, and profound exhaustion. Foundry workers called this conditions the "brass chills," also known as brass-founders' ague and metal-fume fever. When the symptoms struck, workers had no choice but to remain home, unpaid and "sweating it out."[25]

The Massachusetts Board of Health devoted a year in 1910 to examining workplaces and identified a series of health risks specific to foundries. State inspectors reported that foundries "expose workmen to extremes of temperature, to dust and to more or less irritating gases and vapors."[26] Moreover, across the state, only two of over two hundred foundries had exhaust fans to remove the fumes. Twenty-three foundries had no toilets or washing facilities on site (and no sewer connection), a situation that endangered health in a number of ways: exposure to bacteria was a primary problem, but inspectors also witnessed workers eating lunch with hands coated in metal and sand particles.

The Board of Health estimated that nearly one-third of Massachusetts foundry workers had lung, heart, kidney, or other diseases. In the end, few men could last long in the foundries; hence, the constant need for new workers, who were often immigrants. The board's report concluded that "the length of time a man can keep at this work is said to be short ... a year or a year and a half"—before the symptoms "forced him to leave."[27] But for many Veneti, especially older men with limited English-language skills, there were few other options. From the perspective of the foundry owners, there was little concern when these workers left because a steady stream of new job applicants arrived every day. Veneto migration peaked in the period 1900–1915, when the foundries were functioning to fill the needs of the railroads and when the constant demand for cheap labor was at its height.

As already discussed, for women cotton spinning, textile manufacturing, and the garment industry constituted the key area of employment. The Asher Pants Factory offered piecework labor sewing men's clothing. A skilled seamstress could work all day and take home a relatively substantial pay envelope to her parents, but life in a clothing factory, where cotton dust constantly filled the air, was difficult. State Board of Health inspectors cited "exposure to dust generated in the course of manufacturing processes" as a key "effect of industry upon health" and one that magnified the susceptibility to "disease-producing germs, especially to the tuberculosis bacillus."[28] State inspectors particularly focused on relief for women, who were constantly on their feet tending machines, citing the need for "seats for women"[29] on the factory floor. In textile mills women were required to constantly watch the spinning frames so they did not tangle, and workers could not leave unless someone else took their place.[30]

Italian women living in the Cleghorn neighborhood could walk down to Kimball Street, then across an iron staircase that arched high over the Boston and Maine railroad. In a few minutes they were on River Street, where cotton and woolen mills covered the acres on both sides of the river. The Orswell Mill, established in 1893, stood four stories high and employed 350 people tending forty thousand spindles. The massive Fitchburg Yarn mill, with fifty thousand spindles and even more workers, was nearby, on the other side of the Nashua River.

Along the Nashua, the Angel Novelty Company began as a small woodworking shop owner by the Mastrangelo brothers. As mentioned earlier, Francesco became Frank Angel in America, and his brother, a carpenter, lent expertise to their construction of small wooden novelty toys. By the 1930s they expanded into cabinetry fabrication for home construction. The company, situated halfway between the Patch and Cleghorn, drew nearly three-quarters of its employees from the Italian community. The Mastrangelos fostered young Italian workers from families they knew. Angel Novelty was one of the earliest and one of the very few large factories owned by Italians in Fitchburg. Heavy industry had dominated Fitchburg's economy, and the well-established industrialist families, known as the Machine City tycoons, constituted a closed circle.

City government and charitable organizations were dominated by those elite families. As Fitchburg's population expanded and its industry boomed, the crowded, unhealthful conditions that bred disease could no longer be ignored. Illness spread in the factories and tenements, and many of the victims were immigrants struggling to survive. Once the workday was over, laborers retreated to their tenement homes but found no refuge from the diseases of the workplace; these residences and their unsanitary living conditions were associated with the spread of disease—primarily of a bacterial nature—where bathrooms and beds were often shared.

One such bacterial infection, diphtheria, was the deadliest of communicable diseases in the tenements. In children it produces a swelling of the throat lining leather-like in appearance, called bull neck. Transmitted by coughing, it spread easily in this environment and led first to difficulty breathing and eventually damaged the heart muscles, lungs, and other major organs. Diphtheria had a long, deadly history in Massachusetts, having killed over 20 percent of children under five years of age who contracted it.[31] Untreated, the disease can lead to myocarditis and heart failure, and another form of it attacks the skin, producing deep lesions and scarring.

The Massachusetts Board of Health ranked Fitchburg eighteenth in population statewide, with 33,636 residents in 1907.[32] Disease statistics were dominated by the most densely populated cities, like Boston, and industrial centers like Worcester, Fall River, Lowell, and Brockton. An outbreak of diphtheria resulted in the quarantine of the home or tenement, but in 1907 Massachusetts investigators found that individuals who had latent cases (mild with few symptoms beyond a sore throat) were responsible for triggering new outbreaks. New cases were isolated, warnings were posted on front doors, and all cases were reported to authorities in the struggle to halt the disease.[33]

But these were not the only illnesses to be faced. Scarlet fever, a highly contagious streptococcal disease, is also transmitted by coughing and causes a bright red face and tongue. The thickening of the throat leads to breathing difficulties, as well as damage to the heart and other organs. There was little to do for victims at the time considered in this study but quarantine the home (this changed with the advent of antibiotics in the 1940s). Rheumatic fever was also untreatable. The disease primarily struck children, permanently damaging heart valves and leaving victims with an irregular heartbeat. Measles, which spread rapidly in the close confines, could scar and debilitate, but before the development of a vaccine it could also kill its victims. Measles remained a deadly and highly communicable disease. Poliomyelitis, or infantile paralysis, was not a major health threat until it spread widely after 1916. Among those ethnic groups who were infected, Italians ranked low at ninth, with only eleven cases in 1910.[34]

But the most-feared disease was tuberculosis, called the white plague, most often contracted in its pulmonary form. Another common name for it was consumption, derived from the gaunt appearance of its victims, who seem to be consumed by the disease. For decades tuberculosis had taken lives with no cure. The disease could enter a dormant period and then reemerge to weaken its host. It was most often spread by inhalation of particles exuded by carriers, who often contaminated entire tenements. It was difficult to eradicate, moreover, because particulate matter could be picked up on shoes and carried into neighboring homes. Tuberculosis often seemed to run in families but was also driven by exposure to disease materials coughed or excreted in the home or workplace. Poorly ventilated tenements and factories where carriers and their neighbors interacted were hotbeds of the disease. Before antibiotic drugs were developed, the cure was the "outdoor treatment" or the "open-air treatment." Tuberculosis patients were put outdoors in tents and wheeled into sun rooms called solariums, where they were exposed to sunshine and fresh air, which, it was hoped, would aid their recovery.

There was a tragic irony in the prescription given to tuberculosis patients: they needed fresh air and nothing more than light labor in an outdoor occupation. That might have been possible in the Veneto, but not in urban Massachusetts. Finding an outdoor job in industrial New England was not easy, and crowded tenements were the worst place for a tuberculosis patient. Physicians advised leaving all the windows in the home open to facilitate access to fresh air, but for a good part of the year that was not possible in wintry Massachusetts. The typical tenement flat, characterized by scant ventilation, crowded rooms, and very little sunlight, was the antithesis of what tuberculosis patients needed to recover.

Moreover, once a person was diagnosed, the apartment had to be scrupulously cleaned. The removal and destruction of contaminated bedding, carpeting, and even clothes were the first steps to preventing a new infection. A vacated tenement was to be entirely scrubbed down, its walls disinfected and its furniture cleansed of bacteria before new tenants could occupy it. The expense involved in discarding clothing and bedding and starting life anew was simply untenable for many. Massachusetts maintained four state-run public-health solariums where adult tuberculosis patients could be treated with sunshine and fresh air: in Rutland, Westfield, Lakeville, and North Reading. Sixteen Massachusetts cities developed their own hospital-based programs to help residents avoid the expense of relocating to a distant city.

The Fitchburg Society for the Control and Cure of Tuberculosis established the Burbank Hospital Clinic in 1915 where patients could be treated for fifteen dollars per week. The expensive of putting a family member through this cure was prohibitive for most immigrant families. The Fitchburg group was composed of social reformers from the Fitchburg Ministers Union, the Fitchburg Woman's Club, and the Fitchburg Medical Club and was led by Dr. E. P. Miller and Dr. F. H. Thompson of the State Normal School. The society's leaders argued in a fund-raising campaign that Fitchburg must develop its own facilities since only 2,400 beds were available statewide for "50,000 consumptives."[35] Their plan was to expand beyond hospital care and develop a camp for children, as well as dental care facilities. Their pamphlet made the very patriotic point that "good health is a natural right that conditions life, liberty and the pursuit of happiness." In sum, the society's goal was "to free Fitchburg from this great scourge."[36] The Fitchburg volunteers battled the disease: they disinfected homes, conducted public-health programs, tested for the disease, and collected donations of clothing for recovering victims. The

State Board of Health praised the Fitchburg clinic's efforts to improve life for adults and children. The Crocker family donated a solarium complex to the community hospital on Burbank Hill so that patients did not have to move to the state's Rutland facility in western Massachusetts.

Even if patients successfully recovered, there were new challenges to be faced. They risked a relapse unless they could find outdoor work and were often advised to relocate to the southwestern United States' drier climate. Both strategies were often beyond the means of poor residents of the tenements. Infection rates in the city were examined and broken down by ethnicity. Italians remained far from the dominant group. In 1910 of the seventy-five cases, 3 percent were Italians, with the most prominent groups being 37 percent Finnish, 22 percent Irish, and 15 percent Americans. Only Fitchburg's Russian, Polish, Scotch, and Armenian communities had fewer victims than the Italians.[37]

One disease common to both the Veneto and Massachusetts was typhoid fever. In an 1882 report on the living conditions of farm laborers in the Veneto, investigators found cases of typhoid and cholera.[38] Typhoid periodically broke out in Massachusetts during the summer in the early decades of the twentieth century, but the 1910 epidemic in Fitchburg severely tested city and state public-health officials.

In April 1910 the Fitchburg Board of Health identified typhoid among men working in the Crocker, Burbank and Company paper mills along the Nashua River in west Fitchburg. Typhoid cases could arise with little warning to spread rapidly and kill. Contaminated milk and water were most often the sources of contagion. Unpasteurized milk and unsanitary milk production often led to outbreaks, but most often the contamination of water supplies was identified as the cause. Untreated sewage was a particular risk in urban areas where not all homes were connected to sewer services. The disease's incubation period can be up to two weeks, making tracing the source of an outbreak difficult. Symptoms include a high fever, prostration, possibly coma, and death. Before the advent of antibiotics, about 12 percent of those stricken with typhoid died. Recovered victims who worked as food or water handlers risked spreading the disease to others for up to a year after initial infection.[39]

As more people in Fitchburg grew ill in the spring of 1910, city health inspectors examined the water supplies for the Crocker Burbank and Fitchburg paper mills. The mills drew city water for drinking, but both bordered the Nashua River and used its water for cleaning purposes. City water was piped in for drinking in the hot, humid atmosphere, but river water was used for paper production and for washing. The mills converted paper and wood pulp by soaking, heating, and essentially cooking it into slurry, then running the material through heated rollers. In this humid, overheated atmosphere, mill workers constantly drank large amounts of water to offset dehydration.

With three workers felled by typhoid, health inspectors tracked the water supplies that both mills were drawing for washing water from the Nashua River. Finally, they identified the source of the contamination: upstream, in Westminster, a chicken farmer was emptying poultry waste into a stream that flowed into the Nashua and was being drawn into the Crocker Burbank washing-water system. Once the cause had been identified and corrected, the crisis was thought to have ended, but a new outbreak occurred only few months later.

In August, one of the most dangerous months for typhoid, a much more virulent outbreak occurred in the center of the mill district along River Street. Dozens fell ill, and within a week two women, both spinners at Fitchburg Yarn, were dead. City and Massachusetts state health inspectors began testing the victims and soon confirmed typhoid. By August 13 three people from the mill were dead, and the number of cases reached nearly ninety. Although most of the victims came from Fitchburg Yarn's mill, there was no common risk factor. Inspectors continued to interview victims and to test their home water and milk but could not find a common infecting agent. The outbreak lasted so long that one early victim recovered and fell ill again.

While Fitchburg's Board of Health was struggling to identify the cause of the typhoid epidemic, there was an outbreak of diphtheria. A triple-decker tenement on Mechanic Street, crowded with Finnish immigrants, saw nearly all its resident children stricken. The Fitchburg *Sentinel* described the way that Dr. Richard A. Morgner struggled to contain the disease and was "considerably disturbed" as the cases escalated and one child died. The city finally lifted the quarantine it had placed on the tenement, but three new cases were then reported. The city could do little but quarantine the building again, even as Morgner reported that he had "secured anti-toxine [*sic*] to inoculate persons who have been exposed."[40]

Although the exact means of disease transmission were not known, the Fitchburg Board of Health had debated banning communal drinking cups at public fountains in the city but ultimately, inexplicably, took no action. Public water fountains, called "iron mikes," were in use throughout the city, but following the typhoid outbreak and water testing in April 1910 (the outbreak was at its height from July to August 1910), they were implicated in disease transmission. These cast-iron water fountains stood five feet tall, and tin cups were attached to them with chains for public use. Iron mikes were supposedly safe because the water came from city supplies, but it was the communal cups that posed the real danger.

In the midst of the typhoid outbreak, the Board of Health debated whether to remove communal water cups from public water sources, and the private sector took action. Whalom Amusement Park, the largest recreational area in central Massachusetts, hosted thousands of families every weekend; the park offered rides, a dance hall, a playhouse, swimming and boating, a picnic grove, and athletic fields. The Fitchburg and Leominster Street Railway, which owned the venue, removed all communal drinking cups from the park's facilities. Private employers like the Union Foundry, Parkhill Mills, and the Crocker Burbank Company's paper mills removed communal drinking cups, installing new plumbing and bubble fountains for their workers.[41] The bubbler forced water to jet up toward the mouth, thus avoiding the need for a cup and the inherent risk of infection.

The American Medical Association's (AMA) journal published an editorial arguing that common cups must be eliminated and replaced by the bubbler so "the child's lips do not touch any part of the machinery." The AMA also condemned barrooms where drinking glasses received a cursory dip in cold water instead of a thorough cleaning in hot water. Across America a drive to replace communal drinking cups with disposable paper cups was underway. The *American School Board Journal*, a key publication for school administrators, published "The Drinking Cup Crusade," arguing for the use of paper cups to limit the spread of tuberculosis and other diseases. A microscopic examination of drinking glasses in public schools revealed each to be a "prolific spreader of disease." Public drinking cups were banned on trains, in factories, and in schools. Educators were advised to hold "cup smashing days," on which public school students could break the old communal drinking glasses and would then be encouraged to alert their parents to the dangers. In an era when communication with foreign-born parents was difficult, this exercise was seen as a means to facilitate awareness of the dangers of shared drinking cups among immigrant families. Coincidentally, the new paper cups that held the promise of ending the spread of disease were produced with machinery made by the Cowdrey Machine Works in Fitchburg.[42]

But in 1910 none of these remedies halted Fitchburg's typhoid epidemic. On August 18 the *Sentinel*'s headline announced "Typhoid Fever Is Spreading" and reported that two unidentified Italian Americans had been struck down. Investigators had ruled out the possibility that typhoid had originated inside the mill because all employees were provided with clean drinking water piped in from the city's water supply. There was no common neighborhood where the stricken employees lived, since employees of the mill lived throughout the city and used the Fitchburg and Leominster Street Railway to commute to work. Nor did inspectors find a common supplier of contaminated milk or ice deliveries. All the typhoid victims lived in tenements with city water and sewage service, so none were thought to have been exposed to contamination through a privy.

How was the mill handling water supplies for its workers in the August heat? On each floor of the mill, an area was set aside for hand washing and drinking. Drinking faucets were used to fill pails of water, ice was added to keep the water cool, and wooden covers were put in place to keep out dirt. Inspectors tested the water boys for typhoid and did not find any to be carriers. Tin dippers were furnished to scoop water into cups. Nearby were other faucets used for washing, but these were clearly labeled "not for drinking use." But the source of the water for washing was not the city supply; instead, it was drawn from a brook outside the factory.

Finally, health inspectors from the state concluded that the cause had to be inside the mill. They reported that despite safety precautions, "a great many of the operatives remove[d] the cover and dip[ped] in with the cups" and often rinsed their cups "with the water from the faucets intended for washing purposes only." The exterior water source was found to be contaminated by "human excreta" from areas outside the factory.[43] The water source was near a corner grocery store and a house which had no city water or sewage service, and had a privy near the stream. Pollution had made its way into the mill and contaminated the drinking cups. The problem, in the end, lay with the workers. State health inspectors concluded "the operatives were in the habit of drinking from the wash-water taps, as most of the help were foreigners and could not read the signs designating the drinking water."[44]

As reformers had argued for years, assimilating immigrant workers into the American work force must begin with learning English, the primary reason being safety in the workplace. In 1900 Sarah Wool Moore, one of the foremost advocates of Italian assimilation, trained workers in New York State in camp schools and developed a bilingual textbook. *An Illustrated English-Italian Language Book and Reader* emphasized learning safety on the job. Moore rejected standard primer phrases like *See the red hen* in favor of practical work phrases linked to safety. She pointed to the tragedy of Italians who had been injured or killed on the job "simply because they could not understand the warning given."[45] Some chapters of the textbook emphasized vocabulary for Italian women, including terms for house cleaning, laundry, and American foods, along with phrases used to describe illness to a doctor.

In Fitchburg a Young Men's Christian Association (YMCA) program to teach English to workers had been organized by Frederick Fosdick, the city's former mayor and the president of the Fitchburg Steam Engine Company. Fosdick had hired and mentored a number of immigrants in his factory and knew the problems faced in the workplace by those who knew little English. Fosdick, the son of a minister and a Progressive, became an advocate of immigrant education as a path to assimilation. He also led the statewide YMCA program and a drive to organize volunteers to teach immigrants English.

The YMCA's investigation into the problem concluded that "in one large factory in the vicinity of Boston over 2,000 [workers] were found who did not understand the English language. In another between 75% and 80% were born across the sea."[46] George William Tupper, the YMCA's Fall River branch secretary, added, "When there are from five to twenty different tongues spoken in a single factory, it at once becomes apparent that a foreman cannot, effectively, instruct all his men as to dangers which must be avoided." In addition, "illiteracy among these workers" caused more problems since it was impossible to "warn them by means of signs printed, even in their own language."[47] The need for foreign-born laborers to learn English was emphasized to Massachusetts industrialists because, as the report concluded, "Ignorant labor is always expensive."[48]

Ignorance had played a deadly role in the outbreak of typhoid at Fitchburg Yarn. The workers' inability to understand written warnings led to nearly one hundred sickened workers and a handful of deaths. City and state health inspectors had spent months in a costly and nearly fruitless effort to identify the cause. Knowledge of basic English would have prevented or at least mitigated the outbreak. Moreover, it is quite possible that had inspectors realized earlier that some workers could not understand the warnings, they might have identified the source of contamination sooner.

In the end, what cost lives and spread disease was the language problem. Immigrants needed rapid education in the basics of English in order to survive in America. It was vitally important that Massachusetts establish programs to educate the foreign born and to assimilate them into American life. Workers who learned basic English would be safer in the workplace—and on the road to becoming citizens as well.

How would immigrants become Americans? Many in the first generation struggled to hold on to the traditions of the Veneto even as they learned English for the workplace. Social clubs, church socials, and religious groups at Saint Anthony's Church all served their purpose. But it was the second generation whose desire to fit into American life drew them to American sports. Whether new or traditional, sports and games were a means for immigrants and their families to escape the hardships of the tenements and factories.

Traditional Veneto pastimes like hunting and fishing were enjoyable for immigrants to New England and had the added benefit of putting food on the table. Although the Veneti in Massachusetts lived in an urban area, there were large tracts of rural forest and fields on the outskirts of the city where game birds and deer could be hunted. Fishing was impossible in the Nashua River owing to the pollution, but Massachusetts's ponds, lakes, and rivers yielded a rich variety of fish that could supplement the diet. Far from the Italian government's ban on killing songbirds, a few Veneti still used the *arket* (bird trap), putting meat on the table alongside their polenta. Part of Rollstone Hill had been cleared of trees, but there remained acres of woods for hunting game and harvesting firewood. Additional fields, streams, and farms stretched to the north and west of Cleghorn, beyond the dense blocks of mills in the center of town.

Children in the tenements along Leighton and Beech Streets made their own use of Rollstone Hill. In summer they could swim in the unused quarry holes—a dangerous way to cool off. In winter the bare stone hilltop behind their homes became a ski run. A few enterprising young men fashioned skis from wine-barrel staves and launched themselves down the face of the hillside toward Leighton Street. The less daring stood by, watched them slide down the snow-covered granite, and flagged down cars as their friends shot between the tenements and landed on Leighton Street.

Sunday morning meant mass at Saint Anthony's, and some families in Cleghorn walked miles to the church before Holy Rosary Mission was opened on Oak Hill Road. Later in the day there would be dinner and an opportunity to share some time with friends in the neighborhood. On Beech Street Lane the Geremia family built a full-size bocce court in their yard that drew throngs of Veneti family and friends every Sunday afternoon. The athletic skills needed to be a competitive bocce player easily translated to the most popular sports of that era in Massachusetts: candlepin bowling and baseball. Over time, Italians established their own place in the competition and in the business of sports. Italian laborers in Cleghorn flocked to the Palace Bowling Alleys across the street from the massive Independent Lock factory in the evenings. Bowling offered recreation as well as jobs for young Italians.

The game of bocce is played throughout Italy and France (where it is known as boules or petanque). The game begins when one player tosses a small ball (*pallino*) toward the end of a dirt or stone-dust playing field at least sixty feet long. Teams of two players armed with small, heavy balls (4.2 inches in diameter) compete to toss their balls underhand and to land them closest to the *pallino*. The game offers ample opportunity to throw with great finesse or to bomb the opposition by knocking their bocce balls out of the court. In Venice the game was denounced in 1576 because of the frequency of betting. Italy's national hero, Giuseppe Garibaldi, was known to play the game. Bocce was an inexpensive outdoor activity that could be organized on a sandlot or in a backyard, and it has always attracted people to play, wager, and relax in the shade.

Candlepin bowling has been played in New England and the Canadian Maritime provinces for decades. The name comes from its tall, narrow pins. The game uses a small (4.5 inches in diameter), light ball that is delivered with great speed and force. Bowling the ball in this quick, almost explosive game requires the same athletic skills as bocce. The sixty-foot alley, similar in length to the backyard bocce pitch, leads to an area called the pit where fallen pins land. Before the advent of automatic machinery, the pins were reset by young men called pin boys, who sat on a narrow bench above the pit while bowling balls crashed beneath them.

Worcester, the largest city in central Massachusetts, with a population of two hundred thousand, became the birthplace of candlepin bowling in 1880. The city hosted what grew into the world championship of candlepins, the Worcester *Telegram & Gazette* classic tournament. The competition drew competitors from throughout Worcester county, making the dominance by Italians from Fitchburg surprising. But Italian immigrants found the New England style of bowling appealing since it was very similar to bocce, and they could compete in the sport with very little investment. It also became an early venue for Italian entrepreneurs. By the 1930s and 1940s candlepin bowling was dominated by working-class immigrants as competitors, and it was also an entry point for immigrant business owners: top competitors often went on to manage or even purchase alleys. Professional teams in what were known as the Industrial Leagues were often sponsored by mills as a recreational outlet for workers, who were lured by cash prizes. Newspapers avidly covered the sport because its popularity attracted readers, and sports cartoonists drew commentaries on the game.

One of the first sports stars for Italian immigrants in New England was Neno Tagliaferri, known in the sport as Johnny Tagg. Unlike most immigrants, who permanently Americanized their names, Tagliaferri kept his Italian name and used *Tagg* as a stage name. He arrived in Massachusetts in 1907 from Pavia, near Milan in northern Italy, and went to work in a typical immigrant job at an Athol shoe factory trimming shoes. In Pavia he had been a competitive bocce player, so in Massachusetts he transferred his skill from bocce to candlepins. He soon began winning local tournaments and in 1918 won the Worcester *Telegram & Gazette* championship while still in his twenties.

Tagg went on to build a reputation as a fearless player who would accept any challenge and who reveled in playing high-stakes matches. In the 1920s he relocated to Fitchburg, a hotbed of candlepin bowling, and bought the Putnam Street Lanes. In 1926 local papers covered a match in which another bowler challenged Tagg to bowl one-on-one before a crowd for two hundred dollars. The papers reported that Tagg had been "off the alleys for a long time on account of a broken hand but ha[d] recovered"; Tagg put down his half of the bet and won. In another match he fell behind so badly that one spectator said aloud, "Even Tagg can't overcome that deficit." Tagg turned to the crowd and said, "Champions are at their best in the late going"; he then went on to hit successive strikes and win.[49]

The Fitchburg *Sentinel* and Worcester *Telegram & Gazette* often covered Tagg's adventures on and off the field of competition. Sports page headlines like "Stoddard Bowls Tagg for $200" helped build his reputation and his business. Tagg also loved to hunt, raised hunting dogs, and was well known as a competitor in local dog shows. In 1926 the *Sentinel* sports pages proclaimed his latest adventure—"11-Pound Wild Cat Is Killed by John Tagg"—making him something close to legendary. If there was any question as to whether the wildcat had actually been bagged, the reporter noted that the carcass was on display at the alleys, where it had "attracted much attention from bowlers and spectators."[50]

By the mid-1930s the Fitchburg *Sentinel* was devoting a section of the sports page to covering competition in the ten-team Italian League sponsored by local businesses. This reflects an increasing prosperity, despite the Great Depression, that allowed for sponsorship of recreational teams. One team was sponsored by the local padrone, Angelo Seretto, and small businesses like Giacoppe's Market, Fiandaca's Market, Giadone's

Fuel Company, Romano's Contractors, Monte's Shoe Repair, and Padula's Bakery supported competing teams. The list of sponsors reflects Depression-era success stories. Competitors included mill workers, business owners, bakers, and even an attorney, Paul San Clemente.[51]

As Tagg's reputation grew, so did his investment in candlepins. He built an empire of bowling alleys where young Italian immigrants could find work as pin boys and, if they proved themselves, play on teams he sponsored and later work for him as alley managers.[52] For example, four Moretto brothers were all competitive on their neighbor's backyard bocce court, as well as on the candlepin alleys. Their father, Giovanni, had immigrated from Rosà, in the central Veneto, and had established a small grocery store and tailoring business in Fitchburg. He raised nine children alone after the death of his wife and enjoyed competing at the German immigrants' Turnverein gymnasium.[53] His oldest son, Paul, became a top candlepin bowler and won the Worcester *Telegram & Gazette* world championship twice (1943 and 1949). The three younger sons, Albino, Alexander, and Enzo, followed Paul into competitive bowling, sometimes playing in the leagues as a team with their father. Giovanni's daughter, Bianca, competed in the Fitchburg *Sentinel* tournament, placing second in 1943 and becoming a finalist two other times. During the war, when her brothers were overseas, she attempted to organize a family team to compete in the men's league but was unsuccessful at bridging the gender gap.

Candlepin bowling proved so popular in the 1930s that Fitchburg High School organized its own team; the youngest Moretto brother, Enzo, became a leading competitor. Paul continued to dominate the Worcester *Telegram & Gazette* championship until a back injury ended his career. Another son of the Veneto, George Fava from Revine Lago, took Moretto's place as the champion of the *Telegram & Gazette* candlepin competition. George Fava began his bowling career in Fitchburg's Italian League and by 1932 was captain of his team, regularly rolling the highest score. He led the local Venetian Club's team and then joined the Hillside Café team. He also continued to compete in Leominster's bocce league, was a semipro baseball player, and later became a softball umpire. He was an ardent fan of the New York Yankees, a team anathema in New England but one that starred a number of Italian players, including Joe DiMaggio and Yogi Berra. Italian success in baseball bred new immigrant fans.

By the early 1940s George Fava had won the local Fitchburg *Sentinel* championship twice. Twenty years later he was still an active competitor, having made the finals in each of seventeen years, leading the *Sentinel* sports writer to compare his consistency to that of baseball's Warren Spahn. He continued to challenge the best in Worcester and won the title a number of times. He later became the manager of a new bowling alley, the Hub, where he remained the "house pro," willing to take on any challengers until his 1980 retirement at age seventy-three; he was inducted into the halls of fame for bowling and softball.[54] Bowling, more than any other sport, offered not only the enjoyment of recreation and competition but also an opportunity to earn wages, to win prizes, and—for the prominent few—to find a place in the business of sport.

Other sports attracted young Italian men and women in which a professional career might be built. Local schoolboy baseball players lived with the dream of following famous Italian players into professional baseball. Joe DiMaggio dominated the national stage as a Yankee, and his brothers Dom and Vince starred for the Boston Red Sox and the Boston Bees, respectively. In *Beyond DiMaggio: Italian Americans in Baseball,* author Lawrence Baldassaro argued that baseball had a particular appeal to second generation Italian Americans who struggled to fit in because it was seen as such an American game.[55] In recalling the ultimate dominance of Italian Americans in baseball by mid-century, Yogi Berra commented, "People used to say the Yankees won a lot because we led the league in Italians. All I'll say is there's a real good history of Italians in baseball." Even earlier, Ed Abbaticchio had broken in as the first Italian in the majors, playing with the Boston Beaneaters between 1903 and 1910.[56] Boston was also home to the Braves team, and between these organizations young men in that city had no shortage of Italian stars to root for. Among the first Italians in professional baseball, a number were first accepted by the Braves and the Red Sox. Baldassaro observed sports journalists, team owners and even the players themselves persisted in changing or altering Italian names or even replacing them with nicknames, "to avoid the hassles associated with names that unmistakably marked their otherness."[57]

Other sports were often outside the margins. Boxing was a brutal but very popular sport in which young men could find a way to some success. Flavio DeBonis, son of a Revine Lago family, was a slender child when he began boxing at six years of age. After winning the Junior National Championship in 1931 Flavio was given a testimonial by leaders of the Italian-American community. Dr. Anthony Mattia praised him as "a modest, unassuming, clean-living and hard-working little fellow" and Dr. Ferdinand Frigoletto said Flavio had demonstrated that "success is not wholly dependent on physical size." While his father recalled the boy was introduced to boxing by the Edgerly school, a public elementary, at age six. Also present at the celebration were seven other young Italian-Americans who had established careers in boxing, as well as Flavio's manager from Boston.[58] He left school at age fifteen to help his family in their landscaping business but eventually graduated from Fitchburg High in 1931. During his boxing career he competed as the "Fitchburg Firecracker" and advanced to the national championship tournament in New York State in 1930. As a featherweight in national competitions, DeBonis won the Golden Gloves as noted in his Fitchburg Sentinel obituary of Nov 28, 2008, "Flavio was an outstanding amateur and professional boxer winning golden Gloves and Jr. National Championships" in his weight category, and he ultimately also competed internationally.[59]

Young Mike DiPrima was billed as "Fitchburg's Fighting Newsboy" when he began his career as a twelve-year-old competitor. He fought as a bantamweight in the Worcester Golden Glove championships, and although the papers lauded the "clever little Fitchburg scrapper,"[60] the experience of winning by a knockout over competitors in a bout described as "a hard-fought three-round battle[61] must have been a brutal experience. DiPrima fought in 1935 and 1936 against Irish and Italian opponents in Fitchburg, Worcester, Boston, and throughout the Northeast, even as far away as a Schenectady, New York, where he won a Sons of Italy club competition.[62]

In central Massachusetts the first Veneto migrants built a community around social organizations and Saint Anthony's Church with the aim of preserving their traditions, language, and faith. The second generation, the children of those pilgrim migrants, grew up as native speakers of English and saw themselves as Americans. Both faced the hardships of working in foundries and factories, as well as the risks that came with life in crowded tenements. Recreation, especially professional sports, offered them an opportunity to dream yet another American dream. The second generation used sports as a way to find some acceptance in 1920s Massachusetts, even as the political atmosphere turned sharply against Italians with the advent of the Sacco and Vanzetti trial.

NOTES

1. For settlement estimates, see Ernest A. Stolba, "The Italian Race in Fitchburg," Sept. 1, 1909, Fitchburg Historical Society manuscript file 953.40.5. Repatriation statistics from 1911 can be found in *Bollettino dell'emigrazione*, vol. 11; and in *Statistica della emigrazione italiana 1908–1909*, quoted in Caroli, *Italian Repatriation*, 42 and 49.

2. One Italian journalist argued that Libya would attract Italians from abroad; denouncing settlement in America as "these illegal colonies in someone else's house," he concluded, "Today the fatherland is no longer far away." Quoted in Mark Choate, *Emigrant Nation: The Making of Italy Abroad* (Cambridge, MA: Harvard University Press, 2008), 187.

3. Frederick Bushee, "Italian Immigration in Boston," *Arena* 17, no. 89 (Apr. 1897): 731.

4. Mussolini quote in R. J. B. Bosworth, *Mussolini's Italy: Life under the Fascist Dictatorship, 1915–1945* (London: Penguin, 2005), 390.

5. Martin Clark, *Mussolini Profiles in Power* (London: Pearson Longman, 2005), 97.

6. "Decree on Public Safety," Nov. 6, 1926, in Marla Stone, ed., *The Fascist Revolution in Italy: A Brief History with Documents* (Boston: Bedford/St. Martin's, 2013), 59.

7. "A Brief Biography of the Loggia Cristoforo Colombo No. 169 Order of Sons of Italy in America," unsigned, undated manuscript; and "4,000 Italians Boost Membership of Local Society: Big Increase in Victor Emanuel, Third Order Due to Public Works," *Daily News* (Fitchburg), Jan. 3, 1912, in "Italian Lodges" file, Fitchburg Historical Society.

8. Ibid.

9. Alana Melanson, "Sons of Italy to Mark 100 Years in Fitchburg," *Sentinel* (Fitchburg), Dec. 16, 2013.

10. *History of Saint Anthony of Padua Parish*, 47.

11. Ibid., 46–48, 52.

12. Author's interview with Rose Ingemie, 2012.

13. "Summary of the Report on Conditions of Woman and Child Wage Earners in the US," Dec. 1915, *Bulletin of the Bureau of Labor Statistics*, US Department of Labor no. 175 (Washington, DC: Government Printing Office, 1916), 264.

14. Frederick A. Bushee, "Italian Immigrants in Boston," *The Arena*, April 1897, volume XVII, number 89, 734. Covello's forty-five years in NYC schools described in Leonard Covello, *The Heart is the Teacher*, New York: McGraw-Hill, 1958, 166.

15. Sweeney quote in Elizabeth G. Messina, "Perversions of Knowledge Confronting Racist Ideologies behind Intelligence Testing," *Anti-Italianism Essays on a Prejudice*, (New York: Palgrave MacMillan, 2010), 48.

16. Mary Cosentino was born in New York City and moved to Fitchburg later. In the *Sentinel* she was described as "the first pupil of Italian extraction to attend FHS"; see "Asseltas Observed 65th Wedding Anniversary," *Sentinel* (Fitchburg), June 14, 1972. Also see *History of Saint Anthony of Padua Parish* (date of graduation shown there is 1904, an error).

17. A review of the graduation yearbooks between 1921 and 1927 at the Fitchburg Historical Society reveals that by 1927 Italian students represented 3.92% (10 of 255) of the graduating class.

18. Stewart Ralph Roberts, *Pellagra: History, Distribution, Diagnosis, Prognosis, Treatment and Etiology* (St. Louis, MO: Mosby, 1912), 141.

19. Ibid., 41–46; Benjamin Reilly, *Disaster and Human History Case Studies in Nature, Society, and Catastrophe* (Jefferson, NC: McFarland, 2009), 322.

20. Caroli, *Italian Repatriation*, 68.

21. Anthony V. Riccio, *Boston's North End: Images and Recollections of an Italian-American Neighborhood* (Guilford, CT: Insider's Guide Press, 2006).

22. Clarence Spring's calculation; quote from Doris Kirkpatrick, *The City and the River*, 396.

23. Massachusetts Board of Health, *Report of State Board of Health*, Public Documents of Massachusetts, ser. 1910 (Boston: Wright & Potter, 1911), 4:515–517.

24. Hardy's mill began working in 1850 and boomed as the city became a center for paper production, home to more than five companies, each with multiple mills. Ellery Bicknell Crane, *Historic Homes and Institutions and Genealogical and Personal Memoirs* (New York: Lewis, 1905), 75–76.

25. Brass chills was first defined by Edward H. Greenhow, "On Brass Founder's Ague," Feb. 11, 1862; see www.ncbi.nim.com; also see Robert Berkow et al., *The Merck Manual*, 16th ed. (Whitehouse Station, NJ: Merck, 1992), 977.

26. Massachusetts Board of Health, *Report of State Board of Health*, 515.

27. Ibid.

28. Annual Report of the State Board of Health of Massachusetts, 1910, volume 42, (Boston: Wright and Potter, 1911), 512.

29. Ibid., 827.

30. Ibid., 34–56.

31. In colonial Massachusetts, diphtheria epidemics repeatedly killed small children. In the 1735–1741 outbreak, 80 percent of the children in New England died; see Thomas Pervis, *Colonial America to 1763* (New York: Facts on File, 1999), 173–174. Also see the College of Physicians of Philadelphia, "The History of Vaccines" (www.historyofvaccines.org).

32. *Monthly Bulletin of the State Board of Health of Massachusetts*, volume 2, (Boston: Wright and Potter, March 1907), 173.

33. *Monthly Bulletin of the State Board of Health of Massachusetts* (Boston: Wright & Potter, Mar. 1907), 2:202. For diphtheria report, 202.]

34. The 1910 statistics are as follows: among Americans there were 315 cases; among Irish, 65; among French Canadians, 33; and among Italians, 11. See Massachusetts Board of Health, *Infantile Paralysis in Massachusetts during 1908–1910* (Boston: Wright & Potter, 1910), 9.

35. "Work is Checking the White Plague," Fitchburg *Sentinel*, April 29, 1910, 1

36. For a period description of tuberculosis care, see *What You Should Know about Tuberculosis* (New York: New York Department of Health, 1910). The nearest state hospital at Rutland charged four dollars per week but was distant from Fitchburg. The sixteen city hospitals were in major urban areas; *Charities and Commons: A Weekly Journal of Philanthropy* 15 (May 25, 1907): 234. Unsigned article on TB hospitals, *New England Journal of Medicine* 185 (Dec. 22, 1921): 764.

37. "Work Is Checking the White Plague," *Sentinel* (Fitchburg), Apr. 29, 1910, 1.

38. *Jacini Commission*, 4:4.

39. Berkow et al., *The Merck Manual*, 102–103.

40. "Many Exposed to Diphtheria," *Sentinel* (Fitchburg), Aug. 13, 1910, 2.

41. "Don't Practice What They Preach," *Sentinel* (Fitchburg), Aug. 16, 1910, 2.

42. "The Drinking Cup Crusade," *American School Board Journal* 5 (Nov. 1910): 19; "The Public Drinking Cup," *Journal of the American Medical Association* 16 (June 17, 1911): 1818; Dixie Cup Company History, www.academicmuseum.lafayette.edu/special/dixie/company.html.

43. *Annual Report of the State Board of Health of Massachusetts*, volume 42, (Boston: Wright and Potter, 1911), 469.

44. Massachusetts Board of Health, "Report on an Outbreak of Typhoid Fever in One Mill in Fitchburg between July 15 and September 6, 1910,"

in *Report of State Board of Health*, Public Documents of Massachusetts, Series 1910 (Boston: Wright & Potter, 1911), 4:468–473.

45. Leila Allen Dimock describing Sarah Wool Moore's thoughts in *Comrades From Other Lands*, (New York, Fleming H. Revell, 1913), 51.

46. Tupper, 97.

47. Ibid.

48. Sarah Wool Moore, *An Illustrated English-Italian Language Book and Reader* (Boston: D. C. Heath, 1902); Leila Allen Dimock, *Comrades from Other Lands* (New York: Revell, 1913), 50–51; George William Tupper, *Foreign-Born Neighbors* (Boston: Taylor Press, 1914), 40 and 97.

49. "Stoddard Bowls Tagg for $200," Fitchburg *Sentinel*, Dec. 14, 1925, 8. International Candlepin Bowling Association biography Johnny Tagg (www.candlepinbowling.com/hall-of-fame-competitive-ability.html#.JohnnyTagg).

50. "11-Pound Wild Cat Is Killed by John Tagg," *Sentinel* (Fitchburg), Oct. 9, 1926, 8.

51. "Italian League," *Sentinel* (Fitchburg), Apr. 5, 1935, 16.

52. Forty years later, one of Tagg's pin boys spoke at a testimonial in his honor, recalling that Tagg had "give[n] that helping hand" to his young charges. *Sentinel* (Fitchburg), June 1, 1967, 8.

53. The Fitchburg Turnverein, later renamed Turner Hall, was established by twelve German families living in the Leighton and Kimball Street neighborhood, below the Rollstone Hill quarries in 1893. Kirkpatrick, *Around the World*, 82.

54. "Bowling Results on Local Alleys," *Sentinel* (Fitchburg), Mar. 4, 1932, 10; and "Veteran Fava Most Consistent Bowler in Tourney's 18 Years," *Sentinel* (Fitchburg), May 3, 1961, 10. Fava's obituary appeared as "George Fava, 99, Champion Bowler and Standout Semi pro Baseball Player," *Sentinel* (Fitchburg), Nov. 30, 2006.

55. Lawrence Baldassaro, *Beyond DiMaggio: Italian Americans in Baseball* (Lincoln: University of Nebraska Press, 2011), xxxv.

56. Ibid. On Ed Abbaticchio, see www.basballreference.com.

57. Baldassaro, xxxiii.

58. "Flavio DeBonis Bantam Junior National Champ is Given Testimonial," Fitchburg *Sentinel*, April 15, 1931, 9. Obituary Flavio Debonis, Fitchburg *Sentinel*, November 8, 2008.

59. Debonis was praised at the testimonial to raise funds so he could travel to competitions; Dr. Mattia commented, "We hope he will be victorious in the Olympics in Europe." No record of his participation has been located.

"Bantam Junior National Champ Testimonial at Hotel Raymond," *Sentinel* (Fitchburg), Apr. 15, 1931, 9. For his obituary, see "Started Debonis Florist, Flavio Debonis, 95," *Leominster Champion*, Dec. 5, 2008.

60. "Fitchburg's Fighting Newsboy Wins Bout from Schenectady Star," *Sentinel* (Fitchburg), Apr. 6, 1935, 2.

61. "Mike DiPrima, Mel Scalzulli win G.G. Tilts," Fitchburg *Sentinel*, December 3, 1938, 2.

62. "Sports Notes," *Sentinel* (Fitchburg), Oct. 15, 1936, 8; and Dec. 15, 1938, 9.

CHAPTER 6

MAKING AMERICANS

THE ASSIMILATIONISTS

Those migrants who settled in America repeatedly faced the question whether to become citizens or to retain their Italian nationality. Often, their American-born children encouraged them on the long path of learning English, studying in citizenship classes, and applying for naturalization. But the last step toward obtaining citizenship required a renunciation of Italy and its monarch.[1] Some were reluctant to undertake classes after the long workday, some were unwilling to learn more than a little English, and others clung to the dream of returning to the Veneto.

There was an intense American debate about whether Italian immigrants could become citizens. Immigration restrictionists battled to close the "unguarded gates" at Ellis Island, whereas assimilationists countered that Americans must help Italians to learn English and to become citizens. Restrictionists debated whether Italian immigrants could develop the capacity to function as American citizens, as well as whether it was desirable for them to become part of American society. This debate was the obverse of Italy's postunification debate regarding how to forge a national identity by "making Italians" out of people with strong regional identities, but in America there was a fear that they might never "melt" in the melting pot. Moreover, the large numbers of Italian immigrants raised fears that if the newcomers were incorporated into American society they would change it rather than be shaped by it.

There were many signs that the Italophilism of earlier decades, rooted in an appreciation of art, opera, and Italian culture, was being overcome by an anti-Italianism that was not just hostile but violent. Anti-Italian violence in America made headlines with the 1891 lynching of eleven Italian immigrants in New Orleans. This crime was followed by other lynchings as violence against Italians exploded in the south and in western mining areas. Moreover, immigrants were often abused by padroni and employers, as well as victimized in society. Their status as Italian nationals and aliens left them vulnerable in the American justice system.

The origins of the restrictionist movement were centered in Boston and New York, as were the assimilationists. Beginning in the 1880s, a contentious dispute arose about the long-term impact of millions of immigrants on America, and it raged until the 1920s. In 1887 Harvard professor Nathaniel Southgate Shaler wrote "Shall Immigration Be Restricted?" terming aliens "dangerous classes" and comparing their population to animals: "[their] numbers are no larger than those of our bears or panthers or other wild beasts. But [this group] has human intelligence, superimposed upon the instincts of the wild beast; its members have the power and will to work destruction."[2] Shaler's earlier writings during the Reconstruction era had expressed similar doubts about the potential of African Americans to participate as citizens. Shaler applied the same arguments to the case of Italians (and other immigrants), questioning not only their intellect but also their very humanity.

This restrictionist drive was led by a small group of highly educated activists with powerful political and social connections. The Immigration Restriction League (IRL) focused nativist wrath upon immigrants, especially Italians. It was founded in 1894 by an elite group of intellectuals and professors, all members of the Harvard class of 1889: Prescott Farnsworth Hall, Charles Warren, and Robert DeCourcy Ward. Hall held a law degree from Harvard; he had practiced law in Boston, and he led the IRL. Beyond his interest in immigration restriction, he also chaired a committee on eugenics for the American Genetic Association and was an anti-tenement activist in Brookline, Massachusetts.[3] Warren also took a Harvard law degree in 1892, became a professor of law, and won the 1923 Pulitzer Prize for his three-volume history of the Supreme Court. Ward later became a Harvard professor of climatology and was an author of books in his field and on eugenics.

This trio drew to itself a small group of permanent members who made a powerful political impact. The IRL grew more powerful when Madison Grant, an exponent of scientific racism, became its vice president and a key author of its propaganda. Grant, a Yale-educated lawyer and noted conservationist, worked with Theodore Roosevelt to found the New York Zoological Society and was a prominent activist working to protect endangered species, especially the American bison.

As vice president of the IRL, Madison Grant authored *The Passing of the Great Race* (1916), which promoted his own brand of scientific racism. The book found an American as well as a global audience and ran through numerous editions, remaining in print for decades. Eventually it was translated into German and praised by Hitler. Jonathan Spiro, in *Defending the Master Race*, has explained how Grant used skull shape and eye and skin color to evaluate peoples in a contorted racial theory that identified the geographical origins of races he deemed undesirable. Southern and Eastern Europeans were a focus of Grant's drive, as expressed in *The Passing of the Great Race*, was to restrict the immigration of "the Slovak, the Italian, the Syrian and the Jew."[4] Most of all, Grant feared that the intermarriage of these groups with Americans would create what he termed "racial hybrids and some ethnic horrors."[5]

The IRL's 1894 constitution stated its goals, including a pledge to seek "stricter regulation of immigration, to issue documents and circulars, solicit facts and information on that subject, hold public meetings, and to arouse public opinion." The IRL also aimed to keep out particular groups that it deemed unworthy: "a further exclusion of elements undesirable for citizenship or injurious to our national character."[6] The IRL advocated not only tightening standards at Ellis Island but also legislating punitive measures against steamship companies that transported immigrants in the form of head taxes and other financial penalties.

The IRL's efforts to stiffen the Alien Contract Labor Law, enforce health inspections, and broaden the political grounds for rejecting immigrants were very effective. Members of the IRL, especially Prescott Farnsworth Hall and Madison Grant, regularly appeared before congressional committees to testify on labor and immigration issues; they also testified before the Industrial Commission, also known as the Dillingham Commission, on the state of immigrant and native labor. The IRL sought a number of means to restrict immigration and often referenced a poem by one of its members, poet Thomas Bailey Aldrich. "The Unguarded Gates" begins with a warning couched in racial terms: the author calls upon "Liberty! White Goddess!" to shut the doors to those who would "waste the gifts of freedom" and ends by comparing immigrants to the "thronging Goth and Vandal [who] trampled Rome."[7]

A recurring theme in the writings of Hall and Grant was the long-term social impact of intermarriage. This both aligned with the eugenics movement and trod upon more dangerous ground. The IRL not only lobbied at the national level but also sent mass mailings to local politicians and business leaders. Circulars asked whether laborers were needed in the respondent's area and included a checklist indicating which national types were wanted and which were not (The IRL mailed these questionnaires to local town and city governments across the United States to measure their response on the issues in an effort to garner support and possibly material for use in their Congressional testimony). Respondents were encouraged to offer comments on immigration restriction, and their responses reflect the intensity of anti-immigrant emotions.

Similar to Aldrich's "unguarded gates" image, the message seems to allude to the Emma Lazarus poem "The New Colossus," which envisions the "Mother of Exiles" welcoming the "huddled masses yearning to breathe free." Affixed to the base of the Statute of Liberty in 1903, years after the statue's erection, the welcoming message expresses a sentiment that was not shared by all Americans. The mayor of Tyler, Texas, responded in August of 1905 and expressed fear that the "foreign ideas" of immigrants would change American politics and argued against allowing the foreign born to vote "until they know what it means." The Texan concluded, "It is time to recall the invitation of [sic] the oppressed of all nations to seek an asylum here."[8] Some IRL publications focused specifically on Italians, for example, "The Present Italian Influx, Its Striking Illiteracy."[9]

The IRL's key initiative in shutting the gates was the mandatory literacy testing of all immigrants upon arrival; the proposal that succeeded after years of lobbying was known as the Burnett Bill. Massachusetts senator Henry Cabot Lodge, who remained close to the IRL and was a noted restrictionist in Congress, spoke in favor of literacy testing, arguing that it "will bear most heavily upon the Italians, Russians, Poles, Hungarians, Greeks and Asiatics." These groups, he argued, "have never hitherto assimilated and ... are most alien to the great body of the people of the United States."[10] His statement raises the question whether the IRL's goal was in fact allowing for more-literate immigrants or simply finding a successful restrictionist strategy. Opponents argued that the tests were unfair, and others argued that such filtering for the most-literate immigrants might result in the entry of better-read political radicals.

In the IRL files is a letter from the Fitchburg Board of Trade and Merchants Association, members of which rather testily responded to one of IRL President Hall's missives promoting the Burnett Bill by refusing to cooperate: "I shall most assuredly do nothing regarding tending to co-operate with the Immigration Restriction League without the sanction of the Directors of this Association, and I do not believe that it will be necessary for anyone to write the Congressman from this district, nor our Senators," wrote Ralph Redfern, secretary for the board. He closed the note by refusing to forward a list of member names, as Hall had requested.[11]

But the IRL was well received in many quarters in its twenty-six-year battle to make literacy testing the law. The organization's correspondence frequently mentions visits with White House and congressional officials, including one of its key allies, Senator Henry Cabot Lodge, as well as President Woodrow Wilson and his aide, Colonel Edward House. Madison Grant numbered among his personal friends former president Theodore Roosevelt, who requested a copy of *The Passing of the Great Race*. Earlier testing legislation had been vetoed by Presidents McKinley, Cleveland, and Taft. In 1914 lobbying intensified as the Burnett Bill passed through Congress but was vetoed by President Wilson. Congress then overrode his veto. Additional literacy requirements were pocket vetoed by Wilson and overridden again.

Restrictionists like Grant and Hall were driven by deep-seated racial anxieties. Their fears extended beyond the gates of Ellis Island to the consequences of millions of foreigners living in American society and, especially, the question of whom they might marry. Grant argued that the battle was already lost because "the native American is too proud to mix socially with them and is gradually withdrawing from the scene, abandoning to these aliens the land which he conquered and developed."[12] Here Grant's and Hall's personal and status anxieties emerge. Assimilation was a part of this process, but Hall argued that "the alien might be assimilating us instead of our assimilating him."[13] Further, immigrants were seen as a threat even when they did adopt American ways: "These immigrants adopt the language of the native American, they wear his clothes, they steal his name and they are beginning to take his women, but they seldom adopt his religion or understand his ideals."[14] The eugenics movement of the 1920s and 1930s grew out of these fears, and the IRL leadership also played a prominent role in pro-eugenics organizations.

Assimilationists countered this alarmist view by arguing that only the integration of immigrants as citizens able to fully participate in American life, complete with voting rights and military obligations, would lead them to contribute to society rather than dilute its quality. Their contention that education was the path to citizenship, again, emphasized that some way must be found to teach English and civics to working adults. Because most immigrants worked long hours and had limited incomes, this represented a challenge on both sides. Assimilationists had to find a means of establishing and supporting educational programs that would attract the full participation of people who were poor, often undereducated in their native tongue, and struggling to survive in America.

This movement to counter the restrictionists was led by social reformers who argued that immigrants would not adjust to American society without help. They argued that the process of assimilation must begin at the gates of Ellis Island and continue through a program of education that would ultimately lead to naturalization, citizenship, and full participation in American democracy. They accepted a future in which the foreign born and their children would participate in the political process. Assimilationists focused on what happened on the other side of the Ellis Island gates as immigrants transitioned to a life in America. But Hall attacked this view, calling the hope for making Americans of aliens "cheerful conclusions" that made "superficial changes ... entirely inadequate to affect the hereditary tendencies of generations." In the struggle to fight the Great War, he called for "oligarchs" to be given power, contending that units composed of "Nordics" performed better on the field of battle and that immigrants "seriously affected the capacity of the nation to think and to act."[15]

In 1904 Gino Speranza of the Society for the Protection of Italian Immigrants (SPII) criticized the assumption that immigrants would actively pursue assimilation on their own: "Many imagine that the record and strength of the American democracy suffice of themselves to make the foreigner love the new land and engender in him a desire to serve it; that, in other words, assimilation is the natural tendency." But Speranza argued that assimilation required effort on both sides: "Assimilation is a dual process of forces interacting one upon the other. Economically, this country can act like a magnet in drawing the foreigner to these shores, but you cannot rely on its magnetic force to make the foreign an *American*." He concluded that assimilation would fail unless action were taken by Americans to help immigrants move out of New York and into full citizenship: "If [immigrants] herd into great and menacing city colonies, if they do not learn your language, if they know little about your country, the fault is as much yours as theirs."[16] Here Speranza touched on a key issue that restrictionists feared. Large masses of immigrants would remain in urban slums, continue working for wages no American could survive on, and constitute a foreign presence within America.

The most prominent assimilationists in this era worked in the major cities, where immigrants struggled to make their way. The most famous of these was Jane Addams, whose Hull House in Chicago came to symbolize the settlement-house movement. She began with one building and expanded into a complex that offered shelter, education, and training as a way for immigrants to transition into American cities. Addams had traveled in Europe, had visited Italy, and possessed personal wealth to back her ambitions. Along with a number of like-minded reformers, she settled near Chicago's Little Italy and went to work. She authored articles for the *Charities* and other reform journals, as well as the book *Twenty Years at Hull House*, to promote her ideas.

Jane Addams described the conflicted emotions of a young second-generation Italian girl, Angelina, who had arrived with her mother at Hull House but "always left her mother at the front door while she herself went around to a side door because she did not wish to be too closely identified in the eyes of the rest of the cooking class with an Italian woman who wore a kerchief over her head, uncouth boots and short petticoats." After Angelina overheard her mother described as "the best stick-spindle spinner in America," she asked whether it was true. Addams, who had traveled in Italy, assured her it was but was plagued that a woman who had once lived in a world where her work was valued had been "torn from it all and literally put out to sea … [and] now walked timidly but with poignant sensibility upon a new and strange shore."[17] Assimilating to this new society—and keeping the respect of her daughter —was the challenge.

Members of the second generation, citizens by birth and native speakers of English, often found themselves put in the difficult position of bridging two cultures. They lived in the world of their parents, where dialect was often spoken in tight-knit Italian colonies. But once outside the tenements, in the world of school and work, they functioned as native speakers of English. Jane Addams saw the second generation as a key to helping Italian immigrant families connect "with American food and household habits."[18] The settlement-house movement could do much to facilitate the adjustment, and Addams argued that the public schools also "deserve[d] all the praise as Americanizing agencies."[19] Answering the call to educate immigrants in citizenship, Hull House offered classes in English and advice on naturalization.

The path to citizenship was long and required education in English and government. An alien had to file first papers, indicating a desire to pursue citizenship, and then invest time learning the language and studying for an exam, as well as organizing proof of his or her status, dates and places of arrival in the United States, and find others who would appear as character witnesses. It was a long path. Often, men worked through the process, but their wives did not. Children born in Italy had to follow the same route as their fathers.

Publications sprang up to reach a wider audience of persons interested in the strategies of social reform: the *Charities*, the *Commons*, the *Outlook*, and the *Survey*. They featured articles by assimilationists describing the challenges they faced helping immigrants in urban America. Central topics were the development of educational programs, the revelation of abuses in the workplace, and housing issues. Jane Addams, Sarah Wool Moore, Gino Speranza, and many associates of the SPII used these journals to promote assimilation.

One of the earliest leaders of Boston's assimilationist movement was Reverend Gaettano Conte, who organized the SPII in the North End. He labored for a decade, 1893–1903, to ensure its success. Conte had arrived as an Italian Protestant missionary from Naples and quickly established himself as the sponsor of a mission to the impoverished residents of the North End. Conte's efforts in Boston were noticed by a New York activist, Sarah Wool Moore, who asked him for assistance in developing a branch of the society in New York City. Over time, she extended its reach throughout the states of New York and Pennsylvania. Her New York chapter of the SPII was established after she met Conte and had been joined by some of his aides. Gino Speranza became a prominent member of the society, taking the lead in investigating workplace abuses of Italians by padroni.

In Massachusetts concerns that the high percentage of illiterate immigrants who were not naturalized would create a massive underclass and weaken the democratic system were sounded by the Young Men's Christian Association (YMCA). Members adapted Moore's ideas in the context of urban YMCAs to channel immigrants into citizenship. Chief among the organizers of this program was Frederick Fosdick, an industrialist and the mayor of Fitchburg. His brother and business partner, Charles, and their niece, Margaret, a librarian and educator, worked as volunteer instructors.

Their work was eventually taken over by the city of Fitchburg. Margaret Kielty, an educator who was fluent in Italian, managed a city-sponsored Americanization program for adults and a day program for Italian mothers, and from Fitchburg's Americanization Office she worked in the public schools to help second-generation immigrant children become accustomed to English-language classrooms. Her work with Italians in public school classrooms inspired her to develop an English-language primer designed to accommodate immigrants from any foreign-language background.

How much of this work is known today? Jane Addams's efforts at Hull House became a symbol of the assimilationist movement; her books and speeches built her legacy as an advocate for immigrants. But many of her contemporaries and their ideas are far less well known. Conte worked in Boston for nearly a decade before returning to Italy, leaving behind a small collection of papers and a memoir. Sarah Wool Moore declined every opportunity to claim credit for her work and asked others to take a more prominent role in the society she founded. Biographers interested in her early life as a university professor and an artist in Nebraska know little of her later life as a social reformer in New York and Pennsylvania or of her camp-school program. The YMCA program was successful but was overtaken by the rise of large-scale, industry-based Americanization programs. Kielty's Americanization efforts were disrupted by the onset of the Second World War.

The goals of these pioneers of assimilation changed over time. In the early years the problem was assimilating the foreign born, but with the birth of the second generation new challenges arose. How to assist Italian youth growing up in poverty who had few models for English-language development? Assimilationists focused on establishing trust between themselves and immigrants, then on securing them from predators, whether these were the Italian padroni or the immigrants' employers. Assimilationists viewed practical language programs as a vital first step toward integrating foreign-language speakers into American life and ensuring their safety in the workplace. Their aim was not docile workers but good citizens. In addition, these activists also worked to develop teaching methods that could be replicated elsewhere, for they acknowledged the widespread nature of the problem of assimilation. It was also important to reach an American audience and to publicize their successes so as to build some good will in an atmosphere of anxiety driven by xenophobia.

American fear of the foreign was, at the root, a reaction to the changes wrought by the massive influx of millions of immigrants to America between 1880 and 1920. In Fitchburg 74 percent of the population was either foreign born or the children of foreign-born immigrants by 1910.[20] In other words, three of every four persons in the city were recent arrivals, spoke a foreign language, practiced a different religion, and ate different foods. Two sections of the city, the formerly Irish neighborhood of the Patch and once French Canadian Cleghorn in the west, changed drastically. Minority influxes were not new to Fitchburg, for it already held the largest concentration of Finns in America, but the populations of these two neighborhoods abruptly shifted to a blend of Italian, Russian, Polish, Austrian, and German newcomers.

Reverend Gaettano Conte became one of the first and most important assimilationists in Boston. He coined the phrase *the Italian problem* to describe the American view. Conte divided Americans into two groups: "a class that knows Italy well because they travel ... they study" and another that held "too many aversions because they think that all the Italians, are like those encountered in the North End."[21] The poverty and squalor of those slums shocked him. Encounters with Americans also shocked him. On a social visit, one American thought she was complimenting Conte and his wife when she said, "I would never have thought you were Italians."[22] Conte recalled that the woman was "eyeing my gloves and my wife's hat" as she spoke. They later received a social invitation specifying that his wife appear in "the costume you wear in your country."[23]

Conte spent a decade working in Boston's North End, one of America's largest Italian colonies outside New York. He had traveled with his wife, who also did missionary work in the North End, and their two children from Naples to Boston in 1893. As the ship pulled away from the Italian shore, an impoverished laborer also on board shouted, "Long live America!" Conte reflected, "Only God knows what that cry meant and what it hid!"[24] Throughout the long sea voyage he listened as emigrants explained why they had left: "The reply came spontaneously from all of them: taxes, of which 54% weighs on the poor." Conte noted other problems that lay deeper: "the real reason lay in the agricultural crisis ... which had created an unbearable situation for them."[25]

Conte's memoir offers a window on the conditions of Italian immigrants in Massachusetts in that critical decade, 1893–1903, from the perspective of an Italian Protestant missionary.[26] Conte noted a report that in Clinton, home to the Wachusett Dam, Sanitary Office inspectors found eighty-five men and five women asleep in a building with six apartments divided into twenty-one rooms. As he walked through the North End, he heard an Irish resident shout at an impoverished woman searching for food, "Diorty [sic] Italian!"[27] The situation had grown so dire that Conte suspected local Italian shopkeepers might deny their own origins in order to separate themselves from those at the bottom of society. He was eager to address the American perception of the Italian problem and spoke to various groups, trying to respond to the key criticism of Italians, that they had no investment in America and wanted earn cash to take back with them to Italy. Conte pointed out that the typical Italian worker's experience in America was "a sequence of abuses, high handedness, suffering and exploitation, which makes him long for his birthplace."[28]

Speaking to the Round Table Club, a Boston Brahmin institution that met to discuss literary issues, Conte encountered a founding member of the IRL, Harvard professor Robert DeCourcy Ward, who was seeking the group's support for the literacy bill. Conte was shocked to hear Ward express the IRL's rationale for a literacy test for all immigrants at Ellis Island: "We have chosen illiteracy as a pretext as the most suitable way to greatly reduce immigration, not because we think the illiterates the worst kind of people."[29] Conte countered by raising the issue of the eleven Italian victims lynched in New Orleans and the inability of the families of naturalized citizens to claim compensation. Conte argued that the families of the Italians who had become naturalized American citizens suffered more because they had been denied any compensation. He noted that American immigration policy was "full of contradictions" and saw clearly a key weakness in the IRL's restrictionist argument: that the fear of Italians did not stem from what the Italians had done to America but, rather, focused on their potential future impact, on "the wrong we eventually may do to the American institutions."[30]

In his work promoting the protection of the Italian colony in Boston, Conte tried to create a more positive image for Italians. He was especially well suited to meet Protestant Boston's Brahmin elite on an equal footing as a minister of the Methodist Episcopal Church. But within the North End community, it is the humanitarian organizations he established and his missionary work for which Conte is remembered. During their decade in Boston, he and his wife assembled a scrapbook of news clippings and materials related to the organizations they helped establish and promote. The scope of their work included the North End Italian Mission, the Association for Protecting Italian Workmen, and the SPII. Even so, their time in Boston was not without conflict. Conte was at times at odds with others in the community. But as an advocate for Italians, he could readily explain the challenges they faced to the Boston philanthropic community and could garner its support.[31]

The inspiration for the SPII was the turmoil Conte had witnessed at Ellis Island. One Italian he had spent weeks traveling with suddenly panicked before the immigration inspectors and was desperately "searching for a paper which he already ha[d] in his hand." Worse yet, aware that any wrong answer meant being sent back to Italy, the fearful immigrant "says, unsays, contradicts himself a hundred times, tries to get by with lies, and then withdraws each statement."[32] Conte was most shocked by what he encountered outside the gates of Ellis Island. There newcomers were beset by what he called "the first category of vampires," who tried to charge them for pseudo-legal advice, and by "parasites offering to send telegrams to Italy" for a fee; still more "vampires [were] waiting ... hoteliers, porters, even criminals." [33]Conte recalled that the once-naïve immigrants soon learned the system, however. He described one who had arrived as "a simple peasant twenty years ago ... [and] worked with a pick-axe ... [but eventually] became a work supervisor, then a saloon keeper ... then put aside several hundreds of dollars and opened a Bank."[34]Conte went on to relate that the padrone banker's loyal customers trusted a fellow Italian's saloon or bank rather than a New York institution because the owner spoke their language, treated them cordially, and did not express "the general aversion to Italians."[35]

Working through the SPII, Conte contacted the Italian ambassador, Baron Francesco Saverio Fava, and his aide, Egisto Rossi. Conte founded a bilingual newspaper, *The Friend of the People*, and raised enough awareness that two Boston immigration officers were assigned to inspect the *bossatura* system used by the padroni to collect a percentage of workers' wages. The society's work drew publicity and the attention of Sarah Wool Moore in New York who wrote Conte requesting a meeting to discuss the padrone and an expansion of the SPII. The expansion was accomplished in April 1900, only a few months after Washington had shut down the Italian Bureau on Ellis Island. In 1902 Ambassador Fava added his support, along with a grant of five thousand lire from the Italian government.

This enlarged group drew support from the broader Boston community, including prominent professional Edward Everett Hale, and a letter of support was received from Massachusetts governor John Bates. Conte had arrived ten years earlier full of ambition. By 1903 he had achieved his goals, survived a battle in the press, and wanted to return to Italy with his wife to allow their children to grow up there. As Conte prepared to leave, Julia Ward Howe wrote to him requesting that he remain: " It would be really bad luck if your work, which has commenced so well, should come to nothing when you leave Boston. Therefore, with all my heart I beg you to remain if it is possible."[36] She went on to say he was "the right man in the right place" and that he should stay. Her caution was borne out: the Boston group faded while the New York organization established by Moore prospered (even expanding into job sites in Massachusetts). Perhaps a key factor was that American opposition to Italian immigration was centered in Boston. The Boston society survived Conte's departure, and the New York group prospered under the guidance of Sarah Wool Moore, who took it in new directions. Moore knew Italy and Italians firsthand, having studied art in Europe. Later in life she witnessed the abuse of Italian immigrants working on railroad projects near her home in New York State. She devoted the remainder of her life to educating Italian immigrants and fostering their assimilation.

Sarah Wool Moore's remarkable career began in Plattsburgh, New York, where she was born in 1846 to a branch of the Dedham family of Massachusetts. Educated first in New York City, she later studied art in Vienna and elsewhere in Europe, where she developed great skill as a painter. She became an early advocate of arts education in American schools and in 1884 became a professor of art at the University of Nebraska. In 1888 she became the driving force for the organization of the Society of Fine Arts in Lincoln, Nebraska, with the aim of encouraging youth and establishing a museum. The University of Nebraska's art historian called her "as dedicated a disciple of the visual arts as ever wielded a crayon or a camel's hair brush." She taught at the university until 1892 having become head of the art department and an energetic proponent of art education.[37]

At some point, Moore abandoned her life in academia and the arts and returned to New York City, where she became one of the founders of the New York branch of the SPII, along with Charles Eliot and Gino Speranza. In trying to describe what had drawn them to this work, Speranza argued that they were "that type of men and women whom many would have classified as 'dreamers'—settlement workers, reformers, philanthropists!"[38] In 1903 Richard W. Gilder of the SPII wrote a letter to the *New York Times* to solicit support, stating that the "great increase of Italian immigration" necessitated their society. He hoped to protect the "numberless bewildered Italians" and give them "a favorable start." Gilder painted a positive image of the future, where such efforts "will shape largely the physical, mental, and moral future of our countrymen." Unlike the IRL's view that immigrants threatened America, the SPII argued that assimilation must be promoted so as to secure America's future. Gilder connected the Italian past with the American future, pointing out that these immigrants sought a new life "in a land discovered by one Italian and named after another."[39]

The SPII's objectives were first "to offer advice, information, aid and protection" to Italian immigrants, then to assist those "unfamiliar with the language and customs" in America, to help immigrants find "remunerative occupation," and to investigate and remedy "all abuses to which Italian immigrants are exposed." But the society's most central goal was to familiarize immigrants with both their "rights and duties under the Constitution."[40]

The first goal was achieved with the opening of an office at Pearl Street, where immigrants could be guided to as they left Ellis Island. Conte's "vampires" still lurked outside the gates. One scam was to collar immigrants, advise them that there was no train for their destination for days, and then drag them off to a boardinghouse. By the time the naïve immigrants escaped, their money—and sometimes even their luggage— was gone. The reality was that those boardinghouse runners, con men, and thieves formed an aggressive gauntlet that few greenhorns could evade. The SPII defense was called the "corps of uniformed watchers"; they met the greenhorns, gathered Italians together, and marched them as a group to the SPII's Labor Bureau and shelter. But even these volunteers had difficulty fending off the runners, and one SPII publication featured a photo of the group walking along guarded by a New York City police officer. On one particularly difficult trip, Speranza recalled, the society's agents took thirty-six immigrants from the Battery Gates headed to Pearl Street, but only seventeen made it to the office.[41] The others had been literally dragged off by the "vampires."

Some of those who arrived at SPII's offices needed more than the aid of the Labor Bureau and shelter. Among them were the most vulnerable Italian immigrants. Perhaps the most poignant illustration shows an SPII agent standing beside two children; the dramatic caption reads, "Two orphans cared for—Their father died in Italy and their mother drowned herself in mid ocean."[42] The society helped workers avoid the padrone and gang labor and the boardinghouses. This represented a formidable challenge to the well-established padrone system, for it cut out those who had preyed upon Italian immigrants. Speranza observed that the padroni of New York were "actively using their great influence against the Italian Labor Bureau."[43] In addition to labor work, the SPII also focused on the needs of women and children. Moore established a residence in New York for immigrants who needed shelter before they could travel to their final destinations. Boardinghouses not only were places where unsuspecting immigrants had been fleeced, but they also posed special risks for women and children who might be traveling unescorted to join husbands or other family in America.

By 1903 the SPII had developed a membership of over three hundred supporters and raised thirteen thousand dollars in one year to expand its work on job sites in Massachusetts and New York State. The society also investigated alleged labor abuses on job sites. This proved a dangerous undertaking as men like Gino Speranza took the lead in traveling to remote sites to gather evidence. On one trip to West Virginia Speranza noted "the power of friendliness as an assimilative force" with immigrants and, conversely, "the surprise among officials and contractors at the idea that an American society should be taking so much trouble for a few 'dago' shovelers." Among Italians themselves, there was some disbelief because "they could not conceive of private citizens arraying themselves against those whom they feared." In the end, Italian laborers aided the society's investigation and offered testimony against their abusers, going so far as to protect Speranza's team, having "mounted guard over our shanty."[44]

The SPII was supported by philanthropists' contributions, dues, and a grant from the Italian government.[45] Although rooted in volunteerism, it also reflected the Italian state's recognition that it could no longer go it alone after the recent closure of the Italian Bureau inside the Ellis Island complex. When the *New Outlook* published a story on the society's work, Moore asked to remain anonymous; rather than identifying her, the article indicates that the SPII had been established "through the efforts of one patient and devoted American woman who, knowing the Italian people, believed that the qualities of character they bring are of value to our national life."[46] Moreover, the SPII viewed some of its charges as unable defend themselves: "Almost all of them are very ignorant, very child-like and wholly unfamiliar with the ways, customs and language of this country."[47] But the society was also concerned with what happened to them after they left New York City. The SPII's largest project was to establish an educational system, called camp schools, which "promises to be a potent means of assimilating" Italian immigrant laborers in the camps."[48]

It was upon the SPII's linguistic objective—teaching new immigrants to communicate in American society—that Sarah Wool Moore quietly built her legacy. She determined that education for the Italian adults must take place at job sites and proposed to test this approach in Pennsylvania. She lobbied contractors on a public-works project for land and materials to establish a camp school at the job site. She was allowed to begin her work near the Pittsburgh Filtration Plant project and established her first camp school. She focused on teaching English to adult workers and then on expanding the society's educational outreach to other job sites.

Education was Moore's area of expertise, and she possessed knowledge of Italian. Leila Allen Dimock, an associate, recalled how Moore developed her bilingual Italian-English primer: "Several years ago, as gangs of Italian laborers were at work ... a lady from New York might be seen, busily noting down the orders of their boss." Dimock argued that the workers "were injured by accidents simply because they could not understand the warning given."[49] Moore regarded children's English primers as unsuited to adults and useless for their needs. She organized the text to promote simple communication in every phase of life. In the preface of her primer, Moore argued that the Italian had arrived but "did not realize that without our speech he is hopelessly crippled" and cannot "satisfy an employer." The result was that an immigrant would take the lowest available job, where "he gives up his name for a number and becomes one of a gang."[50]

Moore designed the book so that Italians could work through the text guided by an instructor who was not necessarily bilingual. This broadened the pool of volunteer teachers she could draw upon. The volume was amply illustrated, and Moore proposed that her instructors use the text in reverse to learn some of the key Italian equivalents. She organized instructors, often women, to volunteer in remote camp schools at major construction projects, promising that the SPII would prepare them so that "an intelligent American teacher, with no previous study of Italian, can keep up with the class and do good work ... indeed better than an Italian teacher whose pronunciation of English is faulty."[51]

Moore's *Libro illustrato di lingua inglese: An Illustrated English-Italian Language Book*, written in 1902 and reprinted in 1908, was her most lasting effort. There was a strong moral component to the text. Each chapter included reading lessons that also contained useful lessons: "A Brave Man," "Petty Larceny," "Work about the House," "A Letter to Italy," "The Drunkard," and "The Trial." In one story a poor and drunken immigrant fights with his boss and ends up in Sing Sing penitentiary. In another reading, "The Night School," Moore described what she recognized as the Italians' own central goal: "to learn English because they do not desire to live in America like strangers in a strange land."[52] The final lesson was the most important: "A Word of Advice from a Naturalized American" asked readers rhetorically, "Do you wish to live well in America? Then learn the English language, honor the laws of the land, respect yourselves, aid your brothers and never oppress them, have faith in God, bear your troubles bravely, never seek a vendetta, and do nothing to dishonor the good name of Italy."[53] This paragraph sums up Sarah Wool Moore's philosophy and the ideas she wanted to convey to every Italian immigrant.

In 1907 the *New York Times* described how Moore had opened her camp school in a shanty after having "personal experience with the business methods of the padrone near her home in Mount Vernon," where Italian laborers did the pick-and-shovel work on the New York Central Railroad. She lobbied the contractors on the project until she was given permission to establish her camp school. Contractors approached her after one workers' settlement "proved such a menace" that neighboring summer homes near the work camp had been shuttered by their owners. Intrepid in building support, Moore convinced the president of the Pittsburgh Stock Exchange to become "the backer of the Camp School movement in Pennsylvania."[54]

Moore's camp schools were expanded to Wappinger's Falls, New York, and to the Ashokan Dam project in the Catskills in 1908. The impact of large numbers of immigrant labor obviously worried the neighbors of other projects who feared workers might settle and remain in the area. The $161 million Ashokan project was planned to last seven years (1908–1915), and the *New York Times* reported that the site "will be depopulated and eventually all the buildings will be demolished."[55] These circumstances were similar to those of the earlier Wachusett Dam public-works project in Massachusetts, where only temporary worker huts were allowed to be constructed. Both projects were contracted by MacArthur Brothers, a construction company that had its share of labor problems.

The SPII issued a circular[56] claiming that its planswould "forestall the demoralization of drink and gaming ... and the many tragedies of the lonely labor camp." SPII workers hoped women and children would settle in the camps and improve the atmosphere. Housing included facilities for families, a hospital, and company store, as well as Moore's schools for children and adults. The design, the society claimed, would appeal to "the sense of beauty [that] is never lost on the Italian."[57]

A year later, the *New York Times* reporter revisited the site and found that both a kindergarten for the children and a night school for adults were busy, writing that daily "health inspections" took place and that a school garden and several clubhouses had been established. Referring to the site as "the model camp," the newspaper observed that Moore herself had funded the educational project for the first year. Daughter of a wealthy New York lawyer, she had bravely invested her money and her life in the camp-school movement. But Moore needed to show concrete results if she was to build political support for expanding the program to other sites; the long-term goal was to have states and contractors fund the program. One success story was the subject of the *New York Times* headline "Camp Has a Playwright," which marked the professional debut of Giaquinto Malpezzi, a stonemason who had taken up philosophy and had written an original play: *What Is Man?* Malpezzi was a fine example of what camp schools could achieve.

Soon other major job sites had camp schools. Dr. Jane Robbins of Brooklyn, New York, carried the SPII model to a project in western Massachusetts but on the first day found that none of the workers would approach the schoolhouse. Robbins rolled a gramophone out and played a recording of Italian music, and then "one by one a dozen or more wandered in. Dozens more listened ... they wanted first to see what it would be like."[58] Eventually, Robbins won their trust, and she went on to establish camp schools at Lee and other western Massachusetts sites.[59]

By 1910 the *New York Times* had grown even more enthusiastic: "Italian Society Uplifts Immigrants" not only reported that the SPII had continued its work in New York City but also related the success of the Casa per gli Italiani, now a five-story shelter for immigrants with two hundred rooms, each "scrupulously clean as a hospital ward." The reporter noted that the camp schools were "the first schools for adult immigrants."[60] Soon, Moore had expanded into other sites and established a multilingual workingman's library. Perhaps of most interest to New Yorkers was the *Times* report that the camp school had led to a "decrease in police" and "it lessens the number of accidents" on the site.

Moore's strategy was not to control workers but to win their trust and then to teach them enough to ensure their safety and spark an interest in learning English and pursuing naturalization. She aimed to teach Italians useful English vocabulary that included the words of warning used while pouring concrete "in the hole," which was the most dangerous operation on the dam. She also devised a small scale model of the key equipment used on the site. Her students could then operate the equipment as they practiced their language skills and rehearsed safe practices in the workplace.[61] Looking back on the opening years of the SPII's efforts, Speranza argued that much had been achieved "by Americans who knew little, if anything, of immigration work, with little money at their command, and still less moral support to aid them."[62]

The end of Moore's career was as modestly recorded as the rest of her life was. A brief death notice appeared in the New York newspapers on May 19, 1911, describing her passing but offering no details. She had died at one of the camp schools. Other than a few short articles printed in reform journals, she left no personal memoir of her career.[63] Moore's life reflected her devotion to education and to the betterment of Italian immigrants. Leila Allen Dimock offered a brief memorial: "She died at her post … She had literally given her all to the people she loved, denying herself almost the necessaries of life, that she might more freely supply their needs." Dimock summarized Moore's two goals for immigrants and the other in the United States. She observed that Moore "longed to open for them the door to the good things of America," even as she tried "to open the eyes of Americans to the possibilities of the Italian." After a brief funeral, Moore was buried with the simple epitaph: "She lived for others."[64]

Sarah Wool Moore's approach was adopted in Massachusetts and was taken up on a national level as the era of big construction projects was ending; immigrants were concentrated in factory jobs by the 1910s. Eventually, the model of volunteer educators working with immigrants was adapted to urban areas. The Young Men's Christian Association (YMCA) claimed that it had a "sane plan" to deal with assimilation. In 1914 the YMCA also argued that Americans should help immigrants become assimilated. They promised that the YMCA could implement "a sane, simple, and practical plan to meet the foreigner's needs … to take the foreigner by the hand and teach him." YMCA leader Peter Roberts described the new plan his organization had developed to solve what it called the "immigrant problem."[65] The focus was on the states where immigration was having the greatest impact, Massachusetts and Rhode Island, reflecting recognition of the magnitude of the problem in the industrial Northeast.

By 1914 the population of Massachusetts was 3.6 million, of which 64 percent were either foreign-born nationals or their children. Half of immigrants arriving in 1912 had settled in four states: Massachusetts, New York, Pennsylvania, and Illinois. Those destinations were then industrial centers, and George William Tupper of the YMCA authored a report, "The Immigrant Problem," which concluded that it was in the interest of businesspeople to support assimilation. He noted: "Ignorant labor is always expensive. Morality in the workingman is a valuable asset."[66] The YMCA's program differed greatly from the Ford Motor Company and International Harvester programs, which aimed to control the worker in the factory.[67]

The YMCA's program of assimilation in 1914 focused on English-language skills for the workplace and on civics training for naturalization. It reflected the Progressive view of the time, as well as a Christian social-reform perspective. The YMCA presented the program in *Foreign-Born Neighbors*, a book that presents the organization's rationale for helping to assimilate immigrants and to recruit young college men to do the work of tutoring and guiding the immigrants towards English literacy and American citizenship. The focus was entirely on male immigrant laborers, who, the argument went, would become a significant proportion of the next generation of voters.

Charles W. Eliot introduced the YMCA plan by tackling the restrictionists' most potent argument: he quoted "a high authority on heredity and eugenics" from within the IRL (very likely Madison Grant), expressing the latter organization's worst fears: "A Harvard Class does not reproduce itself ... whereas from a thousand Roumanians entering Boston today

... there will come a hundred thousand descendants two hundred years hence." Eliot countered this argument by stating that the "present rates of reproduction" may change, and Americans "have no good reason, physical or mental, for despising the recent immigrant races." He also noted that workingmen feared immigrant labor: "This competition they dread." [68] The YMCA argued for assimilation, defined as "the blending of the best ideals of the Old World with the best ideals of the New."[69] Contending that since its foundation in 1844, the YMCA's watchword had been *service*, Eliot called upon members and young university men to volunteer as teachers. But the numbers of immigrants were rising. They would need more than volunteerism: the YMCA also sought financial support from the business and financial community for its nascent program.

What had been established so far? The YMCA program was both local and international: in thirteen embarkation ports around the world, the association dispatched teams to connect with emigrants and set up City Associations, developing programs throughout major destination cities. Observations made by members of the SPII and the Italian ambassador were echoed in the YMCA's literature: Tupper argued that immigrants without English-language skills required what he called "First Aid" because they were "bereft of speech" and victims of "runners and sharpers, American and foreign-born, [who] pounce upon [them]."[70] As an international organization well established in Europe, the YMCA soon set in place a volunteer network in European ports, including Le Havre and Naples—both key exit points for Italians. Volunteers in the United States then met the same immigrants once they arrived on Ellis Island, in East Boston, and elsewhere. Nationally, the YMCA created what it called Schools for Citizenship. These were developed as part of a four-week course to explain the fundamentals of American government at the local, state, and federal levels. Instructors came armed with materials that included a set of oral examinations to prepare candidates for the hurdles of the naturalization process.

But the association's best work was being done at the local level. Since 1908 civic-minded YMCA members had been recruited to run evening English classes and courses to prepare immigrants for naturalization. The YMCA defined civic education for immigrants as "education which fits a foreign-born man to enjoy the privileges and share the obligation incident to citizenship in the US," and the goal was to "weld into one American civic body the diverse interests represented by many incoming nationalities." Tupper did not see "the lure of freedom and liberty" as enough to accomplish this, but instead the program demanded an immigrant's full commitment: "it presupposes and demands patriotic conviction, intelligent plans and systematic efforts." [71] To that end, the YMCA needed to establish support programs. In western Massachusetts, it identified cities where there were no evening schools (Massachusetts law required them only in cities with populations over ten thousand) and organized volunteers to establish classes. By 1910 these programs were expanding eastward into Worcester County and Greater Boston.

In 1911 the focus shifted to one of the twenty-five cities with the highest foreign-born population when the former mayor of Fitchburg, Frederick Fosdick, became the national leader of the YMCA's Immigrant Department but also an activist on the ground in Fitchburg. He and his brother, Charles, owned a large machine shop, the Fitchburg Steam Engine Company, which employed sixty-five workers, among them many immigrants. The Fosdicks managed a firm that used immigrant labor and lived in a town that had attracted large numbers of immigrants to work in its factories. Both Fosdick brothers and their niece, Margaret, promoted the YMCA program and volunteered their time to it. As a business owner and committed Bull Moose reformer, Fosdick devoted years of his life to the YMCA program and to teaching evening classes for immigrants. As the son of a Unitarian minister, he had been a long-time supporter of Christian Endeavour and other missionary efforts. Charles Fosdick was a local temperance leader and co-owner of the Fitchburg Steam Engine Company, as mentioned earlier. Margaret Fosdick became involved in teaching in the program, as well, and in preparing immigrants for the naturalization process.[72]

Much like Sarah Wool Moore, who feared that immigrants' lack of language skills posed life-threatening risks in the workplace, the YMCA also focused on factory communication. English courses concentrated on dangers in the workplace and on communication about safety issues. Tupper observed that workers' multiple native languages made it impossible for factory foremen to communicate effectively and emphasized, given the high rates of illiteracy, "the inadequacy of trying to warn [workers] by means of signs printed, even in their own language." The YMCA conducted a series of public presentations entitled "The Prevention of Accidents" for managers struggling with high foreign-worker populations, noting that one eastern Massachusetts mill had a staff composed of 75–80 percent foreign laborers, and another had two thousand employees unable to speak English.[73]

When Charles Fosdick died in 1925, his obituary highlighted his commitment to mentoring "those who entered his shop as young men"; he "went a long way in helping them to develop ... both in and out of the shop." Fosdick had accomplished this work by employing immigrants; Veneti like Giuseppe Grava and others had found opportunity in his facilities. The Fosdicks practiced what they preached in the workplace as managers of the Fitchburg Steam Engine Company and, later, of the Willard Screen Plate Company.[74]

What was achieved by the YMCA's volunteers? Little record of the local program remains. I interviewed the daughter of an Italian immigrant who arrived in Fitchburg from the Veneto in 1907. She recalled that her father had attended evening school to learn English from young woman he happily referred to as "*Bella, bella* Miss Fosdick." As an assistant librarian and volunteer educator, Margaret Fosdick helped many Veneti and other Italians adjust to life in Fitchburg and move toward economic betterment and American citizenship. She encouraged them to learn English and guided their transition to American life. Fosdick had particularly encouraged this man to establish a small business and to begin the naturalization process. Giovanni M. had applied himself to English classes and worked as a tailor. In 1922 he filed his first papers for citizenship, and by 1926 he was a naturalized American citizen who owned grocery store that supported his wife and their seven children. He later opened a men's custom tailoring business.[75]

But by the 1920s Massachusetts was riven by harsh anti-Italianism. The arrest of Nicola Sacco and Bartolomeo Vanzetti occurred in 1920, and their trials and appeals continued until they were ultimately executed in 1927. On the national level, Red Scare anxieties and the violence of the 1919–1920 Palmer Raids, which had also targeted alien groups in Fitchburg, only worsened the mood. In Washington the victory of the restrictionists finally arrived with the passage of the first of the Quota Acts in 1920, consolidated in their expansion in 1924. This signaled the final success of the IRL's efforts to limit immigration, and this legislation hit Italian immigration especially hard. These provisions would remain in force for four decades. Taken together, these events show that Italian aliens resident in the United States were vulnerable. Their only protection would be US citizenship. Therefore, in the 1920s pursuing citizenship became an imperative in the Italian American community.

A new office was established in Fitchburg's City Hall in 1928 and charged with promoting Americanization. Margaret Kielty, daughter of an Irish immigrant, had grown up working in her father's drugstore and interacting with a variety of people whose English was limited. Her father's practice of learning enough of a language—even Chinese —to count back change to his customers inspired Kielty to become a linguist and an educator. She learned Italian and, after finishing college in Washington, returned to Fitchburg in 1928 as the field supervisor of Americanization for the city. For nearly half a century she was the city's liaison to its alien population and its chief proponent of naturalization.

Kielty began her work with Reverend Angelo Carpinella of Saint Anthony's parish and with a prominent Italian American businessman,

Joseph A. Padula. Public meetings were held that gathered groups of Italians to hear the Americanization program promoted. In 1928 Kielty made her first foray and addressed four hundred Italians in their native language to describe what the city offered at the nearby Water Street Clinic. She established what she called "mothers' classes" to bring women into the citizenship process and educate them, too, in English. (Joseph Addante recalled that his mother had joined the mothers' classes and had taken him along when he was a five-year-old in 1931.)[76] The speakers urged the audience "to make an effort to learn the English language and to speak it in their homes."[77]

By the 1930s a new issue had emerged. The second generation needed aid adjusting to the school system. Kielty worked with the Fitchburg public schools to create programs to meet this need. By 1932 she had organized night schools on citizenship that were held in the high school and in two neighborhood schools. The program comprised reading and writing in English, as well as a special citizenship class. The goal was to identify individuals who had filed first papers and to prepare them for the formal examination. There were citizenship classes for minors and a separate program for illiterate adults who needed to complete grammar school in the evenings.[78]

Addante recalled Kielty as "a legend in her own time" within the Italian community and as "one of the foremost people in adult education in the US by the time she died." [79]Her legacy, much like Moore's, was the design of an innovative textbook to assist immigrants in developing their English skills. In 1940 she published the method she had developed in her Americanization classes. She adapted the work of a British researcher who had identified 850 key words as the basics for English communication.[80] Kielty and her two co-authors tested methods of teaching these fundamental words in the public schools. The result was a new English primer that was not keyed to any other language and could be used in a class of immigrants from a variety of linguistic backgrounds.

Addante concluded that Kielty's Irish heritage played a role as she became an ambassador of citizenship and worked in the Patch, once an Irish neighborhood, which had become home to many Italian immigrants and businesses. He pointed out that she had "helped bridge the differences between the Italian community and the Irish community at a time when some saw the Italian movement as a quote unquote Latin invasion." Addante himself had grown up working in his father's shoe shop and speaking both Italian and English. "We spoke Italian at home [and] spoke English with our friends without even giving it a thought." But adjusting to school was a different matter, and he pointed out that the neighborhood Nolan School played "a large role in helping ... the newly arrived Italian immigrants to get adjust[ed] to the American way of life."[81]

Once on the path, Italian immigrants established their own means of aiding their compatriots. Many communities in Massachusetts had Italian American Clubs (many founded in the 1930s) and many more *mutuo succorso* societies that promised workers a small insurance payment in case of injury or death (discussed in greater detail earlier). But in Leominster, Massachusetts, a small group of Italian immigrants from Avellino founded their own organization devoted to assimilation and citizenship.

Giovanni Antonucci and a small group worked together to establish the Italian American Citizens Club (IACC) in 1910. Their goal was to work with fellow Italians to guide them on the road to naturalization and citizenship. By the 1930s the group had a twenty-five-man political committee and was actively sponsoring Italian candidates for city council and mayoral races. The club's records show that it invited political candidates to meet with the group to present concerns and that it gradually developed slates of its own candidates. Politicians understood the ability the group had to organize and motivate Italian American voters in the community (the IACC records contained a list of every registered voter in Leominster). The IACC encouraged Italian Americans to apply for positions in local government and to run for the city council. After World

War II the IACC refocused its energies on guiding the second generation of young Italian American veterans into civil service jobs. Many of those aided by the IACC became local entrepreneurs and Italian "firsts" in the fire department and police force.[82]

Over the span of decades, Italians grew from objects of assistance into independent political organizers. At the start they needed help from Americans; Gaettano Conte and Sarah Wool Moore both stand as models of the American assimilationist. Moore adapted the idea that had begun with the Italian ambassador's plan for a transitional service inside the Ellis Island facility—the Italian Bureau.[83] She took the idea that assimilation began at the gates of Ellis Island and created the SPII, later developing a bilingual textbook to teach Italians the language skills they desperately needed. The SPII organized volunteers and financial support to expand the camp school movement. Moore lived the life of sacrifice she encouraged others to follow.

The efforts of the Fosdicks and the YMCA represent the furtherance and national expansion of Moore's pioneering efforts. Restrictionists encouraged xenophobia as they lobbied Congress to shut the "unguarded gates," even as assimilationists quietly built a model to help Italians transition into American life and put them on the path to citizenship. The Fosdicks, the YMCA leaders and workers, and many others struggled to carry the cause forward in Massachusetts at a time when anti-Italianism was growing increasingly more powerful.

But not all who wanted to educate immigrants were idealists. Henry Ford built a program of social control to channel immigrants through the melting pot so they could emerge as flag-waving Americans to work in his factories. The goal was model employees rather than model citizens. Historian Gerd Korman has posited that after the Great War, "the militant wing of the Americanization movement tried to impose its solutions" and altered the YMCA language program to make it a factory-based system aimed at behavior control. The first phrase learned in this language program was *I hear the whistle. I must hurry.*[84]

NOTES

1. The 1906 naturalization oath of allegiance required that the immigrant "entirely renounce and abjure all allegiance and fidelity to every foreign prince, potentate, state, or sovereignty ... of which he was before a citizen or subject." US Department of Homeland Security, US Citizenship and Immigration Services (www.uscis.gov).
2. Shaler (1841–1906), a Harvard graduate and professor of geology at the Lawrence Scientific School, wrote "The Negro Problem," presenting his doubts about African Americans (*The Atlantic Monthly*, November 1884, 696–709). Also see Shaler, "Shall Immigration Be Restricted?"
3. In 1916 Hall promoted local legislation in Brookline, Massachusetts, his summer home, to limit three-deckers and wooden constructions—typical working-class and immigrant housing. Prescott F. Hall, *Immigration and Other Interests of Prescott Farnsworth Hall*, comp. Mrs. Prescott F. Hall, 1922. Manuscript in Cornell University Library and Internet Archive (www.archive.org/details/cu31924064104254).
4. Madison Grant, *The Passing of the Great Race or the Racial Basis of European History*, (New York: Charles Scribner's Sons, 1918, 91.
5. Jonathan Peter Spiro, *Defending the Master Race*, (Burlington: University of Vermont Press, 2009), 151.
6. "Vote on Motion Draft of Article II of Constitution, Amended," Aug. 17, 1894, Immigration Restriction League (US) Records (MS Am 2245), Houghton Library, Harvard University, Cambridge, Massachusetts.
7. Thomas Bailey Aldrich, "Unguarded Gates" (www.bartleby.com/248.689.html).
8. "Jno." as in original: Letter dated August 28, 1905, Jno. H. Bonner, Mayor of Tyler, Texas, Section B Circular Letters, Immigration Restriction League (US) Records (MS Am 2245), Houghton Library, Harvard University, Cambridge, Massachusetts.
9. Publications of the Immigration Restriction League, No. 14, "The Present Italian Influx, Its Striking Illiteracy." Undated, in IRL collection, Houghton Library, Harvard University, Cambridge, Massachusetts.
10. Henry Cabot Lodge, "The Restriction of Immigration," *Speeches and Addresses, 1884–1909* (Boston: Houghton Mifflin, 1909), 245–266, quotes on page 2. Although literacy testing struggled through Congress, eventually it passed in both houses but was repeatedly vetoed by Presidents

McKinley, Taft, and Wilson. In 1917 Congress finally overrode the last veto and made it law.

11. Letter, Fitchburg Board of Trade and Merchants Association to IRL President Prescott Farnsworth Hall, May 4, 1915, letter no. 422, Immigration Restriction League (US) Records (MS Am 2245), Houghton Library, Harvard University, Cambridge, Massachusetts. The Houghton Library is situated in the middle of Harvard yard, and physically connected to Harvard University's Widener Library. It is not in or near Boston, which is on the other side of the Charles River.]

12. Madison Grant, *The Passing of the Great Race*, 91.

13. Prescott F. Hall, "Immigration and the World War," *The Annals of the American Academy of Political and Social Science,* volume 93, January 1921, 191.

14. Grant, 91.

15. *Immigration and Other Interests of Prescott Farnsworth Hall*, 80–81.

16. Gino C. Speranza, "How It Feels to Be a Problem: A Consideration of Certain Causes Which Prevent or Retard Assimilation," *Charities* 12, no. 18 (May 1904): 458.

17. Jane Addams, *Twenty Years at Hull-House with autobiographical notes,* (New York: Macmillan Co.), 1911, 243–244.

18. Ibid., 253.

19. Ibid., 254.

20. Tupper, *Foreign-Born Neighbors.*

21. Reverend Gaettano Conte, *Ten Years in America: Impressions and Recollections,* Italian-English by Gina Servini, edited by William R. and Suzanne K. Conte, (Olympia, Washington: no publisher, 1976), 25. Translation of Gaettano Conte's *Dieci anni in America,* (Palermo: G. Spinnato, 1903). In Massachusetts Historical Society, Boston, Massachusetts as bound typescript in collection Societies for the Protection of Italian Immigrants: documents and illustrations, 1894-1906, call number E184.I8 C6613 1976.

22. Gaettano Conte, *Ten Years in America: Impressions and Recollections; A Discussion of the Italian Emigration in North America at the Turn of the Century,* trans. Gina Servini; Massachusetts Historical Society Collection bound typescript, originally published as *Dieci anni in America* (Palermo: G. Spinnato, 1903), 25–26.

23. Ibid., 25, 3.

24. Ibid., 9.

25. Ibid., 3.

26. For a discussion of Conte's role as an Italian Methodist Episcopal missionary in Boston, see Benjamin Hartley, *Evangelicals at a Crossroads: Revivalism and Social Reform in Boston, 1860–1910* (Hanover, NH: University Press of New England, 2011), 157.

27. Conte, *Ten Years*, 42.

28. Ibid., 81.

29. Ibid., 95.

30. Ibid., 95, 100. For an account of the New Orleans lynching, see Gambino, *Vendetta*.

31. Accusations were made that the Contes had sold donated used clothing, but when he hired lawyers "to prosecute the slanderers ... the antagonists vanished" (p. 193). An examination by the Protection Society's board cleared him in 1903, but after a decade he was ready to return to Naples. Conte, "Memoirs," 189–190, manuscript collection of Reverend Gaettano Conte (one oversize box), Societies for the Protection of Italian Immigrants: Documents and Illustrations, 1894–1906, Massachusetts Historical Society, Boston, Massachusetts.

32. Conte, *Ten Years*, 121.

33. Ibid.

34. Ibid., 129–130.

35. Ibid., 130.

36. Ibid., 121–122, 130, 174–176, 189; and Benjamin Hartley, *Evangelicals at a Crossroad*, 157–158.

37. Fred N. Wells, "The Nebraska Art Association" (1972; web resource), the Regents of the University of Nebraska, 1. See also Sharon L. Kennedy, "Early Nebraska Women Artists, 1880–1950" (www.unl.edu/plains/gallery/gallery.shtml).

38. Gino Speranza, "Solving the Immigrant Problem," *New Outlook*, April 16, 1904, 928.

39. Richard W. Gilder, letter to the editor, *New York Times*, Mar. 23, 1903.

40. Quoted in Gino Speranza, "Solving the Immigration Problem," *New Outlook*, Apr. 16, 1904, 928.

41. Speranza, "Solving the Immigration Problem," 930.

42. "The Society for the Protection of Italian Immigrants" (pamphlet), cover, and page 9, in Houghton Library archive, Harvard University, Cambridge, Massachusetts.

43. Italian Labor Bureau, 930.

44. Speranza, "Solving the Immigration Problem," 931–932.

45. SPII founders were Eliot Norton, William Howland, Gino Speranza, Sarah Wool Moore, Lawrence Abbott, Mrs. Lorillard Spencer, and others. See Speranza, "Solving the Immigration Problem," 928.

46. Unsigned, "Our Italian Immigrants," *The Outlook*, volume 76, April 16, 1904, 911.

47. Gino Speranza, "Solving the Immigrant Problem," *The Outlook*, volume 76, April 16, 1904, 930.

48. Ernest Hamlin Abbott, "The Establishment of Night Schools in the Great Labor Camps," *The Outlook*, volume 88, January 24, 1908, 244.

49. Leila Ann Dimock, *Comrades From Other Lands*, (New York: Fleming H. Revell Company, 1913), 50–51.

50. Sarah Wool Moore, *An Illustrated English-Italian Language Book and Reader* (Boston: D. C. Heath), 1902, iii.

51. Sarah Wool Moore, *An Illustrated Italian Language Book*, (Boston: D.C. Heath, 1902), viii.

52. Ibid., 117.

53. Ibid., viii.

54. "Camp Schools for Italian Laborers," *New York Times*, Oct. 6, 1907.

55. "City to be Built at Ashokan Dam," New York *Times*,September 7, 1908, 9.

56. This English-language circular was quoted by the *Times*, and an earlier 1904 version in the Houghton Library gives an overview of the SPII's services with photographs, a list of donors, and explains what they did at the gates of Ellis Island. They were trying to promote their services to immigrants in NYC, their labor bureau, etc. They wanted to appeal to an American audience because they sought donations as a charitable organization. Their circulars served to justify the efficacy of their work to both audiences. SPII workers also issued circulars, in Italian, to laborers to draw them to the camp schools.

57. Circular quoted in "City to Be Built at Ashokan Dam," *New York Times*, Sept. 7, 1908, 9.

58. Leila Allen Dimock, *Comrades from Other Lands: What They Are Doing for Us and What We Are Doing for Them* (New York: Fleming Revell, 1913), 54.

59. Ibid., 51–55.

60. "Italian Society Uplifts Immigrants," *New York Times*, Feb. 20, 1910.

61. "Italian Society Uplifts Immigrants," *New York Times*, Feb. 20, 1910.

62. Speranza, "Solving the Immigration Problem," 933.

63. Sarah Wool Moore's correspondence with her family during her childhood can be found in the special collections (66.7f) of Plattsburgh State

University of New York. Authors who have written about her life at the University of Nebraska were unaware that she had pursued a second career as an educator of immigrants.

64. Dimock, *Comrades from Other Lands*, 52.
65. George William Tupper, *Foreign-Born Neighbors*, (Boston: The Taylor Press, 1914), xi.
66. Tupper, *Foreign-Born Neighbors*, 21.
67. For comparison, see Stephen Meyer, "Adapting the Immigrant to the Line: Americanization in the Ford Factory, 1914–1921," *Journal of Social History* (1980): 67–82. Also see Gerd Korman, "Americanization at the Factory Gate," *Industrial and Labor Relations Review* 18, no. 3 (Apr. 1965): 396–419. Korman described the way that a linguist in the YMCA program, Peter Roberts, later established factory-based programs.
68. Charles W. Eliot, introduction to Tupper, *Foreign-Born Neighbors*, xiii.
69. YMCA leaflet quoted in Tupper, *Foreign-Born Neighbors*, xv.
70. Ibid., 33.
71. Tupper, *Foreign-Born Neighbors*, 83.
72. "Frederick Fosdick, Ex-mayor Is Dead" *Sentinel* (Fitchburg), July 7, 1924; "Charles Fosdick, Long Active in Business and Civic Life of City," *Sentinel* (Fitchburg), June 11, 1925.
73. Tupper, *Foreign-Born Citizens*, 97.
74. "Charles Fosdick, Long Active in Business."
75. Interview with the author, June 2012.
76. Joseph Addante, Sogni d'Oro oral history interview, Fitchburg State University archive, Fitchburg, Massachusetts.
77. "Urged to Prepare for Citizenship, Italian-Speaking Residents Are Offered Assistance" *Sentinel* (Fitchburg), Feb. 13, 1928, 3.
78. "Night Schools on Citizenship Open Monday," *Sentinel* (Fitchburg), Oct. 14, 1932; "Never Too Late To Learn," *Montachusett Review*, Mar. 1, 1972.
79. Joseph Addante, Sogni d'Oro oral history interview, Fitchburg State University archive, Fitchburg, Massachusetts.
80. Margaret E. Kielty, "Reporter Adopts Standard English"; Mary Guyton and Margaret E. Kielty, *From Words to Stories: A Reading Book in Simple English for Men and Women; Beginner's Book in English Education* (New York: Noble & Noble), 1951. Mary Guyton was the Commonwealth of Massachusetts's supervisor of adult education. Guyton and Kielty's research was based on the work of C. K. Ogden of Cambridge, England. See Margaret E. Kielty, "Reporter Adopts Basic English to Report Basic English Story; Only 850 Words in New Language," *Sentinel* (Fitchburg),

Feb. 9, 1940. Kielty asked the reporter to allow her to write the article using only the 850-word vocabulary. Joseph Addante, Sogni d'Oro Oral History.

81. Joseph Addante, Sogni d'Oro Oral History.
82. Records of the Italian American Citizens' Club, Leominster, Massachusetts, 1910–1964, Fitchburg State University archives. The organization later was involved in supporting John Volpe for statewide office as Massachusetts's first Italian American governor.
83. Teresa Fava Thomas, "Arresting the Padroni Problem in America, 1881–1901," *Altreitalie: International Journal of Studies in Italian Migrations in the World* (Jan.–June 2010): 57–79.
84. Korman, "Americanization at the Factory Gate," 396–419. See also Meyer, "Adapting the Immigrant to the Line." Meyer has pointed to Ford's emphasis on "the Gospel of Work" as a key lesson.

CHAPTER 7

THE 1920S

A NEW WITCH HUNT IN MASSACHUSETTS

The era of the Great War represented the peak of immigration to central Massachusetts and a turning point in the way Italians were viewed. In *Imagining Italians: The Clash of Romance and Race in American Perceptions, 1880–1910*, Philip Cosco has examined the shifting American view of Italians in this era, a time when "America's romance with Italy clashed with the threatening reality of Italian immigrant 'hordes' now pouring into the country."[1] There was one view of high culture, which Cosco termed the "storybook Italy" of music, art, and travel stories, typified by Henry James's Italomania. In part, the racial distinctions drawn reflected crude stereotypes of a "Germanic" north and a chaotic south. In contrast, many others—including immigration restrictionists—feared the millions of Italian immigrants and dismissed them with "superficial, often negative stereotypes."[2] Cosco concluded that this sense of threat was rooted in American fears and was "preoccupied with ideas of nationhood *and* manhood."[3] Scientific racism was applied to southern Italians and deemed them inferior.[4]

This racial stereotyping had a geographical component even with respect to Italy itself. As early as 1899, the US Bureau of Immigration divided Italian immigrants into one of two groups: *Italian, North* and *Italian, South* appear on ship's manifest forms. In 1911 the Industrial Commission, also known as the Dillingham Commission, finished its congressional investigation and issued its report on labor and immigration. This forty-two-volume study included one volume entitled the *Dictionary of Races or Peoples* that further codified geographical and racial divisions for American immigration inspectors. This reflected the tensions in America and the growing impact of scientific racism and eugenics theory. The Immigration Restriction League's (IRL) Prescott Hall and Madison Grant were at the forefront of this movement and testified before the Dillingham Commission. This division was not merely a verbal distinction but was entrenched in the record-keeping system at Ellis Island in 1899. Historian Thomas Guglielmo has described the ways that social scientists amplified this message during the subsequent decades as increasingly negative messages about Italians were heard in Congress and echoed in the American popular press.[5]

How did residents of central Massachusetts view their new neighbors? Foreign-born residents and their children represented a substantial part of the Fitchburg population: three of every four persons by 1910. Social reformers called assimilationists argued that these immigrants must not be ignored but should be aided in learning English and becoming citizens. Naturalization and voting rights for a group so large that it was not a minority, however, frightened the average American.

Italophilia did exist in Fitchburg. As the twentieth century opened, many of the industrialists whose fortunes had been built in foundries, factories, and mills had seen a second generation raised to carry on this work. Some members of that second generation, well educated and well traveled, were interested in the art, music, and architecture of Europe, particularly Italy, and had the wealth to indulge in travel and an appreciation for the arts. Their donations to the city reflected the developing tastes of this new generation of the industrial elite who had the financial resources and leisure to explore Italian culture. They also pursued a variety of philanthropic efforts in the community. The Wallace family funded an expansion of the public library, and the Crocker family supported first a new community hospital and then a maternity hospital. These were not single founding donations; most continued over three generations. Fitchburg's public library was expanded with repeated donations from the Wallace family, whose members later also built an independent children's library and established a mobile library collection to reach poorer neighborhoods, as well as a planetarium and two skating rinks.

At the turn of the century music and art flourished in Fitchburg and reflected an elite taste in European music, especially Italian operatic materials and popular music. Music educator Augustine Strickland Belding grew up the son of the wealthy family that had established the Belding Shoe Factory and patented a leather shoe tip that became the source of their fortune. The business expanded, opening offices in Boston and a large business block and a factory in Fitchburg. Augustine Belding and his wife traveled in Europe and returned to build a mansion in Fitchburg, where he offered music lessons and sponsored public musical performances. Belding helped the city establish a military band and compiled a sophisticated library of sheet music, including operatic, classical, and popular works for use in his profession. Among these are works by Puccini and Carcciolo, along with *Un giorno in Venezia*, a collection of popular folk tunes from the Veneto.[6]

Italians also taught music and performed in the area in the 1920s. An Italian American music teacher, Frank L. Fava, arrived in Fitchburg in 1917 and offered lessons in piano and other instruments. [7] Rocco Pandiscio immigrated to Fitchburg in 1898 from Avellino, Italy, fought in the Great War, and then began an operatic career. He returned to Italy, where he studied in Milan before making his 1925 debut in Naples. By 1928 Pandiscio was a regular at the Metropolitan Opera House in New York City and at Boston's Symphony Hall.[8]

One member of the Wallace family took an especial interest in music and more than doubled the local public library's music collection, with an emphasis on Italian works. In 1905 Boston opera critic Francis H. Jenks died; he had contributed to Grove's *Dictionary of Music and Musicians* and had written for the *Boston Transcript*. His extensive music library was purchased by Henry Wallace for the Fitchburg Public Library. The benefactor was Herbert Wallace, son of Rodney Wallace, who had donated the funds for the first public library and was described as "Fitchburg's own musical god-father" for his role in establishing the original music collection. The Wallace Collection was described as ranking "in completeness and value, next to the Harvard College and Boston Public Library collections" at the time.[9] It included an extensive assemblage of Italian operatic music, including Puccini's works.

Alvah Crocker, the entrepreneur who had built the first rail connection to the city and a paper mill, educated his son, Alvah Crocker Jr., at the Groton School and Harvard before bringing him into the family business. But young Alvah dreamed of a career in architecture and left management of the Crocker Burbank Paper Company to his father and younger brother. Alvah married and then lived in Europe during the early 1900s. He studied at the École des Beaux Arts in Paris, where he pursued a graduate degree in architecture until the beginning of the Great War.[10]

Eleanor Norcross, daughter of the Fitchburg's mayor, aspired to become an artist, and after studies in America, she traveled to Italy and eventually settled in Paris. She spent years at study and was successful in exhibiting her paintings. Each summer she returned to Fitchburg to visit family and brought home artwork to fill her father's home. Norcross invited friends to see her collection, which she desired to share with the public. Upon her death, the Fitchburg Art Museum was established with a generous donation of money for the design and construction of the museum and the gift of her substantial personal art collection.[11]

Other industrial elites, including John Parkhill, Alvah Crocker, Henry Coggeshall, and Arthur Lowe, donated land for public parks where their employees could enjoy green space and a better life outside the grim tenements. In 1906 the Parkhill family took a large parcel of land and built a picnic area, swimming pool, and sports complex for public use adjacent to in the Cleghorn tenement neighborhood, where his textile-mill workers lived. Parkhill's son-in-law and mill manager, Arthur Lowe, donated a public playground in 1909 along Elm Street, in an area of densely packed four- and five-story tenements near two public schools. Lowe continued to offer financial support to create recreational opportunities for children and said that Fitchburg "cannot expect boys and girls to grow where grass won't grow."[12] Industrialist Henry Coggeshall bequeathed his summer home, along with 221 acres of land and Mirror Lake, to establish the city's largest park and a bird sanctuary in 1909.

In 1917 members of the Crocker family expressed concern about the health of public school boys and announced they would hire architects to design and provide construction funds to establish an athletic complex for the public high school. The athletic fields, tennis courts, field house, and stands were completed and then sold to the city for two cents. Designed by one of America's top architectural firms, the Olmstead Brothers of Brookline, Crocker Field was the gift of Alvah Crocker and his wife, whose two sons were then serving in the American army in France. They intended the gift "for the spiritual and moral development of our boys," Crocker said at the complex's dedication in early June 1918, as America mobilized for the Great War.[13]

Italians of the community had their own social and cultural aspirations, but they began on a more practical level. In Fitchburg various regional groups established their own clubs: immigrants from the Veneto organized the Venetian Club and the Carlo Alberto Society in honor of the monarch from Savoia who first tried to liberate the Veneto from the Austrian Empire. The Carlo Alberto Society began as a small group of Venetian friends who met to play cards in a rented room on Beech Street, near the quarry. It gradually gained members from the broader Italian community and formalized its meetings at Leclair's Hall, and small contingents of members represented the group in the city's parades and at the funerals of deceased members. The society provided a means for older men to socialize and to represent their identity in the larger community.[14] Similarly, immigrants from La Marche established the Marconi Club a short walk from Saint Anthony of Padua Church in 1916.

Italian religious societies blossomed through the church as well. A men's group, La Congrega di Sant'Antonio, and a woman's sodality, La Sodalizia Maria Sanctissima del Carmine, were both organized in 1908. These groups provided social outlets that brought Italians from a variety of regions together in the church. The women's group worked with the Venerini Sisters to offer evening classes in lace making and sewing for young women. The increasingly large numbers of southern Italians arriving in the 1920s led to the organization of a Madonna della Cava Society by immigrants from the province of Enna. They established a tradition of religious processions and expanded the population of the church. No other Italian-speaking church existed in the region until Saint Anna's was established in Leominster by Avellinese immigrants in 1935.

Social clubs began as a means of providing some security for Italian workers, as *mutuo succorso* organizations. Robert Antonucci, past president of Leominster's Corfinio Club, recalled it as a recreational gathering spot for families from one central Italian town, though it had originated as a *mutuo succorso* society: "They gave you five dollars if you were sick and twenty dollars to the family if you died." These social clubs brought together people from the same *paese* who spoke the same dialect.[15] As time passed, the Venetian Club, the Corfinio Club, and similar groups developed more permanent quarters, which often included bocce courts. The second generation joined their elders as families attended get-togethers in the clubhouses or public halls that replaced the early male-only public spaces so similar to those in their ancestral Italian towns. Once established, these Italian social clubs began to play a political role, as well. Italians who had been regionally grouped in the clubs also came together in larger organizations, like the Sons of Italy Charles Albert Post.

The opening decade of the twentieth century was a time when Italian culture was appreciated even though Italian workers were held in lower regard. Enrico Caruso was famous throughout the world, and many Italian Americans saved to purchase a Victrola and RCA Victor records of their operatic hero. Italian music and fine arts created a counterimage to the negative view in America of Italian labor.

Another contemporary factor in reshaping the Italian image was the emergence of Italy as an ally of Britain and France in 1915. The Great War began in 1914, engulfing Europe, but the United States and Italy both took a neutral stance. Italy remained on the sidelines when the Austrian military invaded the nearby Balkan region, but in 1915 the king abruptly took the fateful step of joining Britain and France. The field of battle between Italy and the Austrians was the Veneto. From the start, the war went badly for Italy. The Austrians literally held the high ground, and the Italian military was tasked with attacking uphill against well-defended positions. The Austrians also drew support from the German military, which sent troops, heavy artillery, and poison-gas shells.

The immediate consequences hit the Veneto very hard as Austrian and German troops poured down the Alps and defeated the Italian forces in a decisive battle at Caporetto. The morale of the Italian army was crushed further after poison gas was used against its troops in October 1917. Although Italian soldiers were equipped with gas masks, these were useless against the particular mix of gases that the Germans deployed. Austrian forces, driven out of the region a half-century earlier, settled into a brutal military occupation of the Veneto. Much of the population in urban areas fled as the Austrians arrived, but in the mountains and rural areas people remained as Austrian troops took control of their lands.[16]

Much of Italy's northeast was occupied by Austrian forces, Italian troops were forced back to the far side of the Piave River, and most of the Veneto fell under military occupation for a year. The Veneti immigrants in the United States did not know the fate of their parents, siblings, and friends who were living under the brutal Austrian occupation. Civilians were hanged, and summary punishment was meted out against anyone suspected of providing information to the Italian military. Worse yet, the Italian army had fallen so far back that its forces clung to the banks of the Piave River in hopes of defending Venice, Vicenza, and Verona.

By 1918 nearly eight hundred thousand Veneti were living under occupation by an Austrian military almost equal to them in number. The occupying army not only doubled the region's population, but it doubled the demand on food supplies at a time when food shortages and malnutrition were already endemic. Austrians troops requisitioned food and animal fodder but then resorted to what historian Mark Thompson called the "plunder and pillage" of "everything edible." First farm animals, then vegetable crops, wine, olive oil, hay, and even clothing and bedding were taken.[17]

Once the US Congress declared war in spring 1917, in response to president Woodrow Wilson's request, America and Italy became allies against the same foe. But Wilson was not necessarily a friend of Italy or of Italians. As a scholar at Princeton University, Wilson had written *A History of the American People*, in which he described southern Italians as "men of the lowest class ... out of the ranks where there was neither skill nor energy nor any initiative of quick intelligence." He went on to compare them unfavorably to the Chinese, who were at the time banned from entering the country by the racist Exclusion Acts. Wilson wrote that the Chinese were "more to be desired as workmen if not as citizens, than most of the coarse crew that came crowding in every year at the eastern ports."[18]

Italian immigrants in America were caught up in the rapid mobilization of American troops. In Fitchburg, whether draftees or volunteers, a substantial turnout buttressed the American expeditionary forces: of the 2,100 men who served, 23 percent (491 in number) were either Italian or Italian American.[19] Even those who had not applied for American citizenship were subject to the American draft. They also could fight with the Italian military, but in 1918 that was not an appealing prospect.

Italian commander General Luigi Cadorna had ordered frontal attacks on the Austrian lines that destroyed morale, and then he carried out a merciless decimation policy on units whose troops were reluctant to fight. Italian immigrants in Fitchburg were called up for the draft, but there were additional categories for married men with children and for foreign nationals. Draft classifications were 1A for men fit for military service; a separate agricultural class; 2B for registrants married without children; 3B for registrants with dependent, aged, or infirm parents; 4A for men married with children; and 5F for resident aliens who claimed exemption. Of fifteen Fitchburg aliens claiming exemption in November 1918, only three were Italian.[20]

Washington needed manpower for immediate training and deployment overseas, and the local draft board began drafting; not only those aged eighteen to twenty-four but virtually every man was called to report. The original age range of nineteen to thirty-six was extended in 1918, and draft records for Fitchburg show that Veneto immigrants, often in their forties and even fifties, were called to report. As the Wilson administration strove to mobilize America and to ship a large force to fight in Europe, a military cantonment, Camp Devens, was established near Shirley, Massachusetts. The camp rapidly expanded as it added an airfield, training facilities, a POW-holding area, and a military hospital.

The local Italian community rallied in support of the war effort. Five social clubs banded together and raised money for the bond drive. The Sons of Italy and the Carlo Alberto Society were among the groups who held a parade and worked to support the fourth Liberty Loan. The *Sentinel* announced, "Italians to Aid in Loan Drive" and praised their patriotism, noting, "Practically every prominent Italian resident of the city is to participate." Frank Robino and Joseph Padula led the combined group, which included nearly every social club in the city: the Victor Emmanuel Society, the Cristoforo Colombo Society, the Carlo Alberto Society, the Marconi Club, and La Societa Salemitana. They worked together in a three-week campaign to raise money for the Liberty Loan.[21]

In Europe the sons of Fitchburg's industrial elite were serving as officers in the army and were featured in the *Sentinel*'s war reporting. The paper printed letters they sent home from the front. Douglas and Alvah Crocker Jr. of the Crocker Burbank Paper Company, George R. Wallace Jr. of the Fitchburg Paper Company, and one of its employees, William Hamilton, sent home letters describing their dramatic experiences and professing their support for the war effort.

Alvah Crocker Jr. had moved his family home from Paris, volunteered for the army, and set off with the Signal Corps to fight on the battlefield that had been his home. Shortly afterward, his parents held a ceremony to announce that they would build Crocker Field for the public school boys of the city. Less than two weeks later, they received word that Alvah, their oldest son and the heir to the Crocker fortunes, had been killed in a military accident in Brest, France.

George R. Wallace Jr., vice president of the Fitchburg Paper Company, served with a regiment of field artillery and rose to the rank of major in 1918. His parents promoted the war effort, and his wife, Alice, led the local Red Cross volunteer program to make surgical dressings for field hospitals in France. As the war drew to a close, Wallace wrote home in late October 1918, and the *Sentinel* featured him in a full-page article titled "With the Boys behind the Guns." Wallace proudly wrote that he and his men were "working hard so all the world may live in peace."[22]

William Hamilton, who had emigrated from England to the United States in 1914 and worked for the Wallace family at the Fitchburg Paper Company, was featured on the "Boys in Service" page. He served as an infantryman on the western front and was gassed on the battlefield but survived. A letter from Hamilton arrived in Fitchburg in December 1918 describing the US Army's final pursuit of the Germans on the western front; it was printed under the headline "Last Drive Was Tough, but US Soldiers Got There." Hamilton modestly alluded to "some marvelous escapes." As the war drew to a close, he recalled, "You should have heard the barrage on Nov. 1. The Boche used plenty of machine guns to try to stop us." He praised American toughness, arguing that US troops stood up better than Germans under shelling: "We can take our medicine ... when the barrage is lifted [we] would fight." The letter describes the soldiers sitting "in our little foxholes" under German barrages but never mentions the gas attack Hamilton suffered. He reported that his mother in England was receiving food aid and wrote that American assistance sent to British civilians had helped her cope with shortages: "If not for American foods she would not know how they lived."[23]

After the war the *Sentinel* regularly published articles honoring those who lives had been lost. In 1927 a full page headed "Lest We Forget" ran a roll of honor, listing the names of the war dead. They were almost entirely from outside the immigrant community. One Italian name, Michele Cousi from the Veneto, was on the honor roll.[24]

And what of those young Italian American men who had returned to Fitchburg from the war? Their stories remained untold until 1938. The DiCicco family had arrived in 1886 and settled on Water Street; Carmine worked as a granite cutter in the quarries. His son Luigi was twenty-one years old when he was drafted in May 1917; his draft registration card listed him as a natural-born citizen. He was a medical student at the University of Vermont when he left for Europe as a member of the infantry. DiCicco later completed his medical studies and became a physician in Fitchburg. In 1938 he was elected the commander of the Italian American World War Veterans Post and hosted a special gathering to encourage naturalization. After two decades, Fitchburg's police chief and city clerk joined the veterans to acknowledge their contribution.

The Fitchburg *Sentinel* described DiCicco as "a man who had helped many fathers of the group to get their citizenship papers," and patriotism was his subject that night on February 23, 1938, when he gave a speech and was in charge of the ceremony. He also introduced other speakers because he was the newly elected commander of the war veteran's post. He observed that the Fitchburg Italian War Veterans Post held "the oldest charter in Massachusetts," granted in November 1919. He then enumerated their contribution to the Great War, a little-known sacrifice: nearly a quarter of Fitchburg's soldiers in the Great War were Italian American.

The impact of the war on the homeland had been devastating, but in the end the Italian military also distinguished itself. Italy began to erase its early defeats and pressured the Austrian front in 1918. The hope in the Veneto for liberation from the Austrian occupation was eventually rewarded when the king appointed a new general, Armando Diaz, to lead the repulsion. Revine Lago and Vittorio Veneto in the central Venetian region became the site of the last great battles of the war. The quiet mountain village of Revine Lago, ancestral home to a number of immigrants in Fitchburg, was held by Austrian forces that turned San Matteo Church into a stable for their horses, confiscated blankets and clothing by force, and requisitioned food from families. Starvation ensued. The Austrian military set up a forced-labor system to construct a road over a mountain pass near the town to help them bring reinforcements into the Veneto. Italian forces, buoyed by new recruits and a contingent of new FIAT armored tanks, moved up the valley to attack Austrian headquarters at Vittorio Veneto. An Italian airfield and teleferic supply system was established to aid in the push against the Austrians and their German allies.

The *Sentinel* headlined the Italian successes on May 4, 1918: "Italian Front Aflame ... Heavy Fighting and Expected Offensive." By June 21 the report came that the Italian offensive was having an effect: "Italians Throw Back Another Austrian Effort." If the Austrian front in the Veneto was not held, Germany would be vulnerable to an Allied push northward, and the Germans could not hold out on both fronts. Soon word leaked that armistice negotiations were underway between Italy and Austria in Padua: "huns beg again," shouted the *Sentinel* in a two-inch tall headline. In late August 1918 Italian forces moved on the Austrian headquarters at Vittorio Veneto, forcing occupying troops them to abandon the town and retreat.

Italians had won the battle on their front, but the *Sentinel* headline of October 28 managed to omit them: "Austria Yields to Her Enemies — Willing to Make Separate Peace." The Italians had removed Germany's key ally from the Veneto and from the war. A few days later, on the first of November, came the headline "in utter defeat"; the article detailed the staggering losses as the Austrians surrendered.[25]

It would take time for the news from the Veneto to reach relatives in America, but in Lago, that small mountain town with a population of less than two thousand, forty-seven soldiers had been killed in the fighting. Worse yet, 115 civilians had either starved to death or been killed by the Austrians. A nun, Sister Elettra Veronesi, tersely recorded the occupation's impact in her diary: "The church has been taken as a stable for horses ... they occupied the school ... the people die of famine." She concluded, "*Fame, fame, fame*" (hunger, hunger, hunger).[26] The victory over Austria came at a very high cost to those civilians who had been stranded in the war zone after the Italian retreat in 1917.

Among the first witnesses to the devastation were members of the American Red Cross team that arrived at the end of hostilities. Homer Folks described what he saw in the Veneto in *The Human Costs of War*; he calculated that one-third of the population east of the Piave River had been displaced (about a half-million persons) and that they were spread across Italy in need of housing and food. In the Veneto the Red Cross discovered that not only had food been confiscated but clothing and bedding as well, and there were few provisions to aid the hungry. The Italian government could not cope. The occupiers had removed glass from the windows of buildings and shipped it to Austria, leaving homes open to the winter winds in late 1918. Roads and bridges had been destroyed, and the Red Cross had great difficulty getting food and clothing into the mountainous Veneto. On a visit to Conegliano, just south of Revine, the Red Cross team found that only three thousand people remained of a prewar population of thirteen thousand. There was no bread or flour;

women had harvested *radici* or dandelions to survive. An estimated two hundred thousand homes in the region had been destroyed.[27]

Italians in Fitchburg, especially those from the Veneto, could take pride that they had been central to the Allied victory. On November 3 the Austrian armistice was signed in Padua, Italy, and General Armando Diaz issued his famous Victory Bulletin in which he trumpeted the significance of the Italian victory. The Austrian withdrawal removed Germany's last and most important ally from the war. Germany held out for only a week after the Austrian collapse. Italians thought they were positioned for a glorious victory at the peace table, but the euphoria dissipated quickly. Prime minster Vittorio Orlando found that the peace would not assure Italy as much of the prized territory on the borders of the Veneto as promised in the Treaty of London by Britain and France. Woodrow Wilson's relationship with Orlando suffered when his Fourteen Points ignored Italian irredentist claims on the Istrian Peninsula and because of his reluctance to allow Italian claims on the south Tyrol region to west of the Veneto.

But even as the fighting drew to a close, a new deadly threat appeared in the form of an epidemic that spread among soldiers and civilians weakened by war as a devastating strain of influenza swept the world in a pandemic. "Spanish flu" began its cruel swath of destruction during the same week that saw the Italian victory. Initially, the disease was confused with less virulent forms of influenza; it was called *la grippe* and mistaken for pneumonia, but it spread faster and killed many more people than those illnesses did. Victims were often in the early decades of life: astoundingly, typical influenza victims in 1918 were healthy adults in their twenties or thirties. Pregnant women were especially vulnerable. Death came within a few days and for some in a matter of hours.

In mid-September 1918 central Massachusetts was ground zero for the pandemic. Camp Devens in Shirley was decimated as influenza and pneumonia killed thousands in a matter of days. Disease ripped through the tenements of Fitchburg, and the city had to open a temporary hospital in the Crocker family mansion, as well as two temporary orphanages, called refuge homes, to deal with the influx of children who had lost both parents.

A full accounting of the dead has never been made. The Fitchburg *Sentinel* usually printed a full list of the deceased on the last day of each year, but in 1918 no list appeared.[28] The system of burying the dead and recording deaths in Massachusetts simply collapsed under the disease as doctors and officials became victims as well. A close reading of the daily *Sentinel* editions from September to November 1918 reveals general numbers but no exact listings and, again, no traditional year-end tally. Some official estimates list forty-five dead of a total stricken population of over 4,500; but elsewhere, death estimates for the city reach into the hundreds.

John Barry's *The Great Influenza: The Story of the Deadliest Pandemic in History* explains that in Camp Devens and the surrounding towns, as well as in Philadelphia and other major cities, the dead fell so rapidly that the systems for burying remains and even for tallying the losses were overwhelmed. One of the first deaths at Camp Devens was the town undertaker. Matters only grew worse from there. Public funerals, church services, and meetings were banned. One daughter of a Fitchburg resident recalled her father describing the Rollstone Quarry neighborhood after the flu: as the bodies piled up, he joined his neighbors in removing the corpses lest they breed more disease. The city of Philadelphia resorted to digging trenches and burying the dead in mass graves. In 1927 the American estimate was twenty-one million dead around the globe, but in 1991 new estimates moved the figures to over thirty-nine million.[29]

The combination of war and influenza wrought unimaginable hardships on families. The wartime experience of one family divided between Fitchburg and the Veneto illustrates the devastation. Originally from Revine Lago, this family's oldest daughter C. married a young man from neighboring Tarzo whom she had met in Fitchburg. Together, they began a family and moved to Mansfield, Massachusetts, where he worked in a foundry. They invited her brother to join them in Massachusetts and established a home in rented mill housing while she raised two children. In September 1918 she lost her husband and her brother, both in their late twenties, to influenza. By the following spring, she had been reduced to living in a boardinghouse in Fitchburg, where her third child was born in March 1919. Within a year she returned to her parents' tenement and moved in with her three children, joining her five younger siblings. By 1920 twelve people were squeezed into the flat, and only three were able to work to support the extended family—but it was the strength of *la famiglia*, the Italian family, that sustained them.[30] Within a few years the daughter married a friend of her late husband from Tarzo and moved out. But the family faced other problems.

They had spent the war years worrying about the fate of one daughter who had remained in Revine when everyone else journeyed to America. This young woman R. had been living with relatives in the Veneto since 1909. She suffered greatly while Austrian troops controlled the town and its people, martial law was in force, and food supplies dwindled. In the fall of 1919 her father crossed the Atlantic to escort the teenager from Revine to Fitchburg, along with another young cousin. In October he booked passage on a steamship to Italy, found the girl—then seventeen years old—and took her and his niece back to America. She arrived to find her eldest brother and her brother-in-law dead and to meet her three youngest siblings for the first time. She had survived the Austrian occupation but never discussed what happened. Her sister-in-law recalled that when later asked about the war decades, she turned away and wept. These new refugees began a new life in Massachusetts but carried the scars of their wartime experience.

This perfect storm of death and destruction struck a civilian population weakened by war and sacrifice, meatless and wheatless days, exhausted by the war effort. Moreover, the war's end had a deleterious impact on the economy of Massachusetts, especially its cotton mills. Fitchburg was home to cotton mills, wool mills, and foundries, all of which had supplied the war effort. Fitchburg's industries had been running at capacity, producing khaki for uniforms, cotton duck for soldiers' leggings, and machinery and tools. Men and women had seen full employment in the mills. As the cost of living rose, so did wages. In a study of the Parkhill Mills, historian Edmund Thomas calculated that the cost of living rose 202 percent during the war and that the Fitchburg mills' wages rose 280 percent. But during those years the American cotton producers in the south had begun developing mills of their own that paid lower wages—and therefore enjoyed lower operating costs.

Suddenly the war had ended, military supply orders were cancelled, and the war economy abruptly dissipated. Factories throughout New England, especially textile mills, shut down as demand shrank and Washington's military orders vanished. Southern cotton suppliers appealed to mill owners to consider relocating the factories closer to the cotton fields. Expanded child-labor and work-protection legislation of the Progressive era made operating in Massachusetts more expensive than elsewhere. By 1922 Fitchburg's cotton mills could not compete with the developing spinning industry in the south.

Parkhill Mills first announced a 22 percent wage cut that was accepted by its workers. Then manager Arthur Lowe abruptly declared an additional 20 percent cut in an effort to realign Massachusetts wages with southern wages. At this point, the Amalgamated Textile Workers of America went on strike, and both sides held firm. Lowe knew his rivals in the south paid wages that were only half his own, but his attempt to erase the disparity did not work. Workers could not live in Fitchburg on such significantly lower wages. Finnish socialists and French Canadian workers led the strike; although Italian workers made up a portion of the strikers, they did not appear as its leaders. After weeks of tension both sides relented: Lowe agreed to hold off on the second wage cut, and workers began crossing picket lines. He then tried to single out the strike leaders and to prevent their return. Eventually, after twenty-nine weeks, it was over; by November 1922 things were back to normal. Parkhill

Manufacturing made a narrow profit in 1923, and then Lowe merged the company with Amoskeag Mills. In 1928 he shut down the Fitchburg mill altogether and shipped the machinery to Amoskeag.[31]

During the 1920s Fitchburg's factory base shrank as jobs in cotton mills were lost to the less-regulated south. Moreover, the Immigration Restriction League's (IRL) twenty-six year battle to limit immigration had finally succeeded, and far fewer immigrants were arriving to take low-wage jobs. The US Congress passed the Emergency Quota Act in 1920 to limit southern European immigration. According to Spiro, the total of each nationality allowed to enter the country was limited to "2 percent of the foreign-born of each nationality according to the census of 1890."[32] This formula was used to calculate the percentage of the Italian immigrants allowed to enter the US based on the number who had resided here in 1890. At first the 1921 Quota Act restricted entry to 3% of Italians based on the 1910 US Census, then in 1924 another Quota Act reduced each nationality to 2% of those present in the 1890 Census. The reason to move to an earlier US Census was to calculate using a smaller population and hence further restrict immigration. A new round of restrictions in the National Origins Act of 1929 left Italian immigration allowed at a rate of only 3,845 persons per year. Then the IRL lobbied Congress to further tighten the restrictions. In 1924 the Johnson Quota Act lowered the number to 2 percent that recorded in 1890, a time when far fewer Italians were entering the US. The Quota Acts allowed only 3,845 Italian immigrants to enter the country each year after 1924.[33] In Fitchburg the immigrant population dwindled so dramatically that the Census Bureau measured negative growth in 1930. The total population of Fitchburg fell for the first time in the 1930 US Census, but this reversed the dramatic growth the city had experienced for more than a half century which was based on an influx of immigrants rather than a dramatic population growth from natives.

Massachusetts—and, indeed, America—was overtaken by a very bitter political mood in 1919. In the space of a year, the Lawrence textile mills went on strike, the Boston police went on strike, and the commonwealth's governor, Calvin Coolidge, put military forces in the streets armed with rifles and bayonets. In Boston's North End a molasses storage tank owned by a military contractor collapsed, killing and injuring many. During the Great War, molasses had been used to produce alcohol for Allied munitions, and according to historian Stephen Puleo, the North End property was considered "a federally protected area" because it had been part of the war effort. Twenty-one people were killed and 150 injured in the tragedy, but as the investigation dragged on the United States Industrial Alcohol Company (USIA) maintained that it was not at fault. Suspicions rested on the Italian community, and newspapers discussed the possibility that Italian anarchists had destroyed the tank. The USIA's lawyer used what was called his "anarchist defense" to protect USIA from liability. For two years, 1920 and 1921, the trial made Boston headlines until the final decision regarding liability was made against USIA.[34] But for months people in Massachusetts had read courtroom testimony positing that Italians had sabotaged the tank.

The entire country was wary of radicals as the 1920s approached. Charles Warren of the IRL had worked with the Wilson administration to draft the Espionage Act, designed to jail anyone deemed a threat to the war effort in 1917. The Federal Bureau of Investigation (FBI), which had looked for wartime saboteurs, was searching for labor radicals in 1919–1920 and finding them in the immigrant community. The entire city of Seattle was shut down by a general strike led by socialist and communist agitators. The US attorney general, Mitchell Palmer, ordered what became known as the Palmer Raids to round up communists and anarchists for deportation. In Fitchburg, government investigators launched a raid aimed at Finnish socialists in a newspaper office in May 1918 and then returned for more arrests in January 1920.[35]

Labor radicalism and anarchism had plagued Massachusetts in particular. Massachusetts was a center for labor agitation because once the Great War ended military contracts were terminated, and this abruptly impacted the cotton and woolen mills as well as machine shops. Workers had made sacrifices during the war effort but then made demands for better compensation at a time when profits sank. Industrialized cities like Fitchburg were especially hard hit by post war drop in demand for products. Massachusetts and New Jersey were two centers of labor radicalism and the key Italian anarchist agitator, Luigi Galleani, moved between the two states. There was tension in the labor sector, coupled with bitterness over wartime sacrifices and personal losses. Immigrants, not just Italians but many other nationalities as well, were frustrated with the reality of life after years of war, disease, and government surveillance. Many, especially those without English-language skills, constantly shifted from one low-wage, unskilled job to another and never advanced. The strike by the Fitchburg Amalgamated Textile Workers of America symbolized the struggles of immigrant workers to hold out. It was ironic that their antagonist was Arthur Lowe, the philanthropist who had built parks for his workers in 1909; he battled them in the 1920s and then left them unemployed.

Moreover, an anarchist group led by Luigi Galleani, an Italian labor radical, settled in Wrentham, Massachusetts, in 1917 and began building a base from which to challenge the capitalist system. Known as the Galleanisti, these Italian radical immigrant labor organizers moved from leading strikes in Patterson, New Jersey, to organizing marble cutters in Vermont and workers in Massachusetts factories. Galleani came under FBI surveillance after publishing a newspaper, the *Cronica sovversa* (Subversive chronicle), which included a seemingly innocuous article, "Le Salute e Voi!" (The health is in us).[36] In reality, it was a prescription for bomb making and terrorism.

Galleani drew among his followers two Italian immigrants, Nicola Sacco and Bartolomeo Vanzetti. Both men individually struggled to find employment and moved frequently around New York, Connecticut and Massachusetts. They fled to Mexico to avoid the draft as did a number of anarchists. At the time of their arrest they were living (separately) in Massachusetts, Sacco in Stoughton and Vanzetti in Plymouth. One a skilled shoe maker and the other a fish peddler, both men had evaded the draft during the Great War by moving to Mexico, but upon their return they faced the dislocations of working life in America. In their writings, they described what immigrants called "the thousand jobs" as they moved from one miserable low-paying post to another. Vanzetti complained about his career in Massachusetts, "I was a 'Dago' to be worked to death." Attracted by Galleani's anarchist dream of a system to replace capitalism, Vanzetti and Sacco spoke on his behalf. On the night of their arrest in 1920, they were on their way to visit another Galleanisto, Mike Buda, who may have needed help disposing of incriminating materials. The pair was arrested and subsequently charged in another crime, the robbery of the Slater and Morrill Shoe Factory in South Braintree, which had resulted in the murder of the company paymaster and the payroll guard.[37]

Sacco and Vanzetti's case moved through the courts until they were condemned to death, and then the appeals continued until their execution in late August 1927. During the appeals process the local, national, and even international press followed every twist and turn in the dramatic story of two immigrants who protested their innocence of the shoe-factory robbery and murders. Yet many of those Italophobes who had feared Italian immigrants in general now had something specific to focus their anxieties on: two radical anarchists who seemed to embody the image of a dangerous immigrant. For others, however, this was a clear case of two men convicted because of who they were rather than what they actually had done.

The mood of Fitchburg's native-born population was reflected in the *Sentinel's* local reporting during the closing weeks of the appeals process, the wire-service reports it reprinted from around the world, and its editorials; one of the paper's two editorial columns, "Here and Now," frequently debated the appeals process. An exploration of the newspaper records of August 1927 reveals events lost in the upheavals of the era, including a wave of violence that stunned Massachusetts and the nation.

The *Sentinel*'s editorials were less sympathetic to Sacco and Vanzetti than those of other regional papers, reflecting the paper's readership: residents of an urbanized and highly industrialized city, substantially Republican in its politics. While debate on the appeals charged the atmosphere, the American Legion veterans held their state convention in Fitchburg. Over one thousand war veterans descended on the city mere days before the executions, filling the hotels and staging military displays and a parade. The *Sentinel* published a two-page spread featuring an image of the newly erected veteran's monument with a black-bordered list of Fitchburg's war dead from 1917–1918. It was probably not lost on readers that a key line of questioning in the trial of Sacco and Vanzetti had centered on their wartime escape to Mexico to avoid the draft.[38]

The *Sentinel* editorials operated from an assumption of the men's guilt and praised governor Alvan Fuller for his "courageous attitude" in denying their appeal; the paper also lauded Fuller's predecessor, Calvin Coolidge, for having used force to bring order during the Boston police strike. An editorial on Sacco and Vanzetti's death sentence stated: "We have not yet read the text of the decision ... it isn't necessary." But the *Sentinel*'s editors did allow that it was time for changes in the appeals process: "The Supreme Court [of Massachusetts] must have power to review questions of fact." On the role of justice Webster Thayer, the editors elided Thayer's notorious comments, admitting that "he may have made an indiscreet remark or two," while countering that the judge himself had been "the target of vicious abuse." More important, the *Sentinel* reported on an enormous wave of violent protest acts across America, in addition to printing wire-service reports about the global protest movement during the appeals process, which began in 1921, and ended with their executions in 1927. Seemingly stunned by the daily swirl of events, the *Sentinel* concluded, "Never in the history of the world had there been such a concentration of mis-directed energy translated into the spirit of willingness to murder."[39]

In fact, each day of August 1927 brought new disasters: subway bombings in New York City, explosions at the homes of people connected to the case, calls for protests and strikes across the United States. A decade after the Bolshevik Revolution, it seemed that Massachusetts was primed to explode. Even today, the seemingly endless series of violent events surrounding the execution of Sacco and Vanzetti is stunning.

How did the *Sentinel*'s editors report the closing appeals, and how did the paper interpret these events? In early August the revolutionary union that had been vilified by the government during the Red Scare, the International Workers of the World (IWW), called for a complete shutdown of the New York City waterfront and then led a Sacco and Vanzetti protest parade that featured a float with effigies of the two men and their judge. The New York City police halted the parade, tearing down the float, and chaos ensued. Three thousand barbers, mainly (one might assume) Italians, called a one-day strike. From Berlin came the headline "Sacco Verdict Stirs German Red," as communist protesters battled police in the streets. Demonstrators in Copenhagen and Paris threatened American embassies.[40]

What was the reaction in Italy? A Roman editorial termed the executions a "tragic jest after seven years of torture."[41] Benito Mussolini, certainly no friend of radicals, sent a personal appeal to Governor Fuller (not mentioned in the *Sentinel*), warning him that the executions "would provide the pretext for a vast and continuous subversive agitation." Furthermore, he argued that although his Fascist government was "strongly authoritarian and [did] not give quarter to the Bolsheviks," it "very often employ[ed] clemency in individual cases." The warning was sent on July 23, but Il Duce's message appears to have had little impact on the governor or on the *Sentinel*. What the Fitchburg broadside did report was that a Fascist newspaper had contended that Italy was stricken by "nameless agony" and that "the Italian people suffocated in its grief."[42]

Then the "subversive agitation" everyone feared struck again. At midnight on August 5, 1927, two subway stations in New York literally exploded. Under a banner headline "New York Calls Out All Police," the *Sentinel* reported that the subway station at Twenty-Eighth and Broadway and a nearby Interborough Rapid Transit (IRT) station had been shattered; storefronts had collapsed, and twenty people had been injured. A day later, the Fitchburg paper reported that police had found their man: Maurice Seigel, a dentist's assistant, was under arrest after acting in what was termed an "unusual and suspicious manner" under police questioning. This was very similar to the argument advanced by Massachusetts police and Justice Thayer against Sacco and Vanzetti that their behavior reflected "consciousness of guilt" because they had been evasive under questioning. Sacco and Vanzetti had tried to blunt this tactic by arguing that the death of Andrea Salsedo in federal custody and the risk of deportation had made them wary.[43]

Later that day the mayor of Baltimore, Maryland, was jolted awake when a bomb exploded on the back porch of his home. The family was shaken, but no one was injured. His wife had heard someone outside and called police just prior to the explosion. This echoed the 1919 bombing of attorney general Mitchell Palmer's home and the Wall Street bombing of 1920. Citizens across the United States again had real reason to fear that a violent explosion might "hit home" in a very real way.

These bombings, perhaps perpetrated by Galleanisti or other Sacco and Vanzetti sympathizers, seemed to confirm the Fitchburg *Sentinel*'s hard line on the executions. The editors questioned whether the perpetrators "were capable of rational mental processes" and argued that they should realize it was futile to protest the coming executions. The editors' argument reversed Mussolini's, contending that anarchists must give up because the state and the nation's power was arrayed against them: "Their acts of violence will have as much effect upon the government of state and nation as an atheist would have upon God by shooting an air gun at the stars." In the end, these new bombings were merely the acts of "the crazed sympathizers of doomed men."[44]

Several more dramatic protests that escalated into riots took place in Boston and Chicago. Edward James, nephew of authors William and Henry James, led a demonstration on Boston Common that was crushed by police and led to his arrest on charges of "inciting to riot and assault on a policeman." Described by the *Sentinel* as "a wealthy radical, [James] pointedly ignored the court's authority during his trial. He refused to stand for the judge, refused to pay the seventy-five-dollar fine, and for contempt received an additional ninety days in jail.[45]

Another Sacco and Vanzetti protest march prompted the headline "Police Rout Chicago Mob, Led by 16 Year Old Girl." The youthful Italian leader, Aurora D'Angelo, was described as "a pretty bobbed-hair high school girl" and was reported to have urged the mob forward while yelling, "On comrades! Mob the police! Strike! Strike! Sacco and Vanzetti must not die!" Cars and store windows were smashed; then D'Angelo and eighty others were arrested as the mob was dispersed by Chicago police. The image of an Italian American schoolgirl leading a mob against the police must have been at least as startling then as it remains today. Her use of the term *comrades* implies that she was probably well versed in the language of syndicalism, and the crowd was reported to have "roared the Internationale."[46]

Next, the *Sentinel* denounced the editors of the Hartford, Connecticut, *Times* and the Springfield, Massachusetts, *Republican*. Both papers had called upon editors across the nation to protest the executions, upholding it as "a duty imposed by conscience" and a "moral protest" that was "the duty of American journalism."[47] The *Sentinel* did not agree. Instead, its chiefs praised Governor Fuller's denial of clemency and expressed doubt that the review of the Lowell committee (headed by Harvard University president A. Lawrence Lowell), which had affirmed the Thayer verdict, could be mistaken. The *Sentinel* then called for "a wholesale deportation" of such persons that would "remove a menace which will sooner or later have to be faced, if it is not checked at the roots." In addition, the writers praised earlier congressional legislation to "erect the barriers" against immigration and argued that "the fence should be erected higher and made tighter."[48]

As touched upon earlier, in 1920 the Emergency Quota Act was passed to temporarily halt any renewed European immigration after the war, but it was expanded and made permanent in the Quota Act of 1924, also known as the Johnson Act. The legislation calculated 2 percent of each ethnic group's representation in America and then used this formula to reduce future immigration, holding it to that number. For Italians that meant that 3,845 would be admitted in 1924, although Rome received four hundred thousand requests. Both acts had been promoted by the IRL, and they were regarded by Mussolini as "inhumane and ungenerous."[49] The second piece of legislation was intended to strike Italian and southern European immigration particularly hard because so few immigrants from those areas had arrived in the United States by that time (the original draft legislation had specified that numbers from the 1900 census be used). This Quota Act stayed in effect until 1964, effectively all but eliminating Italian immigration to the United States.[50]

Two days after their comments on the denial of appeal and the report of the Lowell Committee, the editors of the Fitchburg *Sentinel* returned to attacking other journalists: the *New York World* felt their wrath for having "shown considerable sympathy" for Sacco and Vanzetti and calling for "commuting the sentence to life imprisonment." But more direct anger was expressed toward *World* columnist Heywood Broun, who had written that the Lowell committee's review of the case was so shameful that "the institution of learning in Cambridge, which once we called Harvard, will be known as Hangman's House."[51]

The *Sentinel* quoted the appeal made by "New York's Sacco and Vanzetti Liberation Committee" to Pope Pius XI, which warned the Vatican that "the Pharisees of Massachusetts will kill them" and requested papal intervention. The chances of the Vatican's taking any action seemed remote, yet other reports came in that Americans were preparing to defend themselves. Perhaps the most bizarre response was that of the state legislature of Alabama, which drafted a resolution to appoint one of its US senators, Thomas Heflin, "to protect this country from the Pope of Rome." The front-page story quoted the resolution as demanding that Heflin be given command over "the newest battleship in the American Navy" because "the USA is in grave danger of an attack by the Pope of Rome." Ultimately, cooler heads prevailed in Montgomery, and the resolution was sent to the state Senate rules committee to die.[52]

But as the nation veered from tragedy to comedy, the day of execution grew inexorably closer, and violence escalated further. In East Milton, Massachusetts, one of the Sacco and Vanzetti jurors was nearly killed when a bomb jolted his home and blew a twenty-foot hole where the back porch had been. The *Sentinel* headline read, "Blown from Their Beds by Blast, Family Escaped Death."[53] Boston's Sacco Defense Committee issued a call for a global general strike on Monday, August 22, 1927, the eve of the execution. A general labor strike in Seattle had paralyzed that city in 1920; Americans trembled at the thought that all the country's laborers might draw together and shut down not just industry but public services as well.

After weeks in which the *Sentinel* reports focused on the furious national and international reaction, events in Fitchburg took a violent turn. The local Sacco and Vanzetti Committee, a group that had not previously been mentioned in the paper's reports, requested permission from City Messenger M.F. O'Neil to rent the City Hall auditorium for a public protest meeting. The request was denied. On the morning of August 10, 1927, the mail arrived at City Hall, a pink envelope was delivered to O'Neill's desk, and he opened it to discover a threat: "We will blow up the City Hall and kill you today. Beware." Each corner of the note bore a sketch of a bomb with lit fuse, and at the bottom was a gallows.[54]

The Italian immigrant community, which had posed no problems during the war, emerged in the closing days of the Sacco and Vanzetti drama as a threat. Though the FBI had tracked Finnish socialists, it had not found any prominent Italian radicals in the community. For seven years Fitchburg's elite had been reading about anarchism elsewhere, but now it was clear that at least one person in Fitchburg was willing to threaten violence and perhaps carry it out.

Fitchburg police guarded City Hall, the home of O'Neill, and that of judge Walter Perley Hall, chief justice of the superior court, and then waited. After the Wall Street bombings, mail bombings, and the explosion at Attorney General Palmer's home, it seemed likely that another such attack could very well be carried out by Sacco and Vanzetti's anarchist sympathizers. Judge Hall's Fitchburg home had been the focus of the desperate appeal of the Sacco and Vanzetti defense team only a few days earlier. The lawyers had rushed to Hall's residence by train to request a new trial but had missed Hall, who, unbeknownst to them, had caught the early-morning train to Boston. The newspapers had all carried the story in headlines, so he could easily have become a target.[55]

In the end, nothing happened. No one blew up City Hall or the judge's home. The threat remained only a threat. In the Boston suburbs justice Webster Thayer rested a bit easier than Judge Hall did in Fitchburg. On the eve of the execution of the men he had condemned, Justice Thayer made a point of sitting on his front porch under police guard in full view of the press. The *Sentinel* reported the arrival of a shipment of trunks from Thayer's Maine vacation home, and its reporter watched as Thayer had his chauffeur drive him to the country club for a round of golf.[56]

In the early hours of August 23, 1927, both Sacco and Vanzetti were electrocuted. The Fitchburg *Sentinel* editorialists drew their own conclusions, arguing that the events should be put in the past: "We should seal the book." The *Sentinel* argued that the defense committee's long battle had brought the case its notoriety: "This delay has contributed toward causing the case to be discussed widely ... which naturally brought variance of opinion"; thus, the "intensity of comment ... increased as the delay was prolonged. The inevitable result was the creation of a most regrettable situation." The editors also focused on the third execution on August 23, that of Celestino Medieros, a Portuguese convict who had claimed to be part of the gang that actually *had* carried out the Braintree shoe-factory robbery and murders (the paymaster, Parmenter, and his guard Berardelli, were both killed in the robbery). Medieros had admitted his own guilt but refused to name his accomplices, later identified as the Morelli Gang. The *Sentinel* editors claimed, "If, in the future, others will not allow you to forget the murder case ... it will be well to ask again: Why did the world hear so much of the two murderers and so little of the third?" The *Sentinel* editors were proved correct in the long run; today the confession of Medeiros is regarded as a key factor in connecting the Morelli Gang to the murderers in the Braintree robbery.[57]

The *Sentinel* reported that the last words of Nicola Sacco to his four-teen-year-old son, Dante, at their last meeting were these: "I want you to work for humanity. Never mind gold and riches. Also, remember all the good people who have worked so hard for us ... even though their efforts may prove unsuccessful." Vanzetti, however, asked for revenge, saying, "I will try to see Thayer death...I will put fire into the human breaths.???"[58]

Many assimilationists had worked for decades to help Italian immigrants integrate into American life. But the experience of economic hardship and war radicalized both sides. Americans viewed Italian immigrants as reluctant to fight the war. The IRL's Prescott Farnsworth Hall claimed that the assimilationists had failed: "The World War completely knocked out these cheerful conclusions by revealing the superficial changes constituting Americanization." He based his argument on scientific racism, concluding that no effort could "affect the hereditary tendencies of generations" and that "resistance to the draft law, whether from cowardice, indifference or conscientious objection revealed the difference in attitude"—in other words, the earliest generations of immigrants who had arrived in America were more patriotic and more willing to fight. Hall closed with this derisive comment: "Americanization was built, in many cases, upon quicksand."[59]

But this view, so true to Prescott Hall's writings and speeches over the decades, condemned the hard work of decades that had brought the greater part of the Italian immigrant population fully into American citizenship. He had dismissed the sacrifices of assimilationists and the immigrants themselves who had invested years of their lives studying English and preparing for naturalization examinations. In towns like Fitchburg, they had come forward to support the war effort. Hall also ignored the dramatic sufferings of the Italian people during the war in Italy, as well as the Italian military's role in bringing the Great War to a close by fighting for the Allied side against Germany and Austria.

For the Veneto migrants in America, the First World War and its aftermath took lives in their original homeland and cut off any hopes for returning. Worse yet, war and influenza also destroyed lives in their adopted homeland and left the country stricken by a massive humanitarian disaster. Hundreds of thousands of Veneti were hungry and homeless and had lost family and friends to military occupation, war, and influenza.

Perhaps the worst outcome of this era was that the Sacco and Vanzetti case created a linkage between Italians and anarchism. Xenophobia replaced Italophilia in the American mind. There was much more than the Braintree shoe-factory robbery; other Galleanisti were involved in the Wall Street bombings, the Palmer home bombing, and other attacks. The shoemaker and the fish peddler had been poor, hardworking laborers. But they also were followers of a dangerous terrorist, and perhaps their innocuous appearance rendered all Italians suspect. In the following decades, Italians were indelibly linked in the American mind with anarchism owing to the steady drumbeat of reporting about labor radicalism, the Boston molasses-tank trial, and the Sacco and Vanzetti appeals.

By the end of the 1920s a distinct shift could be seen away from the generous spirit of the assimilationists, who had labored to bring Italian immigrants into full citizenship. The Italophilia of many who viewed Italy as a place of culture and respected Italians as artists, musicians, and writers disappeared from American life. Even though Italy had fought with America against a common enemy, the Paris peace negotiations brought little of the gains Rome had expected. The Orlando government and the Nitti government after it collapsed as Benito Mussolini's small Fascist Party began its takeover, attacking socialists in the Veneto and marching on Rome.

Returning to labor in the Veneto was an even bleaker option for immigrants by the end of the 1920s than it had been at the beginning of the decade. The rise of Fascism was built on crushing labor and controlling wages. Farm workers who organized against the Fascist Party were beaten and killed, their unions crushed by Mussolini's squads. Il Duce's allies solidified his control over the government by killing Giuseppe Matteotti, a social reformer and politician from Rovigo who had criticized the Fascists and claimed to have evidence of election fraud. Matteotti came from one of the poorest farming towns in the Po River valley and had spent his career fighting for improved conditions for farm workers and the poor. His concerns reflected the humanitarian crisis in the Veneto.[60]

In America the postwar years of the 1920s had been hard on immigrants who struggled to find work as the once common entry-level, low-wage jobs disappeared. Cotton spinning, which had employed many Veneto immigrants, was no longer profitable in Massachusetts. Mills were shut down and moved south. Fewer jobs were available for unskilled labor. The Emergency Quota Act of 1920, which might have reduced Italian immigration only temporarily, was instead solidified in the Johnson Act of 1924, virtually halting migration from the Veneto to America.

Throughout this period, people had suffered the effects of war, disease, and economic hardship. Labor organizers, churches, and local governments could offer little aid to immigrants. Having left the Veneto to escape hardship and disease, Italians in Fitchburg found a new world where war and disease took on a deadly global dimension. The networks of Veneto friends and family that the immigrants had constructed in America were all they could rely upon as they struggled together to survive. These hardships tested them to their limits. But the world in which they lived had changed, for many Americans, especially the people of Massachusetts, came to view Italians in America far less charitably after the chaos unleashed by the Great War and the Sacco and Vanzetti case. The hostility toward Italians in Massachusetts made national and international headlines for nearly a decade, but its impact on the local level echoed for several. It was not until the fiftieth anniversary of their execution, in 1977, that the injustice was publicly recognized. It was then that governor Michael Dukakis proclaimed a memorial day and declared that the "stigma and disgrace should be forever removed from the names of Nicola Sacco and Bartolomeo Vanzetti." Dukakis called upon the people of Massachusetts to consider the lessons of that tragedy and to not let "intolerance, fear and hatred ... overcome rationality, wisdom and fairness."[61]

Notes

1. Cosco, *Imagining Italians*, 17.
2. Ibid., 7.
3. Ibid., 12.
4. Ibid., 8–17.
5. Thomas Giuglielmo, "'No Color Barrier': Italians, Race, and Power in the United States," in *Are Italians White? How Race Is Made in America*, ed. Jennifer Guglielmo and Salvatore Salerno (New York: Routledge, 2003), 34.
6. The Belding Collection, comprising forty-one linear feet of sheet music for instruments and voice, was originally donated to the Fitchburg Public Library, which transferred it to Fitchburg State University in 1979. For biographic information on Belding, see Belding biographical US Census Fitchburg, Fitchburg City Directories, and *Sentinel* (Fitchburg). *The Fitchburg Directory*, (Fitchburg: Price Lee and Company and Sentinel Printing Co., 1882, 180. *Report of the Fitchburg, Massachusetts Public Library 1909*, (Fitchburg: H.M. Downs Printing Company, 1910), 6.
7. No relation to the author.
8. "The Maestro Speaks and Singers Listen," *Naples Daily News* (Florida), Apr. 1, 1973, 33. Doris Kirkpatrick, *The City and the River*, 227.
9. *The Literary Collector: A Monthly Magazine of Book Lore and Bibliography* 9, no. 6 (June 1905): 208. See also "Our Drama Critics," *New York Dramatic Mirror*, July 23, 1892 (www.fultonhistory.org).
10. "Suddenly in Service to His Country," *New York Times*, July 1918; *Harvard Alumni Directory*, 1910–1919 (Cambridge : Harvard University Directory, 1910–1919).
11. "Eleanor Norcross, 1854–1923: Artist, Collector and Museum Founder," Fitchburg Art Museum website (www.fitchburgartmuseum.org); Anne O'Connor, "Salute to Women: Eleanor Norcross, Artist, Leaves Enduring Legacy," *Sentinel* (Fitchburg), July 31, 2013.
12. "Children Swarming to Lowe Playground," *Sentinel* (Fitchburg), July 7, 1909, 1. On Lowe's continued support, see *Sentinel*, November 2, 1926, 3.
13. "Crocker Field Gift," *Sentinel* (Fitchburg), Dec. 12, 1917; Mark Bodanza, *A Game that Forged Rivals: How Competition between Two New England High Schools Created One of the Greatest Traditions in Football* (Bloomington, IN: iUniverse, 2009), 106–107.

14. Confidential interview with Bianca M., 2012.

15. Author's interview with Robert Antonucci, Nov. 6, 2012. Antonucci described some of Leominster's clubs for Bretarri, for Foggese, and for Abruzzese in the Corfinio Club.

16. Italy was promised Austrian territories in the Alto Adige (South Tyrol) and on the Istrian Peninsula when signing the secret Treaty of London in 1915. Irredentism drove the king's decision. See "The Treaty of London," *Parliamentary Papers* (London, 1920), LI Cmd. 671, Miscellaneous No. 7, 2–7 signed Apr. 26, 1915; and Mark Thompson, *The White War Life and Death on the Italian Front, 1915–1919* (New York: Basic Books, 2010), 299–303.

17. About four hundred thousand managed to flee, but the eight hundred thousand who remained were "people in the villages and countryside [who] stayed and waited for the enemy." Thompson, *The White War*, 348–349. Ernest Hemingway, as a medical volunteer, witnessed the chaos, and it inspired *A Farewell to Arms*.

18. Woodrow Wilson, *History of the American People Reunion and Rationalization* (New York: Harper & Brothers, 1903), 5:212–213.

19. "Speakers Urge Loyalty to US at Charter Presentation Ceremony," *Sentinel* (Fitchburg), Feb. 23, 1938.

20. "Draft List," *Sentinel* (Fitchburg), Nov. 4, 1918.

21. "Italians to Aid in Loan Drive, *Sentinel* (Fitchburg), Sept. 25, 1918, 2.

22. "With the Boys behind the Guns," *Sentinel* (Fitchburg), Nov. 2, 1918.

23. William Hamilton, "Last Drive Was Tough, But US Soldiers Got There," *Sentinel* (Fitchburg), Dec. 28, 1918, 8.

24. "Fitchburg's Departed War Heroes, Lest We Forget," *Sentinel* (Fitchburg), Aug. 11, 1927.

25. *Sentinel* (Fitchburg), Oct. and Nov. 1918.

26. Sister Elettra Veronesi, "La chiesa diventa stalla per i cavalli ... occupate le scuole ... la gente muore di fame," quoted in Luigi Carlet, *Lago Ricordi* (Lago: Parocchia di Lago, 205), 128.

27. Homer Folks, *The Human Costs of War* (New York: Harper Brothers, 1920).

28. "Believe Epidemic in City at Height," *Sentinel* (Fitchburg), Oct. 8, 1918; and "Grip Hospital is Now Closed," *Sentinel* (Fitchburg), Nov. 5, 1918.

29. John Barry, *The Great Influenza: The Story of the Deadliest Pandemic in History* (New York: Penguin, 2004), 186–188; for the statistics, see 238–239; on Philadelphia, see 326–328; Séverine Ansart, et al., "Mortality Burden of the 1918–1919 Influenza Pandemic in Europe," *Influenza and Other*

Respiratory Viruses 3, no. 3 (May 2009): 99–106 (first published online Apr. 9, 2009). www.blackwellpublishing.com/influenza

30. World War I Draft Records, 1918 Mansfield, Massachusetts City Directory, 1920 US Census (www.ancestry.com). Confidential interview with Bianca M., 2012.

31. Edmund Thomas Jr., "The New England Textile Strike of 1922: Focus on Fitchburg," *Historical Journal of Massachusetts* 15, no. 1 (Jan. 1987): 21–28.

32. Spiro, *Defending the Master Race*, 232.

33. Spiro, *Defending the Master Race*, 232.

34. Stephen Puleo, *Dark Tide: The Great Boston Molasses Flood of 1919* (Boston: Beacon Press, 2004), 228–229.

35. Palmer's men were concerned that the Finish Socialist paper *Raivaaja* had been too critical of capitalists and war profiteers; see Jan Voogd, *Maynard, Massachusetts: A House in the Village* (Charleston, SC: History Press, 2007), 445–446. In 1923 Massachusetts assistant secretary of labor Louis Post wrote an article describing Palmer's "ruthless night-raiding" in New England; see Post, "The Deportations Delirium of Nineteen-Twenty," in *The Sacco and Vanzetti Case: A Brief History with Documents*, ed. Michael Topp (Boston: Bedford/St. Martin's, 2005), 81.

36. Galleani document, in Topp, *The Sacco and Vanzetti Case*, 62–64.

37. Vanzetti quote in Bruce Watson, *Sacco and Vanzetti: The Men, the Murders, and the Judgment of Mankind* (New York: Penguin Books, 2007), 14; see also Topp, *The Sacco and Vanzetti Case*.

38. "Fitchburg's Departed War Heroes" and "Lest We Forget," *Sentinel* (Fitchburg), Aug. 10, 1927. A review of the names on the war monument reveals only one Italian, Michael Cousi. This stands in contrast to the larger number of Fitchburg Italians who served and died in the Second World War, during which the Saint Anthony of Padua Church lost fourteen parishioners.

39. "Here and There," unsigned editorial, *Sentinel* (Fitchburg), Aug. 4, 1927, 6.

40. "IWW Plan NY Sacco Protest," and "Sacco Verdict Stirs German Reds," *Sentinel* (Fitchburg), Aug. 5, 1927, 1 and 5; "How Governor Fuller's Decision in the Sacco-Vanzetti Case Was Taken around the World," *Sentinel* (Fitchburg), Aug. 5, 1927, 7.

41. "How Gov. Fuller's Decision in the Sacco-Vanzetti Case Was Taken Around the World," Fitchburg *Sentinel*, August 5, 1927, 7.

42. For the Mussolini letter, see Topp, *The Sacco and Vanzetti Case*, 171 (document 39). For the *Sentinel's* report, see "How Governor Fuller's Decision in the Sacco-Vanzetti Case Was Taken around the World," *Sentinel* (Fitchburg), Aug. 5, 7.

43. "New York Calls Out All Police," and "The Subway Explosions," editorials, *Sentinel* (Fitchburg), Aug. 6, 1927, 1 and 6. The fate of Seigel, a dental assistant and an admitted anarchist immigrant from Russia, is unknown; no *New York Times* account has been found indicating that he was ever prosecuted. See Paul Avrich, "Sacco and Vanzetti's Revenge," in *The Lost World of Italian American Radicalism*, ed. Philip V. Cannistraro, Gerald Meyer, and Paul Avrich (Westport, CT: Praeger, 2003), 163–169.

44. "The Subway Explosions," editorial *Sentinel* (Fitchburg), Aug. 6, 1927, 6.

45. "James Will Go to Jail for Ninety Days," *Sentinel* (Fitchburg), Aug. 8, 1927, 1.

46. "Police Rout Chicago Mob, Led by 16 Year Old Girl," *Sentinel* (Fitchburg), Aug. 10, 1927, 1.

47. "The Sacco Report," and "Here and There," *Sentinel* (Fitchburg), Aug. 8, 1927, 2.

48. "Here and There," Fitchburg *Sentinel*, August 8, 1927, 6.

49. Finklestein, "The Johnson Act, Mussolini and Fascist Emigration Policy: 1921–1930," 40.

50. Immigration Restriction League collection, Houghton Library, Harvard University archives, Cambridge, Massachusetts. Prescott Farnsworth Hall and Madison Grant had great influence on the Industrial Commission (the Dillingham Commission), entering testimony and statistics into the record that were used to justify the Quota Acts. IRL member and senator Henry Cabot Lodge of Massachusetts also supported the legislation. See Monte Finkelstein, "The Johnson Act, Mussolini and Fascist Emigration Policy: 1921–1930," *Journal of American Ethnic History* 8, no. 1 (Fall 1988): 38–55.

51. "Indication of Prejudice," *Sentinel* (Fitchburg), Aug. 10, 1927, 6.

52. "Would Give Heflin Warship with Full Authority to Repel 'Invasion of New York by Pope,'" *Sentinel* (Fitchburg), Aug. 19, 19276, 1.

53. "Bomb Wrecks Home of Sacco Case Juror," *Sentinel* (Fitchburg), Aug. 16, 1927, 1.

54. "Police Guard Public Buildings after Threat," *Sentinel* (Fitchburg), Aug. 10, 1927, 1.

55. "Sacco-Vanzetti Lawyers Make Fruitless Trip Here," *Sentinel* (Fitchburg), Aug. 19, 1927, 1.

56. "Judge Thayer Rests and Reads at Home," *Sentinel* (Fitchburg), Aug. 10, 1927, 7.
57. "Three Are Executed," editorial, *Sentinel* (Fitchburg), Aug. 23, 1927, 6.
58. "World General Strike," *Sentinel* (Fitchburg), Aug. 19, 1927, 4. Avrich wrote that the funeral wreath carried the words *Aspettando l'ora di vendetta* (Awaiting the hour of vengeance); Paul Avrich, *Sacco and Vanzetti: the Anarchist Background,* (Princeton: Princeton University Press, 1991), 212.
59. Hall, *Immigration and Other Interests,* 80–81.
60. Roberto Cavagnaro, et al., *Il Delitto Matteotti* (Rome: Avvenimenti, 1994).
61. Michael Dukakis, "Proclamation on the Sacco-Vanzetti Trial," in Topp, *The Sacco and Vanzetti Case,* 184.

CHAPTER 8

ENEMY ALIENS OR AMERICAN HEROES?

The Depression years were difficult times for all Americans as hardship increased social and ethnic tensions, but for Italian Americans in Massachusetts the atmosphere grew especially bitter. The 1920s had been marked by a series of events that seemed to link Italians to anarchism. An industrial accident in Boston's North End, the collapse of a molasses storage tank used for producing war munitions, was initially blamed on Italian saboteurs. Although the accusation was false, it took years for an investigation to determine the real cause and clear North End Italians. The Sacco and Vanzetti affair dragged on from their 1920 trial until their executions in 1927. During that time Luigi Galleani, an anarchist leader, was arrested in Massachusetts and deported. The Galleanisti, his followers, were very likely involved in a string of anarchist attacks that included the 1920 Wall Street bombing, package bombs sent through the mail, and an explosion at US attorney general Mitchell Palmer's home.

Taken together, these events radically altered the way Italians were perceived in Massachusetts and across America. Any possible growth in the Italian colony of Massachusetts was limited by the 1924 Quota Act, which restricted Italian immigration into the United States to 3,845 people per year. Any potential for new immigration from Italy had ended. After 1924, migrants who had reluctantly left the Veneto in northeast Italy to settle in central Massachusetts knew it was now highly unlikely that anyone else would join them in America . The migrants' transnational lifestyle had been interrupted by the war and by the global economic crisis following the stock market crash in 1929. The days of highly mobile Veneto migrants traveling to America were over. Those who did leave the Veneto with the dream of making a fortune might try Canada or Australia. Although both nations had closed their doors to immigration in the 1920s, they reopened them later after World War II, whereas the United States did not for some forty years.

Veneto immigrants in central Massachusetts and their families had established their Italian colony and built support networks of religious and secular organizations. They had saved and sacrificed to build Saint Anthony of Padua Church and a school. Some immigrants had raised families and by the 1930s had adult children. Some were veterans of the Great War and felt patriotism for their new homeland. Many had suffered the loss of family and friends in the 1918 influenza epidemic. They were torn between two homelands, often with family and friends on both sides of the Atlantic, as fascism grew in Italy and economic hardship increased in America. From a personal perspective, they identified with their region, the Veneto, but in America anyone from the Italian peninsula was an Italian, and large waves of southern migration had expanded the community in Fitchburg and neighboring Leominster, Massachusetts. Now their identity was found in larger umbrella organizations like the Sons of Italy and Italian war-veteran groups.

Occasionally, the Scalabrinians, the northern Italian missionary priests to the immigrant community, visited Fitchburg and ministered to local families. The Scalabrini had established churches in Massachusetts, Rhode Island, and Connecticut in the early twentieth century. The order had been founded by Giovanni Battista Scalabrini, bishop of Piacenza, who witnessed the emigration of many of his parishioners to Brazil. He formed an order to minster to Italians abroad, with a seminary in Bassano del Grappa, the heart of the Veneto. Reverend Giuseppe Chiminello, although stationed in Providence, Rhode Island, made frequent visits to the Veneti of Saint Anthony's parish in Fitchburg.[1]

The Italian government, allied with the United States during the Great War, had made territorial claims at Versailles that were rejected by president Woodrow Wilson. Italy's king had joined the war in 1915 largely to regain Italian-speaking territory from Austria, to expand the Veneto's borders, and to regain the Istrian Peninsula. Wilson voiced his opposition to Italian irredentism and greatly reduced Orlando's gains. This treatment from an ally at war's end led to political chaos in Rome. Benito Mussolini's Fascist Party came to power by focusing public anger on the issue of lands Italy should have gained at Versailles, and his followers attempted to take the Istrian Peninsula by force. Fascists marched on Rome, and Mussolini was appointed the new leader by the king. Mussolini moved quickly against labor protesters and political opponents; he drew support from the business community by crushing labor demonstrations and holding down wages.

By the 1930s Italy had the lowest labor costs in Europe: industrialists cut wages in 1927, 1930, and 1934, and already low farm wages fell by as much as 40 percent. Veneto farm workers first reduced to working as temporary day laborers then found conditions worsening. Agriculture was firmly under the control of wealthy investors who had built large estates and had the Fascist squads to protect their interests, silencing workers. Historian Martin Blinkhorn described the power Fascists wielded against the Veneto laborers and unionists: "The offices of left-wing parties, socialist unions and Catholic peasant leagues ... were sacked ... physical violence and humiliation ... were meted out to left-wing and trade-union activists."[2] The wage cuts for farm and industrial workers ended any hope for Veneti in America to return to labor in the Po River valley.[3]

Fascists attacked and intimidated socialists like Giacomo Matteotti, perhaps the Veneto's best-known politician. Matteotti was born into a wealthy family near Rovigo, one of the poorest agricultural districts in the Veneto; he studied law and became a socialist deputy in Parliament. He promoted prison reform, social welfare issues, and improved working conditions for farm laborers. As the Fascists took control of the Italian Parliament, Matteotti denounced them and pledged to reveal how they had rigged the 1924 elections and misused government funds. Matteotti was attacked by Mussolini's henchmen in broad daylight in June: he was stabbed in the back and buried in a remote grave. His body was not found until three months later, and by then many of his allies had fled abroad. Fascist squads crushed Po valley farm workers and destroyed union halls.[4]

Mussolini looked to America for investment and laid out the welcome mat. American multinational corporations saw a conservative, probusiness regime that received and protected investors. Il Duce's aggressive colonialism in Africa and his support for Franco raised concerns, but he made the cover of *Newsweek* on May 13, 1940, as "Il Duce: Key Man of the Mediterranean." After his declaration of war on France in June, however, he made the cover of *Newsweek* again, this time under the headline "Mussolini Unsheathes His Sword for Axis."[5] Yet president Franklin Delano Roosevelt viewed Mussolini as a stabilizing force even during the Spanish Civil War. It was only after his "stab in the back" attack on France that FDR finally denounced him.

The US stock market crash and bank problems shook financial institutions and caused economic chaos around the world. The Massachusetts economy remained stagnant as FDR's New Deal programs, like the Civilian Conservation Corps (CCC) and the Works Progress Administration, put people to work. The second generation of Italian Americans, comprising youths born during the Great War, was unemployed and often returned to the pick-and-shovel labor of their parents, building roads for the CCC. The corps specified that each laborer earn thirty dollars per month but also that of that, five dollars go to the worker and twenty-five be sent home to his or her family. Italian families were happy to have the additional income, and the method of dividing the paycheck mirrored their belief that teenage workers should turn their pay envelopes over to their parents.

Beginning in 1933 the CCC began training young men from central Massachusetts at Fort Devens in Ayer, and an estimated one hundred thousand were part of the programs. Whereas Mussolini's paramilitary youth programs like the Balilla trained children for war, the New Deal project's youth were called "the tree army" and "soil soldiers," reflecting the CCC's emphasis on conservation and recreation projects. Large areas of Massachusetts had been clear-cut by commercial timber firms that then sold or donated land to the state. These areas might have been considered parks, but they had not been improved. Although Fitchburg was heavily industrialized, it was home to a number of these public reservations and surrounded by other heavily wooded terrain.

In Massachusetts the CCC concentrated its recruiting efforts in the industrialized areas characterized by high unemployment, and Fitchburg fit that profile. The 197th CCC group was formed in the city, and one of its first tasks was to build barracks, or dormitories, that would house the teams of young workers. They were put to work constructing a garage for the team's trucks and a water-supply system, as well as a concrete reservoir. By October 1933 they were building roads, repairing dams, and excavating ponds. The nearby Wachusett Mountain State Reservation was home to old-growth forest and attracted amateur skiers from Worcester. The CCC cut trails for hiking and skiing and built overlook huts and a log cabin for rangers on the trails. In the surrounding area they built roads, ball fields, playgrounds, and a swimming pool. Recreational facilities at Coggshall Park were expanded and improved with new roads and trails cut for hiking. A study of the program's impact over nearly a decade estimated that over twenty million dollars was sent to workers' families during the Great Depression.[6]

The Fitchburg *Sentinel* praised the CCC for helping families avoid starvation and because the city's citizens "benefit[ed] by the beautification and improved recreational facilities ... a secondary return comes in increased tangible assets of the city."[7] Among the more practical projects the Fitchburg CCC accomplished were painting city bridges, improving the access road to the city hospital, repairing the hospital property, and improving the city's sewage disposal plant and city playgrounds. By 1934 CCC workers were laboring all day but also fielding a softball team and a basketball team. In 1935 the CCC boys renamed themselves the Conspicuous Comical Comedians and put on a variety show that attracted a large audience and was a way to give something back to their community.[8]

Many of these young men were from immigrant families in the mostly Italian neighborhoods of Cleghorn and the Patch. The projects they worked on benefited the city, and their earnings helped their families survive. But in September 1938 the CCC played a more dramatic role, rescuing Fitchburg from the damage of a deadly hurricane. The devastating storm swept through New England, killing an estimated six hundred people and causing millions of dollars' worth of damage. In Fitchburg the most alarming aftermath was the tangle of fallen timber. One Fitchburg official called the situation "the greatest fire hazard this city has ever known."[9] CCC teams went to work clearing fallen timber and opening up fire ponds (used to fight fires where there was no water service or hydrants). Coggshall Park had been reduced in the hurricane to two hundred acres of firewood and was a tinderbox ready to explode. Hardware stores sold out of saws, axes, lanterns, and roofing supplies as people struggled to rebuild homes and businesses. Special trainloads of supplies were shipped to the region from all around the country.

Two weeks after the hurricane, in October 1938, although Fitchburg's Chamber of Commerce made no official statement, merchants let it be known they would not be closing for the Columbus Day holiday. The chair of the chamber's mercantile affairs committee told the *Sentinel* that "competitive cities have kept open on Columbus day [*sic*] in the past," and since there had been "limited opportunities lately to be open for business," merchants would not close. Dr. Luigi DiCicco, chair of the Sons of Italy's Columbus Day Planning Committee, protested that the holiday actually obligated merchants to close for only a few hours. The Massachusetts legislature required stores to close after one o'clock in the afternoon, and the parade could not proceed down Main Street if the stores remained open.

DiCicco, a veteran of the Great War, viewed this as both an issue of patriotism and an ethnic problem: "We of the Italian-American Colony, being good Americans, consider this an affront ... action of this kind tends to keep the Americans hyphenated. It makes the people more race-conscious, and defeats the theory that America is the melting pot." He closed by stating, "We had made plans for a parade ... but I am calling off all parade plans. We feel that these people responsible are willing to sell their Americanism for a mess of pottage."[10] As a leader of the Italian American community DiCicco was calling upon the city to celebrate the Italian hero rather than focus on making money. Given the rising power of Fascism in Europe, DiCicco's statement was also perhaps a word of warning that the merchants should consider how their actions might alienate those who had made America their home. The issue of "hyphenated Americans" who would not assimilate had long been a problem, and DiCicco's remarks indicate the frustration of those who had worked hard to do so and to become American citizens.

Italian Americans faced economic hardships in the 1930s and saw the New Deal as a lifeline. Many young men had used the CCC to help support *la famiglia* in hard times, and immigrant families resorted to relief from the government. Fitchburg's City Hall was the site of long bread lines. Immigration historian Donna Gabaccia has described the pressure on immigrants in the struggle and "each family's search for security in a global labor market."[11] For Veneti in Massachusetts, the labor of every member of the family was critical, and there was no advantage in returning to Italy. Young women left school and went to work in dark, dusty clothing factories like the Asher Pants Company, and boys worked for Independent Lock polishing keys. Young men also worked in the bowling alleys, earning small amounts resetting pins for bowlers. The atmosphere was loud and noisy, but money could be earned nights and weekends to supplement other work—unless the boys challenged each other to a game and lost their pay.

Jobs in mills and factories took young Italians from school at a young age, usually fourteen or fifteen, but kept food on the table. As the Depression deepened, Italian families often put students to work even before they had entered Fitchburg High School. Any job, no matter how dusty, dirty, or difficult, was a means for the family to hold on to a tenement apartment. Some families struggled to pay the rent but failed. People who had immigrated across continents left a record of a different address every year in the city directory as they moved from one flat to another trying to find shelter. Some families moved more than once a year.

The struggle to pay for food led some to return to the traditions of the Veneto. Hunting, fishing, and gathering food in the wild had been a way of life, and it was easy to pass those skills down to the second generation. Older Veneti still hunted songbirds, as well as the pheasant, grouse, and rabbits that were abundant in the fields around the city. Armed with a shotgun, young men could bring home some food for the table. In 1939 the *Sentinel* reported that five young men from the neighborhood softball team had gone on "a hunting expedition [and] got an average of .800"— meaning that four of the five had taken home a deer. The neighborhood store, Wagner's Meat Market, proudly displayed a two-hundred pound eight-point buck and three does.[12]

School was simply not an option if parents needed more income from a fourteen- or fifteen-year-old who could earn a paycheck in the mills. Very few Italian families felt they could afford to allow their children to pursue education through high school and into college during the Great

Depression. A few families managed to do so, however; one Fitchburg High School graduate John Oliva returned as its first Italian American sports coach, and in 1931 Nicholas Roberti became the first mathematics teacher of Italian origin at the high school.[13]

Fitchburg City Hall, once the focus of Italian American anger about Sacco and Vanzetti, became the site where many unemployed laborers stood in breadlines and hoped for any monetary relief in the wake of the mill closings. Shantytowns called Hoovervilles, a symbol of homelessness, sprang up across central Massachusetts. The tenements ringing the Rollstone Quarry hilltop housed both workers and the unemployed. For the fortunate ones, a walk up the hill led to a job cutting granite in one of the six quarries, or a walk down the hill and across the railroad tracks led to a factory job in the mills. Anyone with a job was fortunate. Some factories laid off workers and slowed production, but others, like the Parkhill Mills, abruptly closed altogether, throwing thousands out of work.[14] One factory announced a summer break in production and sent its workers home. When they returned two weeks later, they found that the facility had been shuttered.

The tenements in Cleghorn had been surrounded by small Italian markets, barbershops, and other small businesses, as was the Water and Middle Street business district, which was lined with the shops of Italian entrepreneurs. But as the Depression went on, fewer people could afford the goods, and many begged for credit. Kindly merchants extended credit to their customers and then sank under the weight of debt when friends and neighbors could not repay what was owed. In the 1930s a new market emerged, the cash market, which was a new type of market that developed as a wider phenomenon as a reaction to the Depression's impact on small markets who had extended credit in the 1920s. Its policy was clear: pay cash or shop elsewhere. It was the only way for stores to survive at a time when fewer and fewer customers could afford to pay.

One key entrepreneurial group in the Italian community had been the padroni, but in the 1930s the future looked bleak for these enterprising

Italian agents who had provided laborers to job sites, had run boarding-houses, and had offered services to immigrants. First the Quota Acts cut off the supply of new immigrants, and then most public-works projects came under the direction of the Works Progress Administration, the CCC, and a variety of New Deal administrators.

Even so, some notable entrepreneurs survived the Depression in Fitch-burg. Pasquale Seretto established the earliest food and wine importing businesses in central Massachusetts, with a store, steamship ticket agency, padrone labor agency, and bank. He was followed by a number of entre-preneurs who dominated many corners with small stores. One of the first was begun by Ernesto Cravedi, a northern Italian from Piacenza. Ciro Barone and his family established the first Italian-owned pharmacy and over the decades expanded into five drugstores in Fitchburg and Leominster. Some shops specialized in meat and butchering: the Romano brothers established a store and passed it down through generations. Homemade sausage and salami, as well as prosciutto, were made for customers who wanted food that tasted like home. Water Street and Cleghorn's business district were lined with small shops vending Italian goods, fresh fruits, and vegetables.

Two families, the Caravellas and the DiGeronimos, each began with a small store and then expanded across the region. The extended family worked together. By the late 1940s Tom Caravella and his parents had established the Caravella Cash Market. Later, with three brothers and a sister he turned a corner store into a supermarket empire. The Digeronimo family was not far behind. Members of the second generation, born in Massachusetts, native speakers of English, and educated in American schools, were determined to do well. These two families were striving to establish a new business model for the Italian family grocery store which had been a path to economic security for the first generation. The Depression had impoverished kind-hearted store owners who extended credit to poor, hungry neighborhood clients. The second generation, born in Massachusetts and equipped with an American education, was striving to develop a larger store that could support their siblings and succeed in the competition with the larger chain markets, like the A & P, which had emerged as competitors. It was perhaps also in response to the perception that stores specializing in only Italian imported products would find their clientele limited in the coming decades because Italian immigration had been so severely restricted.

Assimilation programs had begun at the turn of the century as volunteer efforts allied with the settlement-house movement and social reform. But by the 1930s the Commonwealth of Massachusetts had largely taken over the effort to Americanize its residents of foreign origin and to assimilate the vast number of aliens who had not taken the path to citizenship. The Massachusetts Bureau of Immigration (MBI) developed Americanization programs for its more than one million foreign residents (of which more than two hundred thousand were Italian) to assist them in becoming naturalized citizens. The MBI also offered English programs for adults and children, as well as special classes for women.[15]

When the MBI was established in 1918, legislation empowered it to build "sympathetic and mutually helpful relations" with immigrants, to protect them "from exploitation and abuse," to "stimulate their acquisition and mastery of the English language ... understanding of American government, institutions and ideals, and generally to promote their assimilation and naturalization."[16] The MBI was also charged with developing a program taught by women for "foreign-born, non-English-speaking women, both in the homes and in industry," to train them in English, as well as in "American ideals and customs," and to provide "specialized training."[17]

In 1928 Fitchburg's Italian community leaders and Reverend Angelo Carpinella of Saint Anthony's Church listened while the leader of Boston's Sons of Italy Grand Lodge spoke of patriotism and citizenship. Margaret Kielty then addressed the audience of four hundred Italian aliens with a pointed message: "racial lethargy is holding back Americanization work." She urged all of those present "to assist in overcoming this handicap."[18]

Kielty was blunt. Time was running out for Italian nationals in America, especially in Massachusetts. Naturalization and citizenship composed the only way to move aliens to safer ground. But older Italians, especially those with limited English skills, were reluctant to act, and the atmosphere a year after the Sacco and Vanzetti executions was bitter on both sides. Naturalization required learning English, passing a test, and taking an oath to abandon all other loyalties, including fealty to the Italian king.[19] For many that irrevocable step was hard to take because it foreclosed any hope of ever returning home. The Americanization Office could offer to guide them through the process, but Italians themselves had to take the initiative and persevere.

Kielty (whose life and work are discussed in greater detail in an earlier chapter) devoted her life to the Americanization effort. She worked for over forty-seven years in Fitchburg's Americanization Office, particularly focusing on female immigrants.[20] Many Italian-born women had watched their husbands pursue citizenship but had not done so themselves; indeed, independent citizenship for women had been possible in the United States only since the Cable Act of 1922. Kielty established an outreach center called the Clinic in the heavily Italian neighborhood of Water Street where mothers could take their children and attend English and citizenship classes. As Christmas approached in 1931, the Clinic hosted a special party for Italian women in the citizenship classes featuring musical entertainment and food. Italian American students from the public schools also appeared before some of the citizenship classes to provide singing and musical accompaniment. The Fitchburg *Sentinel* described the teachers' goal of demonstrating to the adult learners "the significance of the Christmas season and the best wishes of the teachers for the holiday season."[21] Italians knew the significance of Christmas as a religious holiday, of course, but celebrations in the Veneto did not include Santa Claus or the commercialized American emphasis on tree and toys.

In 1932 the evening school program was expanded to provide "elementary instruction for those who have been unable to finish their grammar school education."[22] This program aimed to help illiterate aliens with their most basic educational needs so as to prepare them for entry into the naturalization classes, putting them in a better position for the job market during the Depression. The rudiments of elementary education were needed before a language student could successfully learn English. One of Kielty's students recalled that her mother, who had arrived in Fitchburg from the Veneto in 1917, needed encouragement to learn English, so her daughter refused to speak anything but English in their home: "I told her I wasn't going to speak to her anymore. She was going to have to learn to speak in English with me so she could understand."[23]

As Kielty was showcasing her English-language textbook, the global threat of Fascism was set to drive political changes that would affect Italian aliens in America. In May 1940 Congress passed the Alien Registration Law, also known as the Smith Act, to require that all immigrant aliens in America be fingerprinted, be photographed, and carry identification cards. A year earlier Roosevelt had asked the Federal Bureau of Investigation (FBI) to draw up a list of aliens who might be arrested in the event of war with the Axis powers; this became known as the Custodial Detention List. Local post offices were to handle the processing of aliens, but the identification of individuals in the alien community was left to city officials, and Margaret Kielty was given the task of assisting the FBI and local officials.

In August 1940 the program was underway, and the director of the registration program, Ralph Maggs, estimated that two thousand aliens needed to be registered in Fitchburg. Shortly thereafter, Margaret Kielty told reporters that she felt this estimate was "too low and set 3,500 to 4,000 as her own."[24] It was too early in the year for the results of the 1940 census, so officials could estimate based only on the 1930 census numbers and statistics for naturalization cases throughout the decade. Fitchburg's total population had been 40,692 in 1930, reflecting the first drop in population the city had ever sustained and demonstrating the effectiveness of the Quota Acts. The 1930 US Census recorded a small drop between 1920 and 1930 of less than 1%, but considering that Fitchburg's population had steadily risen by double-digits in the preceding decades it indicated a significant alteration in the pattern. An expanding population had been measured every decade since 1790. Of that population 8,960 (22 percent) were foreign-born: 5,083 naturalized American citizens and 3,877 non-naturalized residents, or aliens.[25]

Alien registration was a complex process that required multiple visits to the local post office and had to be completed before December 26, 1940. Registrants were required to appear in person (if they did not understand English, they were to bring someone to translate for them), and they had to fill out seven forms and be fingerprinted. For those who had delayed for years and possibly decades, this was a daunting challenge. One of the first problems most encountered was a question requiring the name of the ship and the steamship line that had brought them to the United States. A second problem was that far more aliens showed up than authorities had estimated because a large number of residents were unsure of their status. Citizenship law had been changed in 1922, and cases of citizenship acquired (or lost) through marriage further complicated Kielty's efforts to sort out who fell under the Smith Act's requirements.

Margaret Kielty's Americanization Office became the center for determining citizenship status. She reported in early September that "the fall season has started off with an unprecedented rush for naturalization papers."[26] For most, however, it was too late. Citizenship had been encouraged for decades, but now the aliens' hopes of speeding through the process with the shadow of war looming were just that: hopes. Ralph Maggs was concerned that the requirement to register might be too difficult for some elderly or ill aliens. The timeline for completing the process was four months, and the penalties were harsh: a thousand-dollar fine and six months in jail. In addition, the people who needed to be reached were mostly elderly foreign-born immigrants—those with limited English skills who were unlikely to be able to read newspaper announcements or understand how to make their way through the process. On December

27, 1940, Fitchburg's officials reached the end of the program with 4,615 aliens registered. Maggs and Kielty agreed that Fitchburg was "practically 100 per cent registered" by that date.[27]

Within a year, the Japanese attacked Pearl Harbor, and Congress declared war against Japan. Hitler and Mussolini, allies of Japan, also declared war against the United States. Italian aliens became enemy aliens. On December 11, 1941, Margaret Kielty was interviewed about the number of enemy aliens in Fitchburg: 370 Italians, 21 Germans. Mayor Woollacott's office confirmed "reports of suspicious persons ... have been turned over to the FBI" and indicated that "many aliens in this city have been investigated."[28]

In neighboring Leominster, "two aliens, one an Italian, were questioned." Kielty tried to alleviate tensions between the government and Fitchburg's Italians: "a great majority of the aliens in this city are law-abiding people who would do nothing to harm this country."[29] She also pointed out that "a majority of the German and Italian nationals in this city are elderly people, many of whom have lived in the city for many years and failed to become naturalized." Kielty was quoted in the *Sentinel* as "She issued a sharp warning to all aliens to conform immediately to the regulation..."[30] Kielty had been working for decades to encourage aliens to complete the naturalization process, but after Pearl Harbor she was faced with the fact that German and Italian nationals were now enemy aliens. After Pearl Harbor they were in a very different and more perilous relationship with the government. Some who had citizenship papers in process in December 1941 were found to have changed their address without notifying the government and Kielty noted these citizenship papers "have recently been withheld" for those "who have violated this law," and she predicted that there "will be a strict rechecking" of those aliens whose papers were in process.[31] But the message was going out via the newspaper to a group of elderly individuals who for the most part did not have English-language skills and were unlikely to read the Fitchburg *Sentinel.*

After Pearl Harbor in December 1941, the roundup of Italians and Germans began, and some people were investigated and interned. Italians and Germans who had already registered were called back to re-register at US Post Offices because their new status was as "enemy aliens."[32] in February 1942 because they had been reclassified as enemy aliens after FDR issued Executive Order 9066, which legitimized use of the Custodial Detention List, detentions, and arrests. The initial list had been used in investigations of some enemy aliens, but in 1942 tighter restrictions were put in place and those on the list were required to carry identification cards. Fitchburg's mayor told the press, "It is, in no sense, to be interpreted as a reflection on the loyalty and good will of the great majority of Germans and Italians in our community. The objective in issuing identification certificates ... is a dual one of strengthening our internal safety and protecting the loyal alien, even if he has become technically an alien enemy."[33]

This was small comfort for elderly immigrants. In 1940 they were required to register, but in 1942 they were to carry an identification card and fell under a new set of restrictions. Each alien was now required to carry a small tan identification card (in some areas, the cards were pink) that bore a fingerprint, photograph, address, age, and signature. In addition, the government required "three unmounted photographs [...] 2 by 2 inches in size" taken within 30 days prior to registration showing "a front view of the face without hat"[34]: one was sent to Washington, one went into the local records, and the third was mounted on the identification card, along with the person's fingerprint.

The annual report to the commonwealth's Division of Immigration and Americanization (which had replaced the old Massachusetts Bureau of Immigration) in May 1940 recorded the information aliens must provide: name, address, date of birth, sex, occupation, employer, relatives, physical appearance, citizenship status (whether they had filed first or second papers), marital status, military and criminal records, when they had entered the United States, how long they intended to stay (any Italian present in the country even for a short time was required to file), and race. The report also notes that the alien "was also required to name any club, organization or society of which he had ever been a member. Registration was free."[35] Obviously, registration came with some high personal costs. The requirement to name clubs and organizations was linked with the secondary purpose of the Smith Act: to identify political radicals. (After the Second World War, the legislation was slightly modified and was used to round up communists in the 1950s.) But in 1940 membership in Italian combat veterans' groups was viewed as an indication of divided loyalty.

Enemy aliens were also put under tight restrictions regarding their movements, possessions, and activities. Their identification cards laid out the rules: aliens planning to move must notify the government in writing within five days of the move. Air travel was restricted. No enemy aliens were allowed enter or travel within military zones. Limits to traveling on boats or ships, especially restrictions placed on Atlantic fishermen, hit Italian communities on the Massachusetts coast particularly hard. Aliens were not allowed to possess guns, shortwave radios and receivers, or cameras (considered tools of espionage) and were placed under a curfew.

Mussolini understood the political power of Guglielmo Marconi's invention and in 1933 established a Ministry of Press and Propaganda to control broadcasts from the Italian national radio service. By 1934 Italy began shortwave broadcasts to North America in Italian and in English. (In the same era, FDR also used the power of radio in his Fireside Chats.) Many Italian Americans owned parlor radio sets that had an extra receiver capable of picking up international shortwave broadcasts.[36] For enemy aliens with such radios the restrictions proved a particular problem and were enforced in a harsh manner. FBI agents had the authority to enter an enemy alien's home and inspect the radio for a shortwave converter, removing it if they found one. Many Italian Americans had listened to Italian national broadcasts on their home radios in the 1930s in the same way that Italian Americans today receive cable and satellite broadcasts of RAI television shows.

If there was any doubt about how Americans would perceive the registration of aliens, it became clear a month later, in March 1942, when the *Sentinel* trumpeted the success of the "Enemy Roundup."[37] What had been going on inside the Italian American community? In 1936 Leominster's Italian American Citizens Club (IACC) had reorganized and opened a new campaign to guide aliens toward naturalization. This group had begun nearly two decades earlier with the goal of making every Italian in the area a US citizen. The new IACC bylaws stated that the group would "encourage the naturalization of Italians, teach them American Ideals and develop in them a proper appreciation of the duties and benefits of American citizenship." It also adopted as its motto "Our Aim: A Better Citizen." Members of the IACC had worked together to sponsor candidates and to appear as character witnesses during naturalization proceedings. In the dark atmosphere of the late 1930s, they recommenced their efforts and organized a political committee to seek support in the local government.[38]

Beginning in 1938 there had been an effort to push for naturalization in the Fitchburg community. On February 23, 1938, fully two years before the passage of the Smith Act, the Italian American World War Veterans held a public meeting with loyalty as its topic and naturalization the goal. Police chief Thomas Godley spoke to the group; he pointed out that he was a veteran of the Spanish-American War and encouraged the Italians to be loyal to America, stating that they had "fought for a good cause" that "must not be abandoned for anything going on in other countries."[39] Mussolini's alliance with the Axis powers and his support for the Fascists in the Spanish Civil War formed Godley's frame of reference, but he was preaching patriotism to a group whose members had already distinguished themselves.

City clerk Sanford Worthington also spoke that day, encouraging the group to maintain "the duty you owe to your nation, state [and] city," and he closed by urging them to "uphold the Constitution of this country and thank God for the privilege of freedom we now enjoy."[40] Reverend

Angelo Carpinella, priest of Saint Anthony's Church, issued his own warning: "Bolshevism and communism are slowly and surely entering life in America. I urge you in America to forget 'isms' and remember the only one for us here is Americanism."[41] From the Catholic perspective, godless communism was even more dangerous than Fascism.

Dr. Luigi M. DiCicco, the Italian American veteran of the Great War and the newly elected commander of the veterans' post, was to present a new charter and install officers for the post, which had been founded in November of 1919 and was the oldest group in Massachusetts. He pointed with pride to the number of Italian Americans from Fitchburg who had served in the Great War, a remarkable 23 percent of the total.[42] Yet as mentioned earlier, a close reading of the local newspapers of that time does not reflect this participation, and it seems ironic that city officials appeared before the group two decades later to encourage them to remain loyal Americans. The accomplishments of the Italian community in the Great War had not made it into the papers, but with war threatening again, the veterans heard a message of patriotism and loyalty. DiCicco was praised, moreover, as a person who had "helped many fathers of the group to get their citizenship papers."[43] In the shadow of war, those who had not yet been naturalized were being encouraged by the city to choose citizenship. The fact that the speakers all focused on loyalty and duty, especially given that this was a ceremony to present the new charter for the Italian American World War Veteran's group, indicates the deepening concern about the political orientation of the second generation of Italian immigrant families and about the alien status of older residents.

How did this community respond when World War II began for Americans? The first-generation Italian immigrants were for the most part too old to serve, although a number of them were called by the draft board. After Pearl Harbor the community responded strongly, as did the vast majority of Americans. These war years were especially difficult because Mussolini's Fascists were the enemy, and many young men were sent to Europe to fight. During the conflict, the priest of Saint

Anthony's Church calculated the impact on the parish and found that 60 percent of the church's families had men fighting in the war. The church bulletin carried a note advising three special weekly prayer services, and the *Sentinel* reported in 1941 "100 Descendants of Italians Here Now In Service."[44] By 1944 the number was six hundred and included a number of women volunteers.

In one Veneto immigrant's family, the Morettos, the four oldest sons volunteered for service after Pearl Harbor. Paul, with a back injury, was rejected, but his his three brothers—Alexander, Albino, and Enzo— enlisted. In 1944 the newspaper that had for years covered their exploits as candlepin bowlers, including Paul's victory in the Worcester *Telegram & Gazette*'s world championship, printed a military report and a sports story: "Bowlers Now Soldiers." The Moretto family, "widely known in bowling circles," had three sons serving in the armed forces: one in North Africa, another awaiting transfer to the Pacific, and a third in France. The story told of the exploits of "well known timber-topplers ... now seeking their strikes and spares with Uncle Sam's fighting forces." Three of the four Moretto brothers were now all in service: Alexander had been shipped first to England and then North Africa. Albino had left a job in the foundries to train in Arizona and had then shipped out across the Pacific. Enzo, the youngest, joined the military after he finished high school. He waded ashore on D-Day and constructed Bailey bridges for General George S. Patton's forces as they fought their way toward Berlin. In the closing days of the war, he was part of the American forces hunting for Hitler.[45]

There were many similar stories in Fitchburg's Italian American community. Whereas the newspapers had covered the exploits of the sons and daughters of Fitchburg's leading old families in the Great War, despite the notable service of the community's immigrant residents, the Second World War was a much more visible venue for the second generation of Italian immigrants. The Saint Anthony of Padua parish had a number of its sons and daughters on the field of battle, and Italian Americans served in large numbers.

Fighting on the Italian peninsula commenced in the fall of 1943 after the king dismissed Mussolini and the Grand Council voted him out. The king's appeal to the Allies was stalled by Winston Churchill's intransigence. Meanwhile Mussolini, who had been imprisoned, was liberated in a bold Nazi raid to establish a puppet regime near Verona, making northern Italy a prime target for the Allies. The Nazis were much more willing to fight the Allies on Italian soil rather than on German territory and turned central Italy into a brutal battlefield. All of 1944 was expended in fighting up the peninsula, and the tourist slogan "See Naples and die" took on a different, sinister meaning for American soldiers.

By early 1945 Allied ground forces were approaching the Veneto, which became the location not only of an infantry battle but also of an air assault. British and American bombers pounded Milan, Treviso, and many rail stations and factories in the north. Italian laborers resisted Nazi masters in factories and sacrificed their lives. The Good Friday bombing of Treviso in 1944 destroyed nearly half the city and killed an estimated one thousand civilians.[46] The Church of Saint Martin (Chiesa di San Martino Urbano) was destroyed in the bombing, and the priest who had organized the boys of the parish into a partisan group was discovered. The Nazis arrested and killed the priest.

In Bassano del Grappa the retreating Nazi SS forces tired of partisan attacks. Commander Karl Franz Tausch was determined to discourage the partisans and to make an example of this town, which was a center of resistance activity and a base for the Italian *alpini* mountain fighters. Tausch ordered that his troops hunt down and capture partisans in a symbolic punishment. Bassano del Grappa is divided by a river, its highest point crowned with a beautiful public park that had been dedicated to the Italian soldiers killed in the Great War. A row of decorative trees lines the crest of this park in the center of the town, each planted in memory of a man from the town. The Nazis hanged thirty-two partisans from the trees, leaving the bodies there in full view of the townspeople. One body had a cardboard sign hanging from the neck that read *bandito*—demonstrating the German soldiers' ignorance of Italian (the term is Spanish). It has been estimated that this particular SS unit killed over four hundred partisans and deported another five hundred to German prison camps.[47]

Even in tiny Revine Lago, a small partisan brigade was organized. When the war ended, Lago (which had lost forty-seven soldiers and 115 civilians to the Austrian occupation in the Great War) had lost another twenty men and a young woman, the leader of Azione Cattolica (Catholic Action), who was killed by machine-gun fire. The partisans recorded an additional thirty-seven fallen.[48]

In May 1945 the Fitchburg *Sentinel* headlined the story of Private Rose A. Posco of the American Women's Army Corps (WACs). She had volunteered in 1943, trained in telegraphy, served in North Africa and Italy, and spent fifteen months moving up the Italian peninsula. In her off-duty hours she and two colleagues gathered wildflowers and decorated the American graves, bravely dealing with the grim aftermath of war. The maintenance of the graves grew into a larger task as the war took more American lives.[49]

Another of St. Anthony's young servicewomen, Maria Batistella, was the daughter of a Revine Lago family. She joined the Women's Army Corps in 1943 and trained as a medical statistician. By 1944 she was stationed in London where she was charged with managing "the movement of hospital trains, evacuation and medical care" for the European theater, and in 1945 she became one of the first WACs to arrive on the French coast. A photograph of S.Sgt. Maria Battistella made the front page of the *Sentinel*, as she marched at the head of a military parade in Paris. Directly above the photograph was the dramatic headline "Bomb Shatters Jap Morale; Believe Hiroshima Obliterated." It was finally during the Second World War that the men and women of Fitchburg's Italian American community had earned a prominent place in the town's record of military service.[50]

In Fitchburg stories of the destruction raised deep concerns about whether Italy could recover from such massive destruction to its civil society and infrastructure. A group gathered to organize a local branch of the American Medical Aid to Italy Committee, which grew from FDR's request for a study by American Relief for Italy. The local committee heard a report from the national organization that "half the children born in Italy die before they reach their first birthday." The report also noted that "the general death rate in Rome in 1945 had increased 100 per cent." Worse yet, tuberculosis cases had tripled during the war. Archbishop Richard J. Cushing of Boston called upon Massachusetts parishes to support the effort, and the Church of Saint Anthony of Padua organized a committee of volunteers to raise funds and collect supplies.[51]

As the war drew to a close, Italians in Fitchburg also learned about the heroism of their soldiers overseas. Lieutenant Leonard J. Lanzilotti had joined the National Guard in 1935 and went on active duty with the army in 1942 as an infantry commander. As the fighting waned in Aachen, Germany, he volunteered to negotiate the surrender of a four-story fortified building (*donker*) that was the holdout of a substantial German force. Lanzilotti entered and met the commander, who threatened to shoot him before Lanzilotti advised him to observe the American tanks ringing the building. The lieutenant averted what would have been a bloody battle and achieved the surrender of 3,500 Germans without firing a shot. A short while later, while his unit was in the Huertengen Forest, he was captured and sent to a Nazi prison camp. Patton's forces liberated the camp months later, and Lanzilotti returned home to his family, some seventy pounds lighter. He finished his military career with the Silver Star, a Purple Heart, the Bronze Star, and a Combat Infantryman Badge.[52]

But not everyone who left returned home, and the parish of Saint Anthony of Padua paid a heavy price. The first of the war dead was Gino Pallozzi, whose mother had immigrated from Revine Lago in the Veneto and ran a small grocery store in Fitchburg. His father worked in a cotton mill. Gino was born in 1916 and graduated from high school in 1933.

He joined the US Army's coast artillery and was posted to California, where he was taken ill and died. In the Pacific theater Alphonse DiNardo, son of an Italian grocer, worked for the Internal Revenue Service (IRS) as a tax collector in Boston and served as Chief Yeoman for the U.S. Navy on a destroyer escort, the USS *Underhill.* The ship was off Luzon in the Philippines when Japanese aircraft and two midget submarines torpedoed the vessel, splitting it in two. Gino was posthumously award a Purple Heart and his mother became the first Gold Star Mother in St. Anthony's parish.[53] Charles Simontacchi, whose family was from the Milan area, joined the US Marines and died in December 1945 from injuries sustained in the line of duty in the Pacific. Another Fitchburg Marine, Joseph Belluardo, fought in Tarawa, in the Gilbert Islands, and was killed in action on Saipan in February 1945. One of the Italian American community's most promising young men was Livio DeBonis. A graduate of the University of Michigan, he joined the air wing of the US Navy in May 1941. He was on a routine patrol off the coast of Rio di Janeiro in July 1944 when his plane was lost. But for some who died, there was little detail in the newspaper reports. Among them is Anthony Spagnuolo, who enlisted as a private in the Army Air Corps in 1942 and died in a military hospital in Texas in 1945.

Another Fitchburg serviceman, Michael Addorisio, proved difficult to track in the records because his surname had been arbitrarily altered when he enlisted. The US Navy misspelled it as *Addorizzi* and inexplicably refused his requests for a correction, so it has remained spelled that way in the military records, despite his objections. His parents had immigrated to Massachusetts from Avellino in 1913, and he was employed by the Mastrangelo family's Angel Novelty Company as a woodworker. In October 1940 Addorisio enlisted as a gunner's mate and saw some of the worst of the Pacific war on the destroyer USS *Reid* in Kiska in the Aleutians, New Caledonia, Fiji Island, Guadalcanal, Wake, and Leyte Gulf. The ship's records show that the crew "was called to battle stations (condition red) an average of ten times day" as they supported General Douglas MacArthur's retaking of the Philippines. The USS *Reid* was escorting a convoy of troop transports when Addorisio was killed manning a gun against a kamikaze attack on his destroyer. The *Reid* was fighting off a simultaneous attack by twelve kamikaze planes when one crashed into the ship's magazine, causing a massive detonation inside the ship. It sank, losing more than half its crew, in December 1944.[54]

The majority of Saint Anthony's Fitchburg sons died in the European theater. Thomas Bica, born in the tiny republic of San Marino in Italy, earned a Purple Heart fighting with the 119th infantry in the Netherlands, where he died a few months after entering the service in 1944. In December 1944 Samuel Spadafore was killed while fighting with the infantry in Belgium, and Joseph Tisa went missing in action in France in late 1944 (Tisa's death was later confirmed in February 1945). Joseph Testagrossa, a musician and a graduate of Fitchburg High School, had also worked for the Angel Novelty Company; in 1943 he enlisted in the Army Air Corps. His bomber went down over the Adriatic in 1944. [Testagrossa's death was confirmed in December of 1945 and he was awarded a Purple Heart and an Air Medal. Three more young men died in France between October and November 1944: Pasquale Sardo, John Chivilo, and Salvatore Lunetta. All three were infantrymen who died fighting in France. The weight of the losses in Saint Anthony's parish was magnified by the large number drawn from its population of a thousand parishioners, as well as by the fact that their deaths all occurred within a span of little more than a year.

Worse was to come as the fighting centered on the Italian peninsula. Lawrence Cravedi, the nephew of a Great War American veteran from Piacenza, fought at Casablanca, Sicily, Salerno, and Naples and died at Anzio. The parents of Anthony Francavilla had left Avellino for Massachusetts and raised their son in Fitchburg. They received word in May 1944 he had been killed in action in Italy. The last to die in Italy was Paul Cardullo who had enlisted in 1942 and later joined the 756th Tank Battalion, which was engaged at the brutal Battle of Cassino. The Germans held out in the Tuscan monastery for thirty days of fighting.

Cardullo won a posthumous Purple Heart as part of a unit that suffered 640 casualties and saw 111 killed in action.

Did the bravery of these men and women erase the stain of being labeled enemy aliens? The Roosevelt administration was torn as some advised that foreign-born aliens must be not only registered but also interned. On the West Coast, Lieutenant General John L. DeWitt and a number of civilian groups called for the internment of all enemy aliens, and some went so far as to call for the internment of the children of the foreign born. Historian Salvatore LaGumina has written of the emotional ups and down of being an Italian in New York City during World War II.[55]

FDR was most concerned with German Americans as a potential threat, unflatteringly and off-handedly dismissing Italians as "a lot of opera singers."[56] When alien registration began, US attorney general Francis Biddle had tried to soften the blow by stating that it would not entail a "witch hunt or prosecution of law-abiding citizens"; Earl Harrison, the director of registration, had likewise insisted that "no 'witch hunt' of aliens will be tolerated" and that registration "does not carry with it any stigma or implication of hostility."[57]

In Massachusetts, where every student learns about Salem and the witch trials, the concept of a witch hunt is eerily familiar. As the 1944 elections drew closer, some advisers warned Roosevelt of the hazards to Democrats in the Northeast if the Italian American community were alienated. Congressional elections might be seriously affected, and the Democrats could lose their majority. Biddle gave a speech entitled "Americans of Italian Origin" in October of 1942 that sought to mend fences with the Italian American electorate. He quoted Giuseppe Mazzini and spoke glowingly of the Risorgimento and Rome. Denouncing Mussolini as having "hidden himself behind a curtain of German steel," Biddle referred to the roundup of "some 600,000 Italians, technically alien enemies,"[58] and said he knew that in time it would be proved "they were not enemies at all."[59] After ten months of "unprecedented exercise of wartime vigilance," Biddle announced that the government had interned "only 228, or fewer than one-twentieth of one percent!"[60] But the reward came at the end of his address of October 19, 1942: "Italians would no longer be classed as alien enemies."[61]

To Biddle's credit, he did not leave it at that but returned to New York in April 1943 to address the Italian American Labor Council on the same subject, praising Italians whose "first loyalty and love [is] to the land where they had chosen to live." He pointed to Hitler's misuse of Italian troops: "invariably the honor of perishing was given [to] the Italian soldier." Biddle called for the Italians to "cast off this mantle" and abandon their support for the Axis.[62] Even Mussolini had recognized the situation; in July 1943 he wrote to Hitler protesting that "the sacrifice of my country cannot have as its main aim that of delaying a direct attack on Germany."[63] But it did serve that purpose, and the crushing blows that ended the war in southern Europe once again fell on central and northern Italy.

In the end, despite the praise for Italian American heroism and the enormous sacrifices made, it would remain a long time before the position of Italians was fully rehabilitated. During World War II Italian had been deemed the language of the enemy; Italian-language broadcasters, writers, and even instructors were among those rounded up for internment. Public schools shut down Italian-language programs, and radio stations eliminated Italian-language broadcasts. The blow to the image of Italy as the source of art, music, and culture (as well as the physical destruction of the country itself) was immense.

In the postwar era central Massachusetts public schools did not return to teaching the Italian language; colleges and universities that had once run Italian-language programs did not reinstate the subject. The prominence of Mussolini's fascism and its alliance with Nazi Germany had stigmatized Italian language and culture in the 1940s in a way that would not be erased in a decade or two. The second generation, those who went from being enemy aliens to being war heroes, helped to erase that legacy, but it was Italian American social clubs and fraternal organizations, like

Leominster's IACC, that went to work raising funds to pay for Italian-language programs in parochial schools and decades later at Leominster High School. Eventually, their support brought Italian back to area public high schools, but the rebuilding effort continues into the present.[64]

The Fitchburg church lost fourteen young men in the Pacific and European theaters of war. How is one to memorialize those who sacrificed their lives in the war? The parishioners of Saint Anthony's wanted a special memorial for their fallen sons that would honor both the men and their patriotism. An area next to the church was set aside for a tall flagpole above a memorial column. Mounted on the memorial is a bronze plaque bearing the names of the fallen soldiers and sailors. Each Memorial Day members of the Italian American World War Veterans Post place a wreath there after the annual military mass to honor those who died.

The patriotic sacrifices of the second generation of Italian Americans in the far-flung fields of conflict truly altered the negative image of Italians in Massachusetts. From one small parish, young men and women had volunteered to serve their country. Many of them died fighting in the Pacific, off the coast of Brazil, in France, Belgium, the Netherlands, and—even more tragically—in their ancestral home of Italy. Those who returned from the war to build new lives faced the question whether their identity would be that of Italian Americans or simply Americans.

NOTES

1. For Scalabrini's letters, see *For the Love of Immigrants*, ed. Silvano Tomasi (New York: Center for Migration Studies, 2000). For Scalabrinians at Bassano del Grappa, see "Delle fotografie dell'Archivio degli Scalabriniani sull'emigrazione," in *Una valigia piena di America: Antiche immagini fotografiche dell'emigrazione italiana nelle Americhe*, ed. Italian Ufficio centrale per I beni librari e gli istituti culturale, xxxiii and 374. Reverend Giuseppe Chiminello was first assigned to Spirito Santo in Providence, Rhode Island, from 1925 to 1932 (www.liguri.net/lepietremare/2202/viaggio.htm).

2. Martin Blinkhorn, *Mussolini and Fascist Italy* (London: Routledge, 1994), 20.

3. Ibid., 34–36.

4. Cavagnaro et al., *Il Delitto Matteotti*; see also Mauro Canali and Spencer DiScala, "Matteotti's Murder and the Rise of the Totalitarian State," *i-Italy: Italian/American Digital Project*, May 25, 2014 (www.i-italy.org/38083/giacomo-matteotti-s-murder-and-rise-totalitarian-state).

5. "Il Duce: Key Man of the Mediterranean," *Newsweek*, May 13, 1940; "Mussolini Unsheathes His Sword for Axis," *Newsweek*, June 17, 1940.

6. "Apr. 13, 1933 First CCC Enrollees Arrive at Fort Devens," *Mass Moments*, Apr. 13, 2005 (www.massmoments.org/print_moment.cfm?mid=112); Shary Page Berg, *The Civilian Conservation Corps: Shaping the Forests and Parks of Massachusetts; A Statewide Survey of Civilian Conservation Corps Resources* (Boston: Office of Historic Resources, 1999).

7. *Sentinel* October 10, 1933, 6.

8. "Relief Projects," *Sentinel* (Fitchburg), Oct. 10, 1933, 6; also see the paper's coverage in "CCC Softball Team," June 8, 1934, 8; and "Large Crowd Enjoys CCC Entertainment," May 17, 1935, 11.

9. "Supt. Sweeney Asks Extreme Care to Avoid Park Tree Debris Fire," Fitchburg *Sentinel*, October 7, 1938, 1.

10. "Unofficial Announcement ... Merchants Keep Open the Afternoon of Columbus Day," *Sentinel* (Fitchburg), Oct. 7, 1938, 1.

11. Donna Gabaccia, *Italy's Many Diasporas* (Seattle: University of Washington Press, 2000), 82.

12. "Softball Team Shoot Four Deer in Royalston," *Sentinel* (Fitchburg), Dec. 11, 1939.
13. *History of Saint Anthony of Padua Parish*, 72.
14. "Parkhill Mills to be Closed," Fitchburg *Sentinel*, February 29, 1928, 1.
15. Massachusetts Bureau of Immigration, *Who Is Your Neighbor? Objects and Functions of the Massachusetts Bureau of Immigration* (Boston: Massachusetts Bureau of Immigration, 1918).
16. *Who is Your Neighbor?*, (Boston: Massachusetts Bureau of Immigration), 1918, 5.
17. Ibid., 6–7.
18. "Urged to Prepare for Citizenship. Italian-Speaking Residents Are Offered Assistance," Fitchburg *Sentinel*, February 13, 1928, 3.
19. The Basic Naturalization Act of 1906 had codified the oath's language, as noted earlier, to "absolutely and entirely renounce and abjure all allegiance and fidelity to any foreign prince, potentate, state, or sovereignty"; US Citizenship and Immigration Services (www.uscis.gov). See also "Urged to Prepare for Citizenship," *Sentinel* (Fitchburg), Feb. 13, 1928, 3.
20. Kielty worked continuously for forty-seven years in the Americanization Office. "Never Too Late to Learn," *Montachusett Review*, undated, Margaret Kielty biography file, Fitchburg Historical Society, Fitchburg, Massachusetts; "Urged to Prepare for Citizenship," *Sentinel* (Fitchburg), Feb. 13, 1928, 3.
21. "Americanization Classes Enjoy Tree Parties," *Sentinel* (Fitchburg), Dec. 23, 1931.
22. "Night Schools on Citizenship Open Monday," *Sentinel* (Fitchburg), Oct. 14, 1932.
23. Pia Cattel Ballarin, Sogni d'Oro Oral History.
24. "Alien Residents Here May Reach Total of 4000," Fitchburg *Sentinel*, September 12, 1940, 1.
25. On the Custodial Detention List, see Rose Scherini, "When Italian Americans Were 'Enemy Aliens,'" *Una storia segreta*, ed. Laurence DeStasi (Berkeley: Heyday Books, 2001), 10. In addition, see the following *Sentinel* articles: "Will 'Print' 2000 Aliens in This City," Aug. 3, 1940; "Aliens over Fourteen Will Be 'Printed' at Post Office," Aug. 12, 1940; "Alien Residents Here May Reach Total of 4,000" Sept. 12, 1940.
26. "Alien Residents Here May Reach Total of 4000," Fitchburg *Sentinel*, September 12, 1940, 1.

27. At the time, if a woman with US citizenship married an alien, she could lose her citizenship. "Think Alien Population All Listed," *Sentinel* (Fitchburg), Dec. 27, 1940.
28. "FBI Checks Here on 391 Nationals of Germany, Italy," Fitchburg *Sentinel*, December 11, 1941, 1.
29. Ibid.
30. "FBI Checks Here on 391 Nationals Of Germany, Italy — 2 Questioned in Leominster, Many Under Surveillance; Arrests Are Expected," Fitchburg *Sentinel*, December 11, 1941, 1.
31. "FBI Checks Here," page 1.
32. "All Enemy Aliens Must Re-Register Here Feb. 9 to 28," Fitchburg *Sentinel*, January 20, 1942, 1.
33. "All Enemy Aliens Must Re-Register," *Sentinel* (Fitchburg), Jan. 20, 1942.
34. "All Enemy Aliens Must Obtain Certificates of Identification," Fitchburg *Sentinel*, February 2, 1942, 3.
35. "All Enemy Aliens Must Obtain Certificates of Identification," *Sentinel* (Fitchburg), Feb. 2, 1942; *Annual Report of the Division of Immigration and Americanization*, May 23, 1940, 5 (http://archive.org).
36. Shortwave converters could be installed on most home radios by the early 1930s. Alan Wells, *World Broadcasting: A Comparative View* (Norwood, NJ: Ablex, 1996), 80–82.
37. "All But 32 Aliens Registered Here in Enemy Roundup," *Sentinel* (Fitchburg), Mar. 2, 1942.
38. Bylaws of the Italian American Citizens Club, 1936, archive record IACC MS 27, box 1 folder 1, Leominster Historical Society, Leominster, Massachusetts.
39. "Speakers Urge Loyalty to US at Charter Presentation Ceremony," *Sentinel* (Fitchburg), Feb. 23, 1938, 3.
40. Ibid.
41. Ibid.
42. Ibid.
43. Ibid.
44. Headline from Fitchburg *Sentinel* (January 19, 1942, 1) reproduced in *History of Saint Anthony of Padua Parish* (2009), 33.
45. "Bowlers Now Soldiers," *Sentinel* (Fitchburg), Aug. 12, 1944.
46. Giorgio Garatti, "La guerra e il bombadamento del 7 aprile 1944" (diary entry; www.sportrevigiano.it).
47. Today, the town has a small resistance museum near the bridge and a memorial on the Viale dei Martiri. Sonia Residori, "Commemorazione

dei caduti del Grappa," Istituto Storio della Resistenza, Vicenza, Sept. 27 2008 (www.istrevi.it); Federica Magnabosco, "L'eccidio di Bassano Del Grappa" (http://piccolimmaestri.blogspot.com).

48. Carlet, *Lago Ricordi*, 132.

49. "Fitchburg WAC Works Off Duty Decking Graves," *Sentinel* (Fitchburg), May 4, 1945, 1.

50. Fitchburg WAC," Fitchburg *Sentinel*, July 27, 1944, 1. Photograph and headline "Fitchburg WAC In the Front Rank," Fitchburg *Sentinel*, August 7, 1945, 1.

51. "American Aid to Italy Committee Formed Here," *Sentinel* (Fitchburg), June 1, 1945.

52. "Fitchburg Hero of Big Capture Returns Home," *Sentinel* (Fitchburg), May 23, 1945; and "About Town: Lanzilotti Retires," *Sentinel* (Fitchburg), May 15, 1968.

53. "The Italian-American Citizens Club Will Hold a Program on Mother's Day," Fitchburg *Sentinel*, May 5, 1943, 2.

54. USS *Reid* 369 (www.ussredi369.org/History.htm); 1940 US census records; author's interview with Rose Anne Addorisio, 2012.

55. On hysteria in California, see Gloria Ricci Lothrop, "Unwelcome in Freedom's Land: The Impact of World War II on Italian Aliens in Southern California," in *Una storia segreta*, ed. Laurence DiStasi (Berkeley: Heyday Books, 2001), 161–194. On Italian Americans in New York City during the war, see Salvatore J. LaGumina, *The Humble and the Heroic: Wartime Italian Americans* (New York: Cambria Press, 2006).

56. See Gary R. Mormino, *Immigrants on the Hill: Italian-Americans in St. Louis*, (Columbia, Missouri: University of Missouri Press, 2002), 222.

57. "Plans Completed for Alien Registration," *New York Times*, July 31, 1940; and Francis Biddle's radio address of Aug. 26, 1940. Biddle is quoted in "Alien Registration Lauded by Lehman," *New York Times*, August 26, 1940, page 17. Texts of other Biddle speeches on U.S. Department of Justice web site www.justice.gov

58. Biddle, *Americans of Italian Origin*, 6.

59. Ibid., 8.

60. Ibid., 9.

61. Quoted in Jerre Mangione, "Concentration Camps: American Style," in *Una Storia Segreta: The Secret History of Italian American Evacuation and Internment during World War II*, ed. Laurence DeStasi (Berkeley: Heyday Books, 2001), 118. Francis Biddle, "Americans of Italian Origin" (radio address) Oct. 12, 1942. Text available at www.justice.gov.

62. Francis Biddle, "Address to the Italian American Labor Council Four Freedoms Award," Apr. 3, 1943.

63. Mussolini quoted in Martin Clark, *Mussolini Profiles in Power* (London: Pearson Longman, 2005), 288.

64. In Fitchburg, though Saint Anthony's Elementary School continued instruction in Italian, it was not until the 1990s that private support emerged—from the Amelia Gallucci-Cirio Foundation—to return Italian-language education to Fitchburg and Leominster's public schools.

CHAPTER 9

SUBURBS AND SUPERMARKETS

LIFE IN THE 1950S

The trials of the World War II era ended in 1945, and Fitchburg's Church of Saint Anthony of Padua saw its young men and women return from war, many as decorated heroes. The second generation came back with dreams of a suburban life and ambitions for a new lifestyle. A number of them had come to maturity during the war and joined the professions afterward. Postwar prosperity and the GI Bill made it easier for them to succeed.

Many young men and women now had a chance for education and a better life beyond the tenements, foundries, and quarries. War veterans applied for civil service jobs or completed their education with government support as a reward for their sacrifices. The children of grocery-store owners and quarrymen finished their educations and became physicians, dentists, bankers, lawyers, and accountants. Once in better jobs, they moved to new areas where single-family housing promised privacy and comfort, as well as an escape from the old tenements of their parents. Contractors who had employed gangs of Italian pick-and-shovel workers began buying up farmland and developing new suburban homes for eager buyers. A good job meant a fatter paycheck and perhaps a new home and a car.

The days when children returned home with their paychecks, handed them to their parents, and submitted to parental advice were ending. Adherence to *la famiglia* and parental control were challenged as the younger generation considered whom to marry. Because the Cleghorn neighborhood was home to a variety of ethnic groups, marrying someone from the neighborhood often meant crossing an ethnic boundary. In addition, numerous soldiers returned home having found partners who did not fit their parents' image of a potential spouse. The best choice would have been someone from their home *paese* who was known to the family. The next-best option was someone from some other part of Italy, but this was often the cause of great parental anxiety. Whether northerners or southerners, parents often found the idea of marrying from the other end of the peninsula a problem. Some second-generation Italians humorously referred to such unions as mixed marriages. But by far the most troublesome selection, for many parents, was a non-Italian spouse, and a marrying non-Catholic raised serious issues in the church.

Paul San Clemente, a lawyer and second-generation son of the Veneto, described how many of his parents' generation wanted their children to have an education and "become Americans ... they were very eager to have children Americanized." But once the second generation had made the leap, this often led to challenges and tension within the family and within the larger Italian community. San Clemente noted that the social groups in the church, like the Pietro Perzia Society for those from Sicily, had died out in the postwar era "because the children were Americanized and didn't accept parents' traditions." Members of the second generation moved away from the old neighborhoods literally but also distanced themselves socially from the clubs that celebrated regional culture and dialects. Many of these organizations dissipated once the first generation had passed away because, as San Clemente recalled, "there was no momentum to perpetuate the organizations." Having lost the dialect, most children moved away from groups that they associated with the immigrant generation. The Venetian Club, the Carlo Alberto Society, and other groups all began to decline the 1950s. San Clemente pointed out that in his generation, "the tendency to marry Italians was not as strong," recalling that among his own friends, "60 to 70 percent of the marriages were between Irish and Italian." He observed he and his sisters had all married Irish partners and concluded that "intermarriage became common."[1]

San Clemente's generation straddled the divide, but that obedience was eroding. He associated the acceptance of absolute parental authority with respect for the father, which was "stronger among Italians than any other group." But this had faded with what he termed the era's "100 percent assimilation," which led to a "clash more profound and direct." His father had been a strong advocate of education, and San Clemente had earned a law degree. But he saw an even greater change as the third generation matured: "You educate them, bring them up, send them off to college and [when] they come back, they aren't your children anymore."[2]

With marriage came the choice of where to live. The traditional Water Street neighborhood's corner stores were losing business as Italian Americans moved to the suburbs. The old tenements that had housed quarry workers around Rollstone Hill were in decline. The buildings degraded over time as fewer workers competed for space, and the newly married sought a way out of the old neighborhoods below the hill. At the pit where six working quarries had once excavated simultaneously, now only the Rollstone Quarry was active.

A new priest arrived in 1946 at Saint Anthony's parish, the Reverend Nicolas Mongiello, and he faced the changes of the postwar decade. In 1935 the parish had established the Holy Rosary Mission Church in a small wooden hall near the Cleghorn fire station. It was within easy walking distance of anyone in the neighborhood and was staffed by the priests and deacons of Saint Anthony's. Over the decades, hundreds of parishioners had walked from the Cleghorn tenements, but Cleghorn's factories were slowing and its tenements in disrepair. The businesses along Fairmount Street struggled as Italians and French Canadian residents drifted away, and other ethnic groups moved in, accelerating the exodus. The remaining employers were the shoe factories; heavy industries were declining in the face of foreign competition, and the cotton mills had already been moved south.

The Water Street neighborhood, once lined with Italian shops, had seen few new immigrants arrive since the 1924 Quota Acts almost entirely closed off Italian immigration. The demand for Italian imported goods waned as the second generation became less committed to the ancestral foodways. Public schools exposed children to American foods, and small grocers could not compete with the larger chain markets that were established in Fitchburg. The children of parishioners from Water Street were moving to new housing developments in other parts of the city and to leafy suburbs in Lunenburg and other neighboring towns. Italians from the Avellino region had settled in large numbers in Leominster and established and Italian American parish there in 1935. By the postwar era, Saint Anna's had its own elementary school. Additional parishes in the area offered options to Fitchburg's Italians.

Saint Anthony's parish needed to hold on to its Italian American population, and Mongiello pursued three key strategies. First, the church began construction of a $400,000 elementary school in 1946 to attract young families. The Venerini Sisters taught school and offered Italian-language classes, as well. The parish did not choose to compete at the secondary level since there were already three well-established Roman Catholic high schools in the city. Saint Bernard's Central Catholic High School had been established in 1920 by the Irish parish and became co-educational in 1927; it later became a regional high school operated by the Worcester diocese. Holy Family High School, a secondary school for young women, was linked to the French-speaking parish but drew many young women from the Italian community. The third, Notre Dame Preparatory, was established in 1952 as an exclusive all-boys college prep school unaffiliated with the local parishes and staffed by the Brothers of the Sacred Heart.[3] This broad access to private secondary schools reflects the growing commitment to education in this area and the economic power of the Italian community, as well as the larger Catholic community in central Massachusetts. Second-generation Italian Americans had emerged as a professional class and wanted their children to attend college; the presence of a state college for teacher education in Fitchburg made that much more possible.[4]

Saint Anthony's launched a second project in 1950 that targeted the challenge of suburbanization more directly. The second generation wanted modern homes in the suburbs, but the parish wanted to keep them near the church. Father Mongiello and his assistant, Father John Capuano, identified Belmont Hill, less than a half-mile from the church building, as the nearest tract of open land. A large upland meadow owned by the Guglielmi family at the end of Belmont Street stretched up a hillside into acres of undeveloped farmland, where Mongiello planned to build ten single-family homes. The church bought the parcel, and plans expanded as it was subdivided into sixty lots. When the parish announced the project to the press, it was called "Housing for Newlyweds." Model homes were described, and rules for the transfer of property were laid down: lots would be sold to couples only if at least one of the partners was Italian.

At the ground-breaking ceremony, Father Mongiello took the controls of the tractor to begin the earth-moving project. Streets were laid out and named for Catholic saints, including Saint Peter, Saint Paul, and Saint Anthony, along with Mount Carmel Street. Costs were to be controlled, and houses were to be constructed for less than five thousand dollars on a concrete slab or for six thousand dollars with a full basement. Located in what was referred to as "the heart of the Italian district," first ten lots and then another fifteen were set off for homes with central heating, hardwood floors, and full basements. After life in triple-deckers, many young parishioners found the hope of a modern home in a new Italian neighborhood very inviting. Father Capuano was appointed head of the new Saint Anthony's Parish Housing Committee and guided the project along, unlocking the door to the first completed home in 1950.[5]

The original homes were simple, boxy "Cape Cod" cottages with pitched roofs, small yards, and driveways. But the lots were large enough for garages to be added to driveways and for the houses to be expanded a bit. Today some have been nearly doubled and include covered decks and large additions constructed to accommodate expanding families, but the original intent of constructing a development that would anchor a new generation in the neighborhood succeeded. Some homes have been inherited by the third generation, and the parish, as well as its elementary school, has survived the sort of shrinkage that has led to consolidation elsewhere.

The third strategy that the parish of Saint Anthony implemented to draw back those who had left Cleghorn was to rebuild the mission church as an independent parish on a new site closer to the suburbs where so many had settled. Large areas of open land south of Cleghorn bordered the Electric Avenue and Oak Hill Road area. Flat, buildable lots were being carved out as contractors competed in building one-story developments. The small Holy Rosary Mission had been organized to serve Italians who lived too far from Saint Anthony's to attend regularly, but with the exodus from the tenements that site was no longer convenient. The new Madonna of the Holy Rosary Church opened in 1958 with a thousand parishioners. Located on the northern fringe of Cleghorn, in a new neighborhood of modern one-story homes and close to the newly extended east-west state highway (Route 2), it was a short drive from a large suburb, as well as from a private country club called Oak Hill.[6] It was ideally situated to attract those who had already moved away. The church was of a modern design, built on one level, and was surrounded by a large parking lot, symbolic of the way that the car had changed everything.

As a whole, Saint Anthony's strategy was a response to the changing American lifestyle. The old neighborhoods were witnessing an exodus, and Saint Anthony's moved not only to attract the new generation but also to reach out to them nearer to where they lived. Parish leaders hoped that by offering Italian Americans a good school and opportunities for affordable housing, Saint Anthony's would retain a third generation of Italian Americans. For those who had already moved away, Madonna of the Holy Rosary offered another, smaller parish that could be supported by Italians and other Catholics in the suburbs.[7]

The root of the social changes in this era was the challenge of the car-oriented 1950s lifestyle. Ethnic food was something the second generation wanted to escape in the 1950s, and negative stereotypes linked Italian immigrants with garlic and olive oil, leading many second-generation families to adopt American-style food. This era saw corner groceries give way to chain supermarkets; three lined Main Street, and others appeared in Cleghorn, which had been the domain of ethnic grocers. As Italian grocers felt the squeeze in the face of discount chain stores and the appeal of large-scale supermarkets designed for car-driving shoppers, the trend was countered by two families that established successful chains of their own, the Caravellas and the DiGeronimos; these Italian grocers found new ways to attract their old customers as their natural constituency moved away.

Grocery stores had always been a fluid sector of the Italian American economy. In 1919 there were 119 corner stores and markets spread throughout the city of Fitchburg, and eleven of them were owned by Italians. These grocers included French, Jewish, Polish, and Irish corner stores, as well as a handful of well-established markets serving the elites, like the S. S. Pierce and the Great Atlantic and Pacific Tea Company (A&P). The Finnish socialists organized a large cooperative that combined a grocery store, oil-delivery service, and a farmer's feed and grain store. A Polish socialist cooperative and the INTO (Into Co-operative Stores, Inc.) Cooperative[8], with four branches, served other ethnic communities by selling groceries at low cost and offering their members a year-end divided.

The Italian community did not establish a cooperative but witnessed the collapse of the padroni's dominance. Angelo Seretto, discussed in chapter 3, had begun selling roasted peanuts from a cart in 1888, and by 1919 he was head of his own business empire importing Italian products and running an employment agency for Italian laborers. Seretto's business grew so large in the golden days of immigration that he could claim branch offices in Rhode Island and Boston, as well as Naples. His primary competitor was Frank Robino, a young and ambitious immigrant who had landed in 1898 at age fifteen and within a decade progressed from a store clerk to owner of a grocery store, a confectionary, and a fruit shop. Robino then became associated with the Banca Stabile & Co. of Boston. In 1919 he moved up Water Street, practically next door to Seretto, and advertised himself as a real estate agent, bank representative, Italian interpreter, agent for steamer tickets, merchant of Italian newspapers and groceries, and importer of olive oil. But after the 1924 Quota Act, the padroni were no longer needed. Instead of focusing on work with new immigrants, the padroni Seretto and Robino turned to other concerns. And the independent Italian grocers turned most of Water Street into an Italian colony where a variety of entrepreneurial concerns flourished for a generation. Seretto built his empire to an estimated half-million dollars, but his fortune was wiped out in the Depression.[9]

The eleven Italian grocers had struggled to survive until the Depression era. Luigi Carbone and his brother were at opposite ends of Water Street, and Vincenzo Cetrino's variety store sat on one corner of the crossroads at Fifth Street. In the Patch, business rivals were always close by, and another Italian grocery store was on the opposite corner. But the lack of parking along Water Street began to cut into their patronage after the Second World War. In Cleghorn two grocers anchored Beech Street, just below the quarry, and Giovanni Moretto from Rosà in the Veneto had a small shop near Kimball Street offering Italian imports, fresh butchered meat, and candies. He worked with his wife, and they did tailoring as a sideline. Together they supported nine children with the store until 1934, during the Great Depression, when the pressure to extend credit to his unemployed neighbors increased. Moretto ran short of cash, his wife died unexpectedly, and he struggled as a widower to raise nine children, finally falling back upon his skill as a *sarto* (tailor) to establish a new business, which he did by the 1940s. Moretto's store was sold to a new Italian owner, Guido Zilli and Bianchi. Giuseppe Altieri ran a grocery store farther up Beech Street, closer to the Leighton Street tenements and the quarries. The Altieri family bought the Moretto store and converted it into the Hillside Café, which became a popular watering hole for men on their way down the hill from the Rollstone Quarry and for workers from the paper mills hiking up Beech Street after a long shift.[10]

But by 1943 much was in flux. The number of Italian grocers had nearly doubled to twenty stores citywide, even as the total number of stores dropped from 119 to 98. The chain markets and the cooperatives were consolidating, and the days of the specialty grocer were numbered. In the 1950s the Caravella family and the DiGeronimo brothers emerged to compete with large chains like the A&P. By 1964 Fitchburg was home to half the number of markets that had existed a few decades earlier, but most supermarkets were now Italian-owned, and fourteen small grocers still hung on as specialty or meat markets.

Only three families managed to survive as small grocers: the Carbone, Romano, and Giacoppe families. But by the early 1950s the four Carbone brothers' stores were reduced to a single shop, and the two Romano brothers separated when one crossed the Nashua River to establish a meat market on the Irish side of the bridge. Billy Romano carried on the tradition for fifty-nine years, specializing in meats and selling produce from the family's twenty-nine-acre farm in Lunenburg. Romano stored meat, sausage, and fresh turkeys in a giant ice box that required three hundred pounds of ice to keep the meat cool. The Romano brothers had built the store to include a coffee shop next door and owned the building, so they managed to survive the onslaught of the supermarkets.[11]

In Cleghorn's Fairmount Street neighborhood, northerner Emilio Cravedi had a well-established store that operated with a changing group of partners, and eventually his brother joined him. Together they established a second store near the paper mills in west Fitchburg that attracted people commuting to work at the mills. The stores that survived often advertised themselves with the owner's name as "cash markets," reflecting the fact that extending credit to customers had destroyed many small entrepreneurs.

Enterprising sons of corner-store families began expanding their concept of what a store should be. The model of a small corner store filled with Italian imported goods and convenient to the tenements was outdated. The growth in car ownership and the reality of commuting to a job in the city from a home in the suburbs led to centrally located stores with parking and prominent advertising to draw customers from a distance. Among these was Tom's Cash Market, operated by Anthony "Tom" Caravella and his parents on Fairmount Street, in the central business district of Cleghorn. Caravella was interviewed decades after having built his grocery empire for a newspaper piece, "The Saga of Tom Caravella," in which he explained what had spurred him to go into business. In 1937, working for someone else as a grocery clerk, he asked for a raise, was refused, and walked out. He opened a store of his own with the aid of his parents in 1939. Working with his two younger brothers, a sister, and his extended family, he built up the store in Cleghorn to gross two hundred dollars each week. They eventually moved to a larger location closer to the center, but by the early 1950s Cleghorn merchants were feeling the out-migration of their customers.

In desperation, the business district ran full-page advertisements in the local papers trumpeting "Cleghorn Monday" as a shopping day with special offers. But shoppers were drawn to the downtown area, where chain markets like the A&P offered bargains, and to the new John Fitch Highway development, where large discount stores had opened. More traditional stores on Main Street felt the decline as new customers refused to fight for metered parking spots.

In 1953 the Caravella family abandoned the small cash market to establish a chain of their own. Tom Caravella bought an oval-shaped lot where five major roads intersected in front and the Nashua River curved around to the rear. No conventional building could fit on the lot, and the postwar car culture demanded parking space rather than proximity to the tenements. The Caravellas built a round supermarket called Tom's Food World, a modern design that symbolized the new suburban 1950s lifestyle. The Fitchburg *Sentinel* called it a "circular-shaped Arabian Nights structure."[12] It was ideal for the new consumer's car-oriented shopping: the round building was ringed with parking spots, and a roofed walkway protected them from rain. This was not a walking destination but was on the path of drivers traveling from the mills in Cleghorn or in west Fitchburg. Tom Caravella's younger brother, Joseph, took charge of advertising, creating a logo that featured the round store, as well as a "Suzy Shopper" discount club. Brother Dominic managed the produce section, and their sister managed the finances. The Caravellas emphasized hiring from the Italian community and made charitable contributions: at Thanksgiving they hosted a turkey dinner for US Army service members from Fort Devens who lived near their Ayer store. The family operation expanded with construction of the Thunderbird Motor Lodge, Motel Linda, a restaurant, a half-dozen other supermarkets (many of them round) across central and eastern Massachusetts, and a real estate business—all by the flagship store's tenth anniversary.[13]

Perhaps the earliest supermarket in the area was established by the Caravellas' rivals: the DiGeronimo family's Victory Supermarkets had begun in neighboring Leominster and then expanded into Fitchburg. Although they were from Fitchburg, brothers Louis and Joseph had established a grocery store in Leominster in 1923. The first two DiGeronimo brothers celebrated America's victory in the Great War by taking the patriotic *Victory* name and a red, white, and blue flag logo that, like Tom's Food World, appealed to a modern American identity rather than to a traditionally Italian one.

The DiGeronimos divided responsibility for the stores among the next generation's four brothers and eventually among members of the third generation. Victory expanded even more rapidly but focused on supermarkets and real estate. The family had developed twenty stores across central Massachusetts by the 1960s and by the 1970s had adopted a new "market square" store design that attracted the attention of the Harvard Business School. Asked about their success, Anthony DiGeronimo credited "a lot of hard work. I started out working 80 hours a week. Come to think of it, I'm still working 80 hours a week." He also expressed appreciation for his opportunities, from "growing up in the Patch and to ... this kind of success ... only in America."[14]

By the 1950s Italian merchants were moving out of the Water Street area because many of their customers had already left. Barone's Pharmacy, begun decades earlier as a family enterprise, moved away from the area, and the second generation rapidly established separate pharmacies as many members of the Barone extended family earned pharmacists' degrees. They built throughout central Massachusetts until competition led them to sell out to CVS in the 1970s.

Frank Mastrangelo had arrived in Fitchburg at the beginning of the twentieth century and found it hard to do business with people who could not pronounce his name. His first business venture was as Angel the Tailor, in the trade he had learned in Italy, then he invented a wooden ruler-like device that could be used by tailors to calculate the position of cuffs on men's pants, and began selling the tool. After the arrival of his brother Alphonse, a carpenter, both turned to wood working. He transformed himself into Frank Angel, as mentioned earlier, and took over a small wooden-toy factory that he renamed Angel Novelty. But as the demand for postwar housing escalated, Angel Novelty shifted to supplying home construction with custom cabinetry. The enterprise succeeded in competing with carpenters who offered custom-built cabinets for postwar housing by creating a catalog of factory-made products to fill the demand for cheaper, quicker construction. After World War II, with the housing boom in full swing, he invented and patented a wooden combination window that relieved New England homeowners from hanging heavy storm windows. Frank Angel emphasized hiring his fellow Italians, and the business grew rapidly in the 1950s—keeping pace as contractors converted the Fitchburg area's farmland into suburban developments. Angel's designers produced a fresh catalog each year that catered to the changing tastes of a new generation.[15]

The Italian American portion of the electorate was also growing. The 1930s and 1940s emphasis on naturalization had been driven by the political tensions of the war era and enemy alien status. After 1945 many who had initially held on to their Italian citizenship had become naturalized citizens, and their children were voters. In neighboring Leominster, the Italian American Citizens Club (IACC) had been working since 1936 to elect Italian Americans to political office, whereas in Fitchburg the effort was less organized but nevertheless effective. In the postwar era the IACC helped returning veterans to take advantage of the civil service system and to apply for positions in the police and fire departments. In both cities it was the first time that Italians filled those jobs.

Fitchburg's Italian community had seen only small political gains, but in 1949 Peter J. Levanti emerged as the first Italian American candidate for mayor. He had begun as a successful businessman, running an express delivery company, and had then gathered support from two influential industrialists, the Crocker and Wallace families. His opponent, Mayor George W. Stanton, was well established, and Levanti's family recalled that Stanton had "the biggest machine in Fitchburg."[16] But Levanti worked to get out the Italian American vote and received public endorsements from a number of businesspeople in the Water Street community. In November 1949 Levanti became Fitchburg's first Italian American mayor. On a visit to speak to the IACC in Leominster, he praised the organization's political activism and wished aloud that such a group existed in Fitchburg. It did not take long; Levanti supporters went to work and established one. His

candidacy was supported by the Sons of Italy Lodge, and in 1960 Levanti
reached state office at a time when the man who would become the first
Italian American governor, John Volpe, was serving in the State House.[17]

The professions comprised another area where Italian Americans found
that only education, hard work, and persistence would lead to success.
Many of the first Italian doctors and lawyers in Fitchburg were people
who had relocated from elsewhere to the city, but the second generation
made gains in these professions. Italian Americans in Fitchburg could
find a host of familiar faces working as physicians, optometrists, dentists,
accountants, bank presidents, and lawyers, as well as businesspeople.

The Zarella family owned a small grocery store, but because neither
of their two sons wished to carry it forward, it was sold in 1958. Young
William Zarrella worked in the store but dreamed of an engineering
career. After studying at Holy Cross and Clark University, he went
to work for Gulf Research and Development as a leading petroleum
geologist. He was awarded the Man of the Year in his Pennsylvania
hometown, Fitchburg, and resided in Pennsylvania as an adult, afterwards
he went on an international lecture tour as leading petroleum geologist in
1960s. His brother, Lawrence, studied electrical engineering and designed
cell-phone systems for the ITT (International Telephone and Telegraph).
The Rollo family's oldest son, similarly, abandoned the corner store for
medical school and became a surgeon. The Addante Shoe Shop on Water
Street in the Patch was the first employer for young Joseph Addante,
who quipped, "If my father can fix people's shoes, I can fix people's feet."
He studied podiatry and traveled the world, lecturing at the University
of Rome.[18]

Ambitions for advancement were the stuff of dreams not only in
postwar Massachusetts. The destruction and hardships of war had ravaged
the Veneto. Rebuilding would take decades, and many could not find
work that would support their families. The desperation of the 1880s
repeated itself in the 1950s. Ferruccio Moz, a partisan nicknamed "Patria"
who had fought the Nazis and survived the war, struggled in Revine Lago

but could not live on his earnings. Worse yet, the only job he did find was abroad—as was the case for many in the Veneto after the Second World War. It was an ironic, bitter experience for someone who had fought the German invasion of his hometown to be forced by hardship to abandon it to work as a miner in Belgium. Moz survived the Marcinelle mine disaster and then returned to Revine Lago, but the agricultural economy could barely support his family. He died of silicosis in 2012.[19]

Osvaldo Grava from Revine Lago was typical of post-1945 Veneto migrants: his father had died during the war, and his widowed mother struggled to earn enough money to feed her two children. A part of the family had emigrated to central Massachusetts and Connecticut decades earlier, but America had since closed its doors. Grava decided to try Switzerland; he arrived there as an educated young man and steadily built his career. Initially, he was determined to support his mother and to earn enough to return home. But as Grava succeeded in Switzerland, he began to invest in property and collect vintage automobiles and he remained abroad. Others from Revine Lago who labored in Switzerland were not so lucky. The cemetery in Revine has a plaque engraved with the name of one son who worked in construction there and died on a work site.

New immigrants could move beyond Italy via the national airline Alitalia, but America remained closed to Italian immigration. Since the 1920 and 1924 Quota Acts, only 3,845 Italians were permitted yearly, a tiny fraction of the hundreds of thousands who had once arrived for seasonal work and permanent migration. America almost entirely shut out Italian immigrants for nearly a half century. Therefore, Veneto migrants focused their dreams far beyond war-damaged Europe and inaccessible America post-1945: Canada and Australia became the new destinations. Australia received three waves of migrants, and they became dominant in the fields related to construction. During World War II the Australian government had interned Italians and restricted others, but after the war Australia accepted Veneto immigrants who sought to join family members in Australia. Migration historians Loretta Baldassar and Ros Pesman termed this *circular migration*; it boomed in the jet age as mostly male Treviso migrants moved back and forth between the two countries. Eventually, many established homes in both places. The pattern of repression during earlier decades had been repeated in Canada, where immigration from Italy had been restricted after the boom in railroad construction ended in 1927. Thereafter, it was not until 1947 that sponsored immigration was opened for a limited number of new migrants. This allowed assimilated Italo-Canadians to apply for accelerated processing and permission for members of their family to join them.[20] Thus, even though the US Quota Act had disrupted the transnational networks to America that many Veneto migrants had established, by the 1950s there were new destinations. But for those living in central Massachusetts, it was their descendants who carved a new way of life in the postwar era.

In Fitchburg the second generation of Veneto migrants and other Italians had worked together, as families, in a variety of new ventures that abandoned the old business model of their parents. Corner groceries gave way to cash markets and later to supermarket chains. A very few managed to survive the leap, but those who did succeeded spectacularly. The Caravella, DiGeronimo, and Mastrangelo families built large empires by emphasizing the participation of brothers, sisters, and parents and by being attuned to the changing American lifestyle.

By the 1960s the old neighborhoods of Water Street's Patch, Cleghorn, and Rollstone Hill, where an Italian colony once flourished, had been abandoned by the second generation. The priests of Saint Anthony of Padua successfully adapted to suburbanization by building a school, a new housing development, and reshaping the mission church as a new parish in the suburbs. In 1964 on the bicentennial of the City of Fitchburg, Father John Capuano celebrated the success of Italians in Fitchburg; he wrote in the church bulletin that Saint Anthony's Church had a population of 3,255 and that nearly another thousand attended Madonna of the Holy Rosary: "That makes us over 4,000 Italo-Americans among the 45,000 inhabitants of our wonderful city." Capuano then described the contributions of Italian Americans: "During the last war, nearly 600 of our men and women defended the flag." He closed with a sentiment that might be seconded by many descendants of the reluctant migrants after a half-century of struggling to assimilate: "We like Fitchburg. We are glad to be here; we shall continue to contribute to the physical and moral splendor of our city."[21]

NOTES

1. Oral history interview (internal evidence collected by Doris Kirkpatrick) with Paul F. San Clemente, Fitchburg Historical Society, Fitchburg, Massachusetts.

2. Ibid.

3. "History of St Bernard's High School" (updated Sept. 11, 2012; http://stb.echalk.com/site res_view_template.aspx). The Notre Dame school emphasized French culture (elements of its school emblem from the fleur-de-lis) and Italian history (its yearbook noted "the powerful Romans carried their all-conquering aegis" as the "emblazoned escutcheon"); see *The Crusader 1957*, Brothers of the Sacred Heart.

4. Established in 1894 as the Normal School in Fitchburg, with its primary purpose being the preparation of women educators, in 1932 expanded to a four year institution and renamed State Teachers College. In 1965 it undergraduate programs were expanded and it was renamed Fitchburg State College and finally Fitchburg State University in 2010 to reflect its range of professional undergraduate and graduate degree programs.

5. "Church Parish Sponsors Housing for Newlyweds Plan to Build 60 One-Family Units Within 2 Years," and "Parish Sponsors Housing Will Build Homes to Cost not over $6000," undated clippings from the *Sentinel* in *History of Saint Anthony of Padua Parish*, 102.

6. The Fairway Construction Company built one-story ranches bordering the farmland that had become Oak Hill Country Club in 1921. Lillian R. Pratt, "The History of Oak Hill Country Club" (2013; www.oakhillcc.org/history); also see real estate transactions in the *Sentinel*.

7. Over the long term, this strategy worked. When the Worcester diocese consolidated the Fitchburg churches (July 1, 2010), Saint Anthony's remained open, whereas Holy Rosary was consolidated with other parishes.

8. 1919 Fitchburg City Directory, 48.

9. Fitchburg City Directories, 1909, 1919; also see the 1910 and 1920 US censuses; as well as Kirkpatrick, *Around the World in Fitchburg*, 209.

10. Confidential interview with Bianca M.; Fitchburg City Directories.

11. Pat Goguen, "He's Still Minding the Store: Billy Romano marks 59 Years," *Sentinel* (Fitchburg), Dec. 18, 1989.

12. "The Saga of Tom Caravella: Tenth Anniversary" *Sentinel* (Fitchburg), Jan. 21, 1963.
13. "Caravella Brothers Host to Thousands," *Sentinel* (Fitchburg), Nov. 5, 1966.
14. "Shopping Centers Right Spot in Growth of Area," *Sentinel* (Fitchburg), June 30, 1972, 30.
15. Mastrangelo family interviews, Sogni d'Oro Oral History.
16. Second interview, 6.
17. Levanti family interview, Sogni d'Oro Oral History.
18. Joseph Addante, Sogni d'Oro Oral History; and Kirkpatrick, *Around the World*.
19. Ferruccio Moz was interviewed by Revine Lago's oral history project and appeared on RAI television's "Una Mattina"; see "Intervista a Moz Ferruccio" (www.tragol.it/Scuole/emira/indice.htm); and "E morto il partigiano 'Patria' 86 anni," *La tribune di Treviso*, Feb. 23, 2012.
20. Loretta Baldassar and Ros Pesman, *From Paesani to Global Italians: Veneto Migrants in Australia* (Crawley: University of Western Australia, 2005), 28–30.
21. "Saint Anthony's Church" file, Fitchburg Historical Society.

Afterword

The story of the reluctant migrants who left the Veneto is a complex tale composed of many interwoven strands. Their experience of migration was much more intricate than their descendants could ever imagine. Failed efforts to find work in Europe gave way to transatlantic and global migration. Some made repeated efforts to find work in America and spent a season in Chicago or New York, then tried a season in a Belgian coal mine, only to return to the United States and try Massachusetts. Their migration stories are much more complicated than the migrants themselves might want to admit and contain many layers of experience, much of it harsh.

From the perspective of America, the great wave of Italian immigration happened in a narrow window of four decades, 1880–1920, and brought young male unskilled laborers, mainly from southern Italy. For Veneto migrants the story is more convoluted. Some left their homeland and remained in the Americas, Canada, or Australia. Others traveled back and forth in what amounted to global commuting. Others returned and remained in the Veneto, facing the hardships of war twice in the twentieth century, as well as the rise and fall of Italian Fascism.

Many of those who remained in Massachusetts achieved what has been called the American dream; numerous Americans equate upward mobility and wealth with success in life. Often, such progress meant advancement and material wealth, a home, a car, and suburban comfort. For the reluctant migrants there were many different American dreams, and not all of them were dreaming of the United States. Venetians often applied the phrase more widely as they sought a better life—whether in the United States, Canada, or South America.

For northern Italian migrants from the Veneto, the migration experience was not directed by padroni but carried out by small groups of impoverished farm laborers. They sought to escape extreme hardship, but many held on to a dream of returning to the Veneto. The rapid political and economic changes following unification in Italy plunged much of the Veneto into hardship, poverty, and even starvation. Despite the difficulties, many held the hope that making a small fortune and returning would allow them to remain in the Veneto for perhaps another generation. These were the reluctant migrants. They were deeply attached to the dialect, the traditions, and the culture of the Veneto. Traditional life in the foothills of the Alps had remained unchanged for thousands of years until rapid economic and political changes steadily eroded that way of life. The Veneti's strategy to meet the challenge was to seek a solution that involved the least change. Only very unwillingly did they migrate, and then no farther from their homes than necessary.

In the Veneto migration began as seasonal travel, first within Italy, then to neighboring Austria and Switzerland. Those who left were men seeking short-term work on construction or railroad projects and young women who could work as domestic help in cities and as field laborers on farms. They traveled on a rigid schedule and made use of the developing rail system across northern Italy. Women and children saw their work as a means to improve life without the commitment of resettlement. For these reasons, it was acceptable for young women and children to travel alone within the region and even farther afield to Austria.

The next waves of migration grew more transatlantic and permanent, first to Brazil and elsewhere in South America. Skilled farmers and farm managers were recruited, and promises of free land were the enticement. Although men left first, they were most often joined over time by their extended family from the Veneto. Brazil, Argentina, and Uruguay attracted people with specific skills who settled so far from their homes that seasonal commuting was impractical. If they could not return, they would take as many of their family and friends with them as possible and would establish themselves in what became isolated Venetian communities abroad.

These migrants all developed strategies in the struggle to survive and nurtured the dream of returning to the Veneto. But changes in the agricultural economy steadily reduced the probability of returning on a permanent basis. Cutting hay, grains, and vines and subsistence farming could no longer support life in the mountains. In the fields of the Po River valley, the contadini who had owned land or held tenant status found themselves working as temporary day laborers for what constituted starvation wages. Malnutrition, a decline in the quality of housing, and the decay of their very existence all took their toll. Child mortality rose as pellagra ravaged the Veneto.

Transatlantic migration the United States held a greater appeal as steam transport developed; it was an inexpensive alternative that opened the possibility of seasonal commuting. Men and women literally traveled the world. The reluctant migrants became highly mobile migratory birds. They built informal networks that spread information about work opportunities and guided them. Migrants found Massachusetts especially inviting, and it was as if these birds of passage, having once found their wings, were no longer content to stay in one place or in any place. Many lived a transnational life, crossing and recrossing the Atlantic in search of work and wealth.

When the United States Congress severely limited immigration of Italians in 1920 and again in 1924, the response of the Veneto migrants was to seek work elsewhere. Australia and Canada became alternatives, although these countries also limited immigration in the 1920s. The battle to assimilate millions of Italians into American life was disrupted by the bitter years of the Sacco and Vanzetti affair and by events that destroyed the tenuous relationship between native-born Americans and Italian immigrants. As another world war loomed, first-generation migrants were labeled enemy aliens and pursued by a government that dreaded a

new war driven by Fascism. Second-generation Italian Americans proved
themselves during the war to be patriotic Americans.

After 1945 a new generation emerged as Americanized Italians who
had lost the Veneto dialect and their links to the social organizations
that their parents and grandparents had built. Traditions and linkage to
the Veneto faded away in America but did not in Australia and Canada.
In those places, a constant renewal of culture occurred as new Veneto
migrants joined the earlier waves. Both Australia and Canada opened
access to Italian migration after World War II. Australia received large
numbers of immigrants who sometimes owned property in both the
Veneto and Australia. Canada hired workers to help build the Saint
Lawrence Seaway and to expand the nation's rail network. America's
doors remained closed to all but a few thousand Italian immigrants each
year, and Veneto migrants in Massachusetts held to their culture as best
they could with no new influx to renew their connections. Boston's North
End, once home to new arrivals, has lost its *Italianita*, as has the rest of
Massachusetts. The key factor is that new migrants no longer refresh
the contemporary connection to Italy. Restaurants and shops stock the
foods and imports, but the spirit is waning.

In the Veneto the need to migrate was renewed by the destruction of
the Fascist era and the Second World War. Veneti continued to migrate
within Europe, as well as to Canada and Australia. Switzerland, France,
and even Germany became home to workers who sought work wherever
they could find it in war-ravaged Europe. Osvaldo Grava from Revine
Lago is a prime example of a Venetian who worked abroad, intending
to earn enough to support his widowed mother and then return. But
over time he grew to be a part of his adopted home and built a life
in Switzerland. Although wealthy, he remained apart from a place to
which he could have returned. Today, commemoration of those roots
continues in Revine Lago, where the Grava family established a yearly
international reunion in the 1980s that draws home kin from around
the world. Similarly, a global organization to unite migrants from the

Veneto, Veniti nel Mondo, is supported by the Regione del Veneto and based in Canada.

In reflecting on a century of mobility, one might ask whether it was better to leave or to remain. The people of theVeneto suffered malnutrition, starvation, and invasion in both world wars. Was their new life better in North America, South America, or Australia? Anti-Italian hostility abounded in the 1920s and 1940s as America, Australia, and Canada all restricted immigration, labeling Italian nationals enemy aliens in the Mussolini era.

Perhaps the final answer is marked by where emigrants from the Veneto chose to remain. Once they had accumulated substantial savings, many might have returned to the Veneto for good. And some chose to cross the Atlantic again and again. Massachusetts became a destination rather than a place to work for a few months of the year. There were as many American dreams as there were dreamers who saw in America, especially in Massachusetts, a place where those dreams might come true.

FIGURES

Figure 1. Map of the Veneto

Figure 2. Livelet Archeological Museum (Parco Archeologico Didattico)

Author's photograph.
Reconstruction of ancient *pallefitte* housing in the Veneto.

Figure 3. Temporary shelters constructed by Italian workers of the Wachusett Reservoir project, 1897

Massachusetts Department of Conservation and Recreation and Massachusetts Archives, Boston.

Figure 4. Huts constructed by Italian workers on the Wachusett Reservoir project

Collection of the Beaman Memorial Public Library, West Boylston, Massachusetts.

Figure 5. Rollstone Hill, tenements and cotton mills

Fitchburg Historical Society, Fitchburg, Massachusetts.

Figure 6. Sarah Wool Moore teaching English to Italians in her Camp School

The Survey, June 24, 1911.

Figure 7. Derricks on the Rollstone Hill granite quarry

Fitchburg Historical Society, Fitchburg, Massachusetts.

Figure 8. Wedding at St. Anthony's Church, Fitchburg, Massachusetts 1939

Author's collection.

Figure 9. Angel Novelty Company picnic

Collection of Fred Mastrangelo
Largest Italian-American owned factory in Fitchburg, Massachusetts.